DEMAGOGUES, POPULISM AND MISINFORMATION

DEMAGOGUES, POPULISM AND MISINFORMATION

A GUIDE TO COMBATING DARK IDEAS

EDITED BY

CHRIS BROWN
University of Southampton, UK

AND

GRAHAM HANDSCOMB
University College London (UCL), UK

emerald PUBLISHING

United Kingdom – North America – Japan – India
Malaysia – China

Emerald Publishing Limited
Emerald Publishing, Floor 5, Northspring, 21-23 Wellington Street,
Leeds LS1 4DL.

First edition 2025

Reprints and permissions service
Contact: www.copyright.com

British Library Cataloguing in Publication Data
A catalogue record for this book is available from the British Library

ISBN: 978-1-80592-171-4 (Print)
ISBN: 978-1-80592-168-4 (Online)
ISBN: 978-1-80592-170-7 (Epub)

INVESTOR IN PEOPLE

They don't publish

the good news.

The good news is published

by us.

They don' publish the good news (extract) Thich Nhat Hanh

Beyond this place of wrath and tears

Looms but the Horror of the shade,

And yet the menace of the years

Finds and shall find us unafraid.

Invictus (extract) William Ernest Henley

CONTENTS

FOREWORD

Standing Together Against the Egotists

It is an absolute pleasure to write the Foreword to this remarkable book because my life has focussed so much on the areas that it explores. I've written books on the last eight prime ministers – some good, some bad. I have also authored books on trust, artificial intelligence, happiness, character and the purpose of education, and I have run both schools and a university. The chapters within this remarkable book stretch both the mind and the imagination. At times, they seem almost too hopeful and ambitious; at other times, the ideas are so obviously sensible one cannot imagine why they are not widespread in our lives today.

The publication of the book is timed to perfection. Why?

- The rise of Donald Trump, the most lawless President in the US history, who is placing the 250-year-old system in the USA of separation of powers and checks and balances, and the post-1945 global order, under severe test.

- The rise of dictators, including Viktor Orbán in Hungary, Recep Tayyip Erdoğan in Turkey, Nicolás Maduro in Venezuela and a host of autocratic figures across every continent in the world. According to the *Economist Intelligence Unit*, only 26 countries out of some 200 can be labelled 'full democracies' the lowest number since the survey began in 2006. Only 6.6% of the world's population, down from 12.5% 10 years ago, can be said to live in countries enjoying full democratic freedoms.

- A prevailing sense of anxiety across the world about the present and future, with worries about climate change, loss of jobs, the impact of AI, food, water and energy security, the damage done by social media, the rise of violence particularly against women and the vulnerable and the devastation caused by legal and illegal drugs. There are fundamental concerns about the decline of family and religion and their replacement by influencers and figures of shadowy and uncertain morality, the rise of gangs, terrorism, and the resurgence of racism, the loss of communal spaces and civic centres, and places where children could play safely outside.

- The rise of populism, in both left- and right-wing forms, spreading across the world, promoting the idea that the ruling elites are acting in their own self-interest, not that of the population at large. Incumbent governments struggle in difficult economic circumstances to satisfy the aspirations of their people.

- Respect for objective truth has come into question in a way that George Orwell foresaw 75 years ago. Totalitarian countries for centuries have used their power to assert what is true and what is false. The new factor though, and a very dangerous one, is that the most powerful leader of the West, Donald Trump, has no interest in or respect for objective truth. The eclipse of objective truth is magnified by people increasingly finding out about news, not from independent and balanced sources, like the BBC, but from highly partisan broadcast, print and digital sources.

- Ideas have never been more needed. But not every idea is a good idea. Racism, genocide and ethnic cleansing are all ideas, but they are bad and dangerous ideas, which were to the fore to devastating effect in the 20th century. The Republican Administration in the USA since January 2025 has produced a set of novel ideas – clean out Gaza of Palestinians and replace with a ribbon development of gambling and golf resorts, take over Greenland, the Panama Canal and Canada. But these are bad dark ideas. History is full of people wanting to follow and to curry favour with powerful leaders, however, ill-informed and illegal their ideas. The dark web is full of ideas that are very, very dark. The human mind seems to be more drawn to that which is dark than that which is wholesome and good.

- Integrity, trustworthiness and public service are all good ideas that have come under enormous strain this century. A host of scandals in the UK involving politicians and even prime ministers has steadily eroded public confidence. No single prime minister in the last century has so damaged the integrity of the office of PM as Boris Johnson, with his repeated lying and dissembling.

- A tired and redundant system of education is responsible for many of the problems in Britain. It is fixated on exams, which are seen as an end in themselves rather than a means to an end. It is not producing young people who employers say are ready for work. It finds little place for the arts, sports, adventure and character development, yet it is ethical workers who society and employers most need. Teachers are leaving schools in droves because the regimentation and lack of discipline is uncongenial. The mental health of young people is of epidemic proportions. It fails to prepare young people well enough for further and higher education, and focusses on the very cognitive and linear skills that algorithms will always be able to outperform humans on, rather than the human skills, on which AI will never be able to compete with humans.

If all this sounds a bit gloomy, then reading this book will fill you as it does me with hope for the future.

Let me conclude with 10 ideas first expounded in *Trust. How We Lost It and How to Get It Back*[1] which I wrote with a team of 10 brilliant young women and men on the very cusp of beginning their working lives. In no order:

- Set up nature trails across the country.

- Remove all graffiti from public spaces the moment it appears.

- Start a national campaign to remove all rubbish from the sides of roads, rivers, beaches, public spaces and elsewhere, and repair damage to public buildings and spaces immediately.

- All young people to join scout groups from 7 to 16 and all over 18s spend a year in public national service activities learning practical and coping skills and being engaged in activities that will build a better society.

- All pupils at school to enjoy an arts education, sports, physical and adventure activities out of school.

- All young people to be engaged in volunteering activities.

- Parks and green areas to be created on brownfield sites – a minimum of 25% of each town and city to be green space.

- All derelict canals to be restored, rivers, ponds and lakes to be brought back to be full of natural life.

- Britain to appoint a 'top 1000 role-models', figures who have excelled in their chosen fields, to serve for five years, to be national exemplars of ethical behaviour, public service, dedication and hard work.

- Schools to be responsible for discovering not what young people *can't do* – with one-third every year failing at GCSE = but finding out what each and every single young person *can do and loves to do*, showering them with trust, and giving each a pathway to becoming responsible and valued members of society.

Idealistic? Of course. Impractical? No. They have all been proven to work elsewhere. Most important to all is that we must learn that the future is about us, no longer about the egotists, and that we will all flourish by standing together rather than alone as we have done for so much of this vexatious century to date.

Sir Anthony Seldon,
October 2025

ACKNOWLEDGEMENTS

We would like to extend our deepest thanks to all the contributors to this volume. Your insight, passion and commitment to challenging misinformation and promoting an ideas-informed society have made this book possible.

Our sincere appreciation goes to *Emerald Publishing* for their support in bringing this work to life. We are especially grateful to our editor, *Kirsty Woods*, whose guidance, encouragement and editorial expertise have been invaluable throughout the development of this project.

Thank you all for helping us strike back against the dark side – one idea at a time.

NOTE

1. Seldon, A. (2009). *Trust. How we lost it and how to get it back*. Biteback Publishing.

TACKLING THE FOUNDATIONS OF DARK IDEAS

1

INTRODUCTION: STRIKING BACK AGAINST THE DARK SIDE

Chris Brown[a] and Graham Handscomb[b]

[a]University of Southampton, UK
[b]University College London (UCL), UK

PURSUING THE IDEAS-INFORMED SOCIETY

As editors of this volume, we are especially proud of what it represents: a further step towards realising what we term the *ideas-informed society*. This is a concept we return to often in our writing – an ideal, even. It envisions a society in which all members, from school students onwards, actively seek out and engage with enriching, constructive ideas, while also identifying and rejecting harmful or misleading ones.[1] As we write this in mid-2025, clinging to idealism may seem naïve – but can you blame us? The world today is awash with crises: impending environmental catastrophe, a growing migration emergency, worsening obesity and mental health issues, the rise of populist demagogues, attacks on democratic institutions, eroding public trust, and an ever-widening chasm between the privileged and the deprived. Against this backdrop, we argue that fostering an ideas-informed society – rooted in critical engagement with ideas – can serve as a much-needed bulwark. At its core, this means encouraging widespread interaction with positive ideas while actively challenging dark ones. So, let's begin there.

POSITIVE IDEAS AND EMPOWERING THE MARGINALISED

We define *positive ideas* as those that help improve lives and strengthen communities. At the personal level, they might include evidence-based knowledge about healthy living – information that leads individuals to reduce alcohol intake or increase physical activity, thus lowering the risk of preventable illnesses.[2] But positive ideas can also have a long-term, transformative effect. Engagement with enriching ideas builds cultural capital, supporting better educational outcomes, upward social mobility, and personal growth.[3]

An ideas-informed society, at its best, enables lifelong learning across formal, informal, and community contexts. However, not everyone who could benefit from such engagement does so. Our earlier research highlights the existence of tight-knit communities – often characterised by lower educational attainment and routine or manual employment – where idea engagement is minimal.[4] Within these groups, discussing current events or exploring new societal developments is uncommon. And yet, these are precisely the communities that could stand to gain the most from becoming more engaged with ideas, particularly given the specific challenges they face.

For example, post-COVID-19 data from the Centre for Social Justice[5] reveal that 40% of individuals in the UK's most deprived communities now report a mental health condition, compared to just 13% in the general population. Among young people, mental ill-health has risen from one in nine to one in six. Severe school absence has increased by 134%, and nearly 5,000 people died from drug poisoning in 2022 – a 63% increase in methadone-related deaths alone. Meanwhile, people in these areas remain less likely to participate in cultural activities that build capital and support social mobility.[6] While ideas engagement is no panacea for deep systemic injustice, it can equip individuals with the knowledge and agency needed to better navigate and respond to these challenges.

TYPE ONE AND TYPE TWO DARK IDEAS

By contrast, *dark ideas* fall into two broad categories. *Type one* dark ideas are factually incorrect yet widely believed. These include fake news, science denial, and conspiracy theories – such as the suggestion that Donald Trump staged his own assassination attempt in 2024. Such misinformation has become so widespread that UK MPs have now been issued with guidance to identify it. Alarmingly, type one dark ideas are infiltrating illegal schools across England – unregistered institutions operating outside of regulatory oversight. Investigative journalist Tom Ball has exposed how two such schools, Hope Sussex and Universallzidz, teach a curriculum rooted in conspiratorial thinking.[7] Students are taught, among other things, that COVID-19 was a 'PLANdemic', aircraft vapour trails are designed to cause dementia, and crystals can cure serious illness. Though the number of children attending such schools is relatively small – an estimated 126,100 were home-schooled at some point during 2022–2023[8] (and, of course, not all of these are experiencing such conspiracy rooted education) – this still represents a disturbingly large population at risk of internalising and acting on such ideas.

Type two dark ideas, meanwhile, are those that lead to harmful outcomes even if they are not factually incorrect per se. Populist ideologies are a prime example. Around a third of voters across Europe now support far-right or far-left parties. Demagogues such as Trump, Farage, Meloni, and Orbán have mastered the art of rhetoric that pits 'ordinary people' against supposed 'elites', undermining trust in democratic institutions, the judiciary, the media, and experts. Minority rights are rolled back, culture wars rage, and facts are bent or discarded altogether. Truth has become negotiable. In this 'post-truth' era, repetition trumps reality. Social media makes falsehoods feel real. Orwell's *Nineteen Eighty-Four* imagined a Ministry of Truth that fabricated facts to serve the state. Today, that dystopia feels uncomfortably close to home.[9] Populism thrives on *post-truth logic*: emotionally charged arguments, belief-driven narratives, and the dissemination of 'alternative facts' – a phrase coined to excuse blatant untruths from the first Trump administration. This detachment from objective truth is particularly dangerous when paired with science denial. Consider former Australian PM Scott Morrison brandishing a lump of coal in Parliament during a heatwave and reassuring the public, 'It won't hurt you'.[10] Or Conservative MPs in the UK claiming that lockdowns were more harmful than COVID-19 itself.[11]

FAKE NEWS AND DARK IDEAS: NOT NEW, BUT MORE DANGEROUS

Although the current crisis of misinformation feels modern, it has deep historical roots. Fake news and propaganda can be traced back to ancient Egypt, with Pharaoh Rameses the Great allegedly inventing military victories to bolster his image. Conspiracy theories have existed since the Roman Empire – some even blamed Emperor Nero for starting the great fire of Rome. Populist leaders have appealed to emotion since ancient Greece, and scepticism towards science has always existed in forms such as Fortean beliefs.[12] What's different now is scale, speed, and reach. With social media, AI, and digital communication, dark ideas can spread with unprecedented velocity and impact. The consequences are tangible. Tim Farley's 'What's the Harm' project documents over 368,000 deaths, 306,000 injuries, and nearly $3 billion in damages resulting from belief in dark ideas. Add to this the erosion of democracy, public trust, and scientific progress, and the stakes become clear. Action is urgently needed.[13]

THE POWER OF CRITICAL THINKING

In our previous work, we identified critical thinking as key to enabling effective engagement with ideas – and thus central to fostering an ideas-informed society. Specific components include:[14]

- **Curiosity:** A motivational force for learning, best nurtured in supportive environments.

- **Intellectual honesty:** Recognising and confronting personal biases and stereotypes.

- **Intellectual humility:** Acknowledging the limits of one's own knowledge.

- **Intellectual empathy:** Respectfully engaging with perspectives different from one's own.

- **Sophisticated epistemic beliefs:** Understanding that scientific knowledge evolves and is subject to revision.

- **Information literacy:** Evaluating and navigating information sources with care.

- **Generic critical thinking skills:** Logical reasoning, argument analysis, and problem-solving.

To this list, we would add *self-checking* – the ability to pause and ask: 'Is this idea too good to be true?' The appeal of seductive, simplistic narratives – what we call the *lure of the dark idea* – must be consciously resisted. Many of these traits are intellectual virtues. They can be nurtured. And so, in this book, we bring together a diverse group of contributors from across society – policymakers, educators, artists, business leaders, religious leaders, activists, scientists, and more – to explore two urgent questions:

1. How can we confront and respond to dark ideas more effectively?

2. How can we help people develop the capacity to engage with ideas in ways that improve not just their own lives, but those of their communities?

THE DESTRUCTIVE POWER OF MISINFORMATION

Bringing the responses of our contributors together, the book opens with a section titled *Tackling the Foundations of Dark Ideas* – an in-depth exploration of the underlying forces that fuel the spread and acceptance of misinformation and populism. The contributions in this section draw on psychology, education, and political science to examine how and why dark ideas take root, and what can be done to counter them. Following our introductory chapter, the next opening chapter, 'Why Are Some Ideas Easy to Believe on

Little Evidence?', Anna Stone explores why certain ideas gain traction despite a lack of evidence, focussing on the roles of conspiracy thinking, populist rhetoric, and low levels of social trust. She examines how emotional reasoning, cognitive biases, and the erosion of rational discourse make misinformation resistant to correction, and outlines interventions such as analytical thinking, pre-bunking, and critical engagement as possible countermeasures.

Similarly, in 'The Lure of the Shadow', Arif Anis examines the destructive impact of misinformation and conspiracy theories in the UK and the USA, linking false narratives to real-world violence, unrest, and social division. He explores the psychological, technological, and socio-economic factors that enable such ideas to thrive, and calls for collective strategies including media literacy education, platform regulation, and community-based efforts to restore trust in institutions. In 'Can Pro-Climate Advocates Steal Populism's Clothes?', Matthew Paterson explores the evolution of climate populism. While older climate denialism relied on misinformation, new climate populism has shifted towards emotionally charged narratives. These reject net zero policies not by denying climate change, but by framing such initiatives as threats to traditional lifestyles or as impositions from out-of-touch elites. Paterson argues that scientists and activists can – and must – adopt the rhetorical tools of populism to effectively reframe climate action in inclusive and empowering ways. This leads into the next theme which focusses on the power of education.

SCHOOLS ON THE FRONT LINE IN A POST-TRUTH ERA

Education is a crucial site in the fight against misinformation, as demonstrated by the chapters in this second section, *Liberation Through Education*. In 'Science Literacy Beats Misinformation', Andrew Morris argues that widespread scientific illiteracy leaves individuals vulnerable to poor reasoning and populist manipulation. Drawing on an experimental science course for adults, he makes the case for inquiry-based learning – both in formal education and lifelong learning settings – as a way to cultivate curiosity, critical thinking, and an appreciation for science's relevance to daily life. Then, Lee Jerome, in 'Defeating Misinformation Through Classroom Deliberation', questions the idea that media literacy alone is sufficient. He argues instead for a deeper transformation of classroom culture, one that prioritises deliberative democracy. In such environments, students are invited to discuss, evaluate, and respectfully challenge ideas – an approach that helps build resilience to misinformation and supports the development of political literacy. David Lambert's chapter, 'Getting Down to Earth', responds to the challenges posed by post-truth politics, climate change, and anti-science sentiment. Drawing on Bruno Latour's concept of 'Down to Earth' politics, Lambert argues for a radical rethinking of education – one that embraces epistemic diversity, prioritises truthfulness, and centres 'powerful knowledge' as a counterweight to ideological noise and misinformation.

TRUST AND KNOWLEDGE SHARING

The next group of chapters, under the theme *Misinformation and the Power of Knowledge*, examine the intersections of trust, expertise, and communication across business, law, and media. In 'Data-driven Misinformation', Anna E. Premo, Alexander Ratkovsky, and Martina A. Rau explore how flawed use of data within businesses can lead to misleading conclusions. Through a fictional case study of a banking executive misinterpreting customer data, they demonstrate how critical thinking and organisational culture are essential for ensuring that data insights are accurate, actionable, and ethically sound. Sir Les Ebdon, in 'Confronting Media Outrage and Restoring Trust and Evidence-based Debate', explores how the rise of sensationalist media and algorithm-driven social platforms has undermined public trust and fragmented civic discourse. He advocates for systemic responses, including ethical journalism, transparency in AI and algorithms, and education that emphasises critical engagement with information. The concerns of Robin Ellison, in 'Populism and its Impact on the Rule of Law', centre on warning against knee-jerk legislative responses to populist demands. He shows how such reactions often lead to ineffective or even harmful laws, and calls for a more measured, evidence-based approach to policy-making grounded in legal principles. In this section, the last chapter titled 'It's Darwin!: An Evolutionary Lens on Knowledge and Truth', Steven Warmoes explores how truth, trust, and cooperation are essential to societal flourishing. Using a Darwinian lens, he examines how trust enhances knowledge sharing and reduces deception, arguing that future success – both individual and collective – will depend on superior knowledge, social trust, and shared values.

LIVING IN A WORLD OF POLITICAL TURMOIL

Our next section, *Demagogues, Democracy and Political Action*, focusses on how misinformation interacts with democratic systems and political behaviour. In 'Extremism Is the Point: How Our Society and Politics Fosters Dark Ideas', barrister Sam Fowles argues that the UK's political and media systems are structurally configured to reward misinformation and extremism. Through detailed analysis, he shows how attention-seeking and deception dominate public discourse, marginalising truth and evidence, while reinforcing the power of an oligarchic elite. In Gopal Subramanium's chapter, 'Preserving and Sustaining Democracy in an Age of Disinformation', he reflects that although almost half the world's population was involved in national elections in 2024, these electorates were not able to be make informed choices because of the insidious proliferation of disinformation and the promotion of Dark Ideas. He warns of the stark danger that many nations appear to be moving to a form of elective despotism. He paints a graphic picture of the contemporary world where the populous turn to hero demagogues, with internet technology fuelling untruths. Legal action to ban disinformation and dark ideas runs the risk of undermining the nature of democracy and free speech. Instead, Gopal sets out an action plan of measures with implications for social media technology and governments.

Meanwhile, Ben O'Laughlin and Alister McKimmon, in 'Living with Shade: Ambiguity Does Not Mean Only Darkness in World Politics', explore ambiguity not as a flaw but as a strategic tool in global affairs. They argue that uncertainty is central to how states and institutions operate and suggest that individuals must become more comfortable with ambiguity to better understand and navigate political complexity. In 'What Would the Suffragettes Think?', Vivienne Porritt traces the enduring influence of patriarchy and misogyny despite progress in women's rights. She connects historical activism to contemporary issues like political misogyny, sexism in education, and online abuse, calling for renewed feminist engagement and collective action from all genders to advance true equality.

FAITH, NATIONALISM, AND DARK IDEAS

The chapters grouped under *Populism, Faith, and Belief* examine how religious communities and spiritual ideologies intersect with political populism and misinformation. First, John P. Bradbury explores in 'Faith Communities and National Populisms: Seeking Integrity in the Grey Areas', the ways faith communities can both enable and resist national populism. Drawing on historical and contemporary examples, he shows how churches can become either echo chambers for nationalist rhetoric or havens of resistance and dialogue. Also exploring this theme, Andy Braunston, in 'Responding to (Christian) Nationalism', investigates how Christian Nationalism has been deployed to justify exclusionary policies in the USA, Russia, and Hungary. He critiques the political misuse of Christian teachings and instead calls for a faith-based politics rooted in truth, justice, and inclusivity. Beverley Clack's chapter. 'Embracing Uncertainty in a Chaotic Age', powerfully draws on the thinking of Dietrich Bonhoeffer to advocate for a more reflective and humane approach to public life. She urges readers to embrace uncertainty, reject passive obedience, and cultivate everyday virtues as a form of resistance to authoritarianism and ideological rigidity.

PERSONALLY FACING UP TO THE DARK

Our final section, *Personally Facing Up to the Dark*, explores what individuals can do to resist misinformation and build resilience. Lesley Saunders' moving chapter, 'Writing into the Dark: Dementia and the Cultivation of Human(e)ness', offers a deeply personal reflection on the experience of illness – particularly her husband's dementia – as a lens for grappling with dark ideas. Through literary and poetic inquiry, she argues that engaging with inner darkness can foster greater empathy, challenge dominant narratives, and deepen our humanity.

The book closes with a call to action from Lynn Wood, founder of IdeaSpies, in the chapter titled 'Taking Control: Be More Selective in Choice of Media'. In her contribution she outlines a manifesto for reclaiming our media diets. While humans may be drawn to negative news, Lynn argues that individuals and institutions can shift the balance by promoting stories of hope, innovation, and possibility. Positive news, she contends, is not naïve – it's necessary. As the epigraph that opens this volume reminds us:

> They don't publish the good news. The good news is published by us.

ENDNOTES

1. Brown, C., & Luzmore, R. (2025). An educated society is an ideas-informed society: A proposed theoretical framework for effective ideas engagement. *British Educational Research Journal*, *51*, 969–989. http://doi.org/10.1002/berj.4110

2. Campbell, D. (2023). *'Dire need' for labels on alcohol and ads about unhealthy eating to cut avoidable cancers*. Retrieved March 17, 2024, from https://www.theguardian.com/society/2023/sep/16/dire-need-for-labels-on-alcohol-and-ads-about-unhealthy-eating-to-cut-avoidable-cancers

3. DiMaggio, P. (1982). Cultural capital and school success: The impact of status culture participation on the grades of U.S. high school students. *American Sociological Review*, *47*, 189–201.

4. Brown, C., Groß Ophoff, J., Chadwick, K., & Parkinson, S. (2022). Achieving the 'ideas-informed' society: Results from a structural equation model using survey data from England. *Emerald Open Research*, *4*, 4. https://doi.org/10.35241/emeraldopenres.14487.1

5. Centre for Social Justice. (2023). TWO NATIONS: The State of Poverty in the UK: An interim report on the state of the nation.

Available at: https://www.centreforsocialjustice.org.uk/wp-content/uploads/2023/12/CSJ-Two_Nations.pdf, accessed on 24 June 2025

6. DiMaggio, P. (1982). Cultural capital and school success: The impact of status culture participation on the grades of U.S. high school students. *American Sociological Review*, 47, 189–201.

7. Ball, T. (2023). Hope Sussex school trains next generation of conspiracy theorists. *The Times*. Retrieved November 8, 2024, from https://www.thetimes.com/uk/healthcare/article/hope-sussex-school-trains-next-conspiracy-theorists-zbv6fnf57; Ball, T. (2024). Exposed: the 'illegal school' teaching children conspiracy theories. *The Times*. Retrieved November 8, 2024, from https://www.thetimes.com/article/exposed-the-illegal-school-teaching-children-conspiracy-theories-htcdtnm6h

8. Department for Education. (2024). *Elective home education*. Retrieved November 8, 2024, from https://explore-education-statistics.service.gov.uk/find-statistics/elective-home-education

9. Handscomb, G. (2024, February). Truth, lies and the thinking Christian. *Reform*, magazine of United Reformed Church.

10. Hamilton, C. (2017, February 15). *That lump of coal*. CSU News, Charles Sturt University. Retrieved April 2, 2025, from https://news.csu.edu.au/3172970/features/society/that-lump-of-coal

11. Craig, J. (2020, November 11). *Coronavirus: Scores of Rebel Tory MPs launch anti-lockdown campaign group*. Sky News. Retrieved April 2, 2025, from https://news.sky.com/story/coronavirus-scores-of-rebel-tory-mps-launch-anti-lockdown-campaign-group-12129631

12. See https://pinebarrensinstitute.com/what-is-fortean.

13. French, C. (2024). *The science of weird shit: Why our minds conjure the paranormal*. MIT Press.

14. Brown, C., & Luzmore, R. (2025). An educated society is an ideas-informed society: A proposed theoretical framework for effective ideas engagement. *British Educational Research Journal*, 51, 969–989. http://doi.org/10.1002/berj.4110

2

WHY ARE SOME IDEAS EASY TO BELIEVE ON LITTLE EVIDENCE?

Anna Stone

University of East London, UK

WHY THE LURE OF *DARK IDEAS* MATTERS

This chapter will focus on some of the underlying psychological reasons why people find it easy to believe certain ideas in the absence of objectively convincing evidence. It is the lack of good evidence that makes the belief something that requires explanation; if there is convincing evidence in support of a phenomenon or a theory then belief is readily justified. You will never be asked to debate the existence of gravity, for example. Some of the beliefs to which people may be drawn could be termed *dark ideas*, characterised by fake news, conspiracy theories, and emotionally manipulative populism.

Understanding belief in *dark ideas* matters because it can lead to negative consequences for the individual and for society. In contrast, well-informed citizens can take sensible decisions on, for example, health care to protect themselves and others, or on protecting the environment. If we are going to succeed in convincing people to engage with beneficial ideas then we need to understand how to counter the lure of *dark ideas*.

There is a wealth of literature and recent research in this area, far too much to cover in one chapter, so I will focus on three broad psychological topics. The first is the social sources of knowledge and why we prefer to listen to unqualified friends and family rather than experts. The second topic discusses the difference between emotional and rational thinking, the different functions of beliefs, and how rational/analytical thinking can defend against the lure of fake news and conspiracy theories. The third topic considers theories explaining why we cling to our ideas so strongly and are so resistant to changing our minds. Together, these three broad psychological reasons may shed some light onto the lure of *dark ideas*.

SOURCES OF KNOWLEDGE

Trust in Those We Know

We often seem to prefer to place our trust in personal acquaintances rather than the opinions of experts. For example, Haran and Shalvi, in their research into the *implicit honesty premium*, found that people are more inclined to trust advice when they think the person giving the advice is being honest.[1] It is easier to regard the people we know as honest compared to a distant scientist, someone we have never met and about whom we know little, and who speaks in technical terms. Along similar lines, Rivas explained how voters prefer to 'go with their guts' and trust information from private individuals, even when knowing it is likely to be less accurate, rather than publicly available information.[2] The tendency to trust family and friends for medical advice, rather than qualified medical people, has been widely noted. For example, Warner and Procaccino reported that 87% of women cited family and friends, and 75% cited the internet, as a primary source of health information.[3]

Our knowledge of social processes can shed light on the influence of belief sharing in social groups. According to Moussaïd and colleagues,[4] we are swayed by the beliefs of those people to whom we feel close, and we tend to hold attitudes for which we have been rewarded, for example, by the approving responses of friends and family. This will, over time, tend to lead us to express the opinions with which we know those close to us agree. This predisposition to express opinions congenial to those around us can lead to the internalisation of those opinions.

Conspiracy Theories and False Consensus

Conspiracy theories typically explain events of great social significance. We are likely to discuss the events, and explanatory theories, with friends and family and colleagues, so there is a heightened potential for us to be swayed by their beliefs.[5] Bena and colleagues observed that repetition (or familiarity) increases the perceived truth in conspiracy theories.[6] The theories we share with friends and family are likely to be repeated, providing reinforcement, and this is reinforcement from people to whom we are close, and we know we are more likely to trust than more distant experts.

The concept of *false consensus* can help to strengthen our beliefs (also known as egocentric attribution or looking glass perception). The idea of *false consensus*, according to Ross and colleagues, is that our estimation of the popularity of our own choices and beliefs is higher than the estimation given by someone with a different view.[7] For example, Wojcieszak looked at communications in 60 different online chat groups (text-based) with randomly selected participants.[8] They met monthly for a year and discussed the topics of gun control, the death penalty, and teaching morality in public schools. There was a correlation between the person's own views and their perceptions of other people's views, so that if the individual was in favour on a topic, they perceived others to be more in favour than they actually were. Furthermore, this tendency increased with the strength of views. Underlying processes include biased recall, whereby the stronger our attitude, the more likely we are to remember the occasions when someone agreed with us, and the motivation to justify our own beliefs by pointing out how many others agree with us. In voluntary social groups, a *false consensus* could be produced by our preference to surround ourselves with people who think like us.

It is particularly interesting that the perceived level of agreement between own and others' opinions was weaker if the contrary views were delivered in person, perhaps because of the more immediate and memorable impact of a real life encounter. Now that so many of our interactions take place online there is reduced scope for real life meetings to break our false consensus views.

Distrust in Institutions

The disposition to trust people we know is accompanied by a general distrust in institutions. For example, Leal and Drochon[9] reported the results of a YouGov poll of over 11,500 people in 8 European countries and the USA. There were worrying levels of distrust in important institutions: 77% distrusted journalists, 76 distrusted government, and 74% distrust company bosses. An encouraging note is that 57% in the USA and 64% in the UK still had trust in academics. There is a growing body of evidence that this distrust in institutions lies behind some of the recent conspiratorial thinking. For example, Kim and Kim[10] found that trust in government was negatively related to belief in conspiracy theories. Similarly, Jedinger and Masch[11] and Srol and colleagues[12] reported a relationship between trust in political and medical institutions and lower belief in conspiracy theories around COVID-19.

Van Prooijen and colleagues[13] discuss how distrust and conspiracy theories go hand in hand. Those who distrust scientific institutions, for example, may believe that the dangers of climate change are systematically exaggerated in order to introduce measures to control the population. Those who distrust the medical establishment may believe that the corona virus was deliberately spread to justify restrictions on individual liberties. In this way, lower trust can erode the social contract and lead to reduced pro-sociality, increased inter-group conflict, polarisation and extremism.

Bartlett and Miller[14] offer a further reason for the particular resistance of conspiracy theories to counter-evidence provided by institutions; the experts in those institutions are part of the conspiracy. For example, if part of the conspiracy belief structure is that the government is in control of the media, then no information or ideas published in outlets generally regarded as reliable need to be accepted.

Altogether, there is good evidence and theoretical reasoning to suggest that the tendency to trust personal acquaintances rather than experts and to distrust institutions can pose serious challenges to health and wellbeing of the population and the world in general.

EMOTIONAL AND RATIONAL THINKING

How We Deal with New Knowledge

Our thinking and decision-making processes are often conceived as comprising two distinct aspects: emotional and intuitive versus rational and analytical, according to Witteman and colleagues.[15] These two aspects generally work together. When it comes to deciding what to believe on particular topics, however, either a rational-analytical or an emotional-intuitive thinking style may dominate. This stems from the principle that some of our beliefs serve rational functions and some support emotional goals. For example, belief in the efficacy of vaccines supports our health, while belief in a religion is more likely to fulfil an emotional and meaning-constructing role in our life. Sperber[16] discussed how emotional beliefs may fit better with our overall worldview, or they may enable us to maintain good relationships with our friends and family and community, or they may provide a source of meaning and solace. The idea that beliefs can be held for either rational or emotional reasons could perhaps explain why we can hold seemingly contradictory beliefs at the same time.

In principle, when new knowledge is gained we should consider it alongside our existing knowledge and perhaps modify our set of beliefs. In practice, we may reject the new knowledge and leave our belief unchanged. Griffin and Ohlson[17] compared emotional and rational beliefs from the perspective of their relative resistance to re-evaluation and change in the light of new evidence. They observed that beliefs based on empirical data and logical reasoning tend to be more accepting of new information and more likely to change accordingly. They attributed this to the greater logical coherence of explanatory beliefs, which facilitates the active assessment and consideration of new information.

In contrast, a more emotionally-based belief is less firmly founded on empirical data and logical reasoning, which renders new information less likely to be identified as a challenge and less likely to inspire reassessment of the belief structure. Thus, an emotional belief can remain unchanged in the face of new information as long the emotional goals are still being achieved. This implies that if conspiratorial thinking, or fake news, or emotionally appealing populism, meets an emotional goal for the individual, perhaps by fitting neatly within their perceived political or economic worldview, then it may be accepted uncritically and may be particularly difficult to challenge.

How to Resist Conspriratorial Beliefs

This leads us to identify various means by which we can help ourselves and others to entertain lower levels of conspiratorial beliefs. One of the most important, and identified by numerous researchers, is analytical and open-minded thinking skills. For example, O'Mahony and colleagues[18] found that fostering an analytical mindset or developing skills in critical thinking are the most effective means of changing conspiracy beliefs. The literature review by Gagliardi,[19] and individual studies by Binnendyk and Pennycook[20] and by Kim and Kim,[8] confirmed that a propensity for analytical thinking is negatively related to conspiracy beliefs. Newton and colleagues[21] confirmed these findings, and went further to report that actively open-minded thinkers are likely to have lower levels, while intuitive thinkers are likely to have higher levels, of beliefs in conspiracies and misinformation.

Analytical thinking and open-mindedness seem like positive approaches, which begs the question of why they are not more commonly employed. Shah and colleagues[22] presented an interesting framework to explain what makes everyday scientific reasoning so challenging. They pointed out that stories in the press often include personal anecdotes and appeals to one's own personal experiences to make an emotional connection with the reader. This has the effect of engaging emotional-intuitive thinking and disengaging analytical thinking. Combined with a general lack of understanding of how to evaluate the quality of scientific research and the accuracy of its presentation, and a general mistrust in institutions, this can lead to a failure to appreciate good evidence when it is presented in the public domain.

Appeals to emotion can be used to promote good ideas as well as *dark ideas*. For example, Toomey[23] suggested that appeals to emotion, intuition, and values, can help to persuade people to support conservation effort to protect ecosystems, habitats, and species. Rather than communicating in a dry scientific style, and relying on conceptual reasoning and evidence to persuade people, she proposes that we should engage people on an emotional level and encourage people to reason in social groups. Along similar lines, Brosch[24] also found that emotion was a major cause of changing behaviour in relation to climate change. It should be stressed that it is dangerous to appeal to emotion alone – emotion should go hand in hand with reason and verifiable evidence.

Finally, the technique of prebunking, explored by Lewandowski and colleagues,[25] can be used to inoculate people against attempts to persuade them into conspiratorial thinking. Informing people about an attempt that may be made to persuade them into a particular line of thinking can help to put them on their guard and enable them to take a more critical approach. For example, explaining how the tobacco industry for so many years presented arguments confusing the true causes of cancer enables people to spot attempt to confuse the reality of man-made climate change.

Increased use of analytical thinking, prebunking, and inoculation, can help us to resist attempts to persuade us to accept fake use and conspirary theories. Being on our guard for attempts to use our emotions to manipulate our beliefs can also enable us to take a open-minded and critical review of information.

CLINGING TO OUR IDEAS

The Role of Dogmatism in an Uncertain World

The third topic considered here is the question of why we cling to our ideas so strongly and disregard other people's views; in other words, what function does dogmatism serve for us? There are a number of answers to this which will be briefly explored.

One answer lies in the negative effects of uncertainty and the advantages arising from the relief of anxiety. Research by Farias[26] and colleagues described how, when people are threatened with uncertainty, they strengthen and cling to their already-held beliefs. The participants in this study were rowers, either in regular training or about to enter a race, thus utilising naturally occurring variation in levels of anxiety and uncertainty. The finding that participants under conditions of uncertainty cling more strongly to their existing beliefs was observed for both religious belief and belief in science (which were negatively related to each other). This is particularly interesting, because while we already knew that religious belief can relieve stress and anxiety, and compensate for a perceived lack of control, this study might suggest that the same applies to belief in science.

Dogmatism, Belief, and Moral Certainty

Whitson and colleagues[27] also investigated the effect of anxiety on belief structures by asking participants to experience either an emotion that generally makes people feel uncertain, about the world (worry, fear, hope, or surprise) or an emotion associated with certainty (anger, happiness, disgust, or contentment). This manipulated the participants' sense of uncertainty. Participants experiencing one of the emotions related to uncertainty reported higher levels of belief in conspiracies and the paranormal. The interpretation was that the experience of uncertainty, or of a lack of control over outcomes, often activates a need to see the world as orderly and controlled. A conspiracy belief can provide this sense of order and stability and thus alleviate the distress. Other researchers have observed similar findings: for example, Kim and Kim[10] reported that anxiety, lack of control, and negative emotions in general, are positively related to belief in conspiratorial thinking; and Srol[12] also found that a lack of control was associated with belief in COVID-19 conspiracies.

Dogmatic beliefs are something to cling to in an uncertain world. Our core beliefs give us certainty and stability, which we find especially valuable when we are made to feel uncertain.

Kossowska and colleagues[28] presented evidence that a dogmatic attitude towards our beliefs can help to relieve anxiety, and, like Farias[26], this was observed both in religious people and atheists. A dogmatic approach to beliefs may mediate the relationship between intolerance of uncertainty, a trait on which people vary, and either religious belief or atheism. When a person high in intolerance of uncertainty feels anxious or threatened they can become more dogmatic about their beliefs as a way of relieving their anxiety.

There are negative consequences to dogmatism, though. Social problems can arise when dogmatic believers, under conditions of uncertainty, become prejudiced towards groups perceived to threaten their values. In the Kossowska[28] study both religious people and atheists with high intolerance of uncertainty held more dogmatic beliefs and displayed more prejudice. They sought to protect their beliefs by showing prejudice towards others who do not share them.

An idea somewhat related to dogmatism is that of moral certainty. If our belief is based on a strong moral foundation it will be particularly resistant to change, because we are reluctant to compromise our moral positions. When we are sure we are morally correct, according to Philipp-Muller and colleagues[29] and Skitka and colleagues,[30] our beliefs must also be correct.

Motivated Reasoning

The last topic to be considered is motivated reasoning. This comes in various forms, all of which concur that a belief is established first, and only later are evidence and reason are used to support and justify the belief. This is known as 'top-down' rather than 'bottom-up' reasoning. Gagliardi[19] reviewed the literature and found good evidence for the *confirmation bias* as a means of maintaining conspiracy belief. *Confirmation bias* refers to the tendency to pay particular attention to ideas and information that agree with our existing beliefs and to ignore those that do not. According to Gagliardi[19], this is particularly strong when the belief is central to one's identity or fills psychological or ideological needs. For example, people are generally adverse to changes imposed by others, and especially to changes that appear to threaten their way of life. If we accept the reality of climate change, then we will have to make changes – to car use, meat consumption, fast and disposable fashion, and many other examples. There is clearly an incentive to dismiss climate change as a conspiracy in order to justify continuing with a preferred way of life. A closely related idea is that people are influenced by their emotional commitment to their beliefs and experience a desire to defend those beliefs.[22]

Membership of social groups is essential for most people and provides a source of identity, validation, and emotional support. Membership of a group may depend on observing and conforming to the core beliefs of the group.[14] For someone whose social group has a core ideology of conspiratorial ideation, either in general or focussed on specific concerns, the powerful emotional nature of belonging to the group would restrict the ability to take in contrary views. This would limit the extent to which an individual member would be motivated to engage in any reasoning that could challenge their sense of belonging to the group.

A strategy that people may use to enable them to maintain their existing ideas is to listen only to congruent views, or to people who can be relied on to express generally congruent views. In a study by Frimer and colleagues,[31] people with ideological commitment (e.g., towards same-sex marriage) were willing to forgot the chance to win a cash prize if it required listening to views in opposition to their own. The participants anticipated that hearing from people with opposing views would cause cognitive dissonance, resulting in frustration, increased effort, and potentially damage the relationship with the other party. This applied equally to political liberals (left-inclined) and conservatives (right-leaning) though other studies have found that conservatives show this effect more strongly.

A CONCLUDING REFLECTION

This has been a quick tour of some of the psychological explanations for why our conspiratorial ideas can be so resistant to change. Other ideas have been omitted for reasons of space and the choice of which topics to include was the author's alone. It is freely admitted that other, equally valid, choices could have been made.

Of course, the individual processes considered here – social influences, distrust of institutions, emotional and rational thinking, dogmatism, the control of anxiety, and motivated reasoning – are not bad things in themselves. They can, however, lead to the adherence to damaging ideas and the rejection of more positive thinking. These processes are perhaps best in moderation and when balanced with commitment to listening to experts, rational thinking, and willingness to change our minds.

ENDNOTES

1. Haran, U., & Shalvi, S. (2019). The implicit honesty premium: Why honest advice is more persuasive than highly informed advice. *Journal of Experimental Psychology: General, 149*, 757–773. https://doi.org/10.1037/xge0000677.

2. Rivas, J. (2018). *Our experiment into how voters think shows that they go with their guts*. The Conversation. https://theconversation.com/our-experiment-into-how-voters-think-shows-that-they-go-with-their-guts-90241.

3. Warner, D., & Procaccino, D. (2007). Women seeking health information: Distinguishing the web user. *Journal of Health Communication, 12*, 787–814.

4. Moussaïd, M., Kämmer, J. E., Analytis, P. P., & Neth, H. (2013). Social influence and the collective dynamics of opinion formation. *PLoS One, 8*(11), e78433. https://doi.org/10.1371/journal.pone.0078433

5. Swami, V., & Coles, R. (2010). The truth is out there. *Psychologist, 23*, 560–563.

6. Béna, J., Rihet, M., Carreras, O., & Terrier, P. (2023). Repetition could increase the perceived truth of conspiracy theories. *Psychonomic Bulletin Review, 30*, 2397–2406. https://doi.org/10.3758/s13423-023-02276-4.

7. Ross, L., Greene, D., & House, P. (1977). The false consensus effect: An egocentric bias in social perception and attribution processes. *Journal of Experimental Social Psychology, 13*(3), 279–301. https://doi.org/10.1016/0022-1031(77)90049-X.

8. Wojcieszak, M. E. (2011). Computer-mediated false consensus: Radical online groups, social networks and news media. *Mass Communication and Society, 14*(4), 527–546. https://doi.org/10.1080/15205436.2010.513795.

9. Leal, H., & Drochon, H. (2018). *Brexit and Trump voters more likely to believe in conspiracy theories, survey study shows.* https://www.cam.ac.uk/research/news/brexit-and-trump-voters-more-likely-to-believe-in-conspiracy-theories-survey-study-shows.

10. Kim, S., & Kim, S. (2021). Searching for a general model of conspiracy theories and its implication for public health policy. *International Journal of Environmental Research and Public Health, 18,* 266–293.

11. Jedinger, A., & Masch, L. (2024). Need for cognitive closure, political trust, and belief in conspiracy theories during the COVID-19 pandemic. *Frontiers in Social Psychology, 2,* https://doi.org/10.3389/frsps.2024.1447313.

12. Šrol, J., Ballová Mikušková, E., & Čavojová, V. (2021). When we are worried, what are we thinking? Anxiety, lack of control, and conspiracy beliefs amidst the COVID-19 pandemic. *Applied Cognitive Psychology, 35*(3), 720–729.

13. Van Prooijen, J-W., Spadaro, G., & Wang, H. (2022). Suspicion of institutions: How distrust and conspiracy theories deteriorate social relationships. *Current Opinion in Psychology, 43,* 65–69.

14. Bartlett, J., & Miller, C. (2010). The power of unreason: Conspiracy theories, extremism, and counter-terrorism. *Demos.* Retrieved August 29, 2010, from https://demos.co.uk/wp-content/uploads/2010/08/Conspiracy_theories_paper.pdf

15. Witteman, C., Van den Bercken, J., Claes, L., & Godoy, A. (2009). Assessing rational and intuitive thinking styles. *European Journal of Psychological Assessment, 25*(1), 39–47.

16. Sperber, D. (2000). Intuitive and reflective beliefs. In P. Engel (Ed.), *Believing and accepting* (Philosophical Studies Series, Vol. 83). Springer. https://doi.org/10.1007/978-94-011-4042-3_13.

17. Griffin, T. D., & Ohlsson, S. (2001). Beliefs versus knowledge: A necessary distinction for explaining, predicting, and assessing conceptual change. *Proceedings of the Annual Meeting of the Cognitive Science Society, 23.*

18. O'Mahony, C., Brassi, l. M., Murphy, G. & Linehan, C. (2023) The efficacy of interventions in reducing belief in conspiracy theories: A systematic review. *PLoS ONE, 18*(4), e0280902. https://doi.org/10.1371/journal.pone.0280902.

19. Gagliardi, L. (2023). The role of cognitive biases in conspiracy beliefs: A literature review. *Journal of Economic Surveys, 39,* 32–65. https://doi.org/10.1111/joes.12604.

20. Binnendyk, J., & Pennycook G. (2022). Intuition, reason, and conspiracy beliefs. *Current Opinion in Psychology*, *47*, Article 101387. https://doi.org/10.1016/j.copsyc.2022.101387.

21. Newton, C., Feeney, J., & Pennycook, G. (2024). On the disposition to think analytically: Four distinct intuitive-analytic thinking styles. *Personality and Social Psychology Bulletin*, *50*(6), 906–923. https://doi.org/10.1177/01461672231154886.

22. Shah, P., Michal, A., Ibrahim, A., Rhodes, R., & Rodriguez, F. (2017). Chapter Seven – What makes everyday scientific reasoning so challenging? In B. H. Ross (Ed.), *Psychology of learning and motivation* (Vol. 66, pp. 251–299). Beckman Institute and Department of Psychology, University of Illinois. https://doi.org/10.1016/bs.plm.2016.11.006.

23. Toomey, A. H. (2023). Why facts don't change minds: Insights from cognitive science for the improved communication of conservation research. *Biological Conservation*, *278*. https://doi.org/10.1016/j.biocon.2022.109886.

24. Brosch, T. (2021). Affect and emotions as drivers of climate change perception and action: A review. *Current Opinion in Behavioral Sciences*, *42*, 15–21. https://doi.org/10.1016/j.cobeha.2021.02.001.

25. Lewandowsky, S., & van der Linden, S. (2021). Countering misinformation and fake news through inoculation and prebunking. *European Review of Social Psychology*, *32*(2), 348–384. https://doi.org/10.1080/10463283.2021.1876983.

26. Farias, M., Newheiser, A. K., Kahane, G., & de Toledo, Z. (2013). Scientific faith: Belief in science increases in the face of stress and existential anxiety. *Journal of Experimental Social Psychology*, *49*(6), 1210–1213. https://doi.org/10.1016/j.jesp.2013.05.008.

27. Whitson, J. A., Galinsky, A. D., & Kay, A. (2014). The emotional roots of conspiratorial perceptions, system justification, and belief in the paranormal. *Journal of Experimental Social Psychology*, *56*, 89–95.

28. Kossowska, M., Czernatowicz-Kukuczka, A., & Sekerdej, M. (2017). Many faces of dogmatism: Prejudice as a way of protecting certainty against value violators among dogmatic believers and atheists. *British Journal of Psychology*, *108*(1), 127–147. https://doi.org/10.1111/bjop.12186.

29. Philipp-Muller, A., Lee, S. W. S., & Petty, R. E. (2022). Why are people antiscience, and what can we do about it? *Proceedings of the National Academy of Sciences U.S.A.*, *119*. https://doi.org/10.1073/pnas.2120755119.

30. Skitka, L. J., Hanson, B. E., Morgan, G. S., & Wisneski, D. C. (2021). The psychology of moral conviction. *Annual Review of Psychology, 72,* 347–366. https://doi.org/10.1146/annurev-psych-063020-030612.
31. Frimer, J., Skitka, L. J., & Motyl, M. (2017). Liberals and conservatives are similarly motivated to avoid exposure to one another's opinions. *Journal of Experimental Social Psychology, 72,* 1–12.

3

THE LURE OF THE SHADOW

Arif Anis

DESTRUCTIVE NARRATIVES AND THE FORMIDABLE POWER OF DARK IDEAS

The proliferation of misinformation and conspiracy theories, significantly amplified by digital platforms, poses a considerable challenge to social cohesion, public trust, and safety globally. These narratives, often rooted in fear, suspicion, and the simplification of complex events, can transcend online spaces to incite tangible real-world harm, ranging from harassment and property destruction to political violence and contributions to mass atrocities. This chapter examines three distinct case studies from the UK, across Europe, and the USA which exemplify this dangerous phenomenon. Each case study investigates the factual circumstances, the nature of the falsification or conspiracy, the mechanisms of its spread via social media, and its subsequent real-world consequences. By analysing these cases – the 5G/COVID-19 conspiracies, the Pizzagate scandal in the USA, and the 2024 UK riots stemming from a tragic incident in Southport – and through a comparative analysis of misinformation in authoritarian and democratic societies, this chapter illuminates the patterns, mechanisms, and impacts of digitally fuelled false narratives, connecting them to the broader themes of psychological susceptibility, platform dynamics, trust erosion, and the urgent need for effective countermeasures.

Firstly, in July 2024, a false story ignited a firestorm across Britain. Reports circulated widely on social media after a man named Eddie Murray claimed that that a group of young girls had been brutally murdered in a dance class in Southport by a migrant, a class which he claimed that his daughters were part of.[1] Although subsequent investigations as to the validity of his daughters being in the same class and witnessing the incident proved his claim to be entirely fabricated, the narrative had already taken root, and soon, another lie formed – that the man responsible for the act was a Muslim immigrant named 'Ali-Al-Shakati'.[2] Thus, In cities such as London, Manchester, and Birmingham, enraged individuals poured into the streets in large numbers to riot, many of them being far-right protesters hoping to push an anti-immigration agenda, using the incident in Southport as fuel.[3]

Across the Atlantic, the notorious Pizzagate conspiracy experienced a disturbing resurgence in the United States. Originally emerging during the 2016 election cycle, the theory alleged that a popular pizzeria in Washington, D.C. served as a front for a secret child trafficking ring involving prominent political figures, such as Hillary Clinton.[4] Despite exhaustive official investigations that debunked the claims, the conspiracy gradually evolved into a narrative that incited real-world violence. In one alarming episode, a man – radicalised by excessive exposure to the online myth – stormed the establishment in question armed with a rifle, later firing a shot and causing an evacuation of the restaurant.[5]

In mid-2019, the global deployment of 5G mobile networks commenced amidst some public speculation regarding potential health effects, despite a lack of scientific evidence supporting adverse impacts. Concurrently, the COVID-19 pandemic emerged and spread globally in late 2019 and early 2020.[6] In the UK, the pandemic led to nationwide lockdowns starting in March 2020. During this period, public health authorities and governments relied heavily on communication networks, including mobile infrastructure, for disseminating information, enabling remote work and education, and facilitating contact tracing and emergency services.[7] The confluence of the 5G rollout and the COVID-19 pandemic provided fertile ground for conspiracy theories linking the two phenomena. The actual situation was distorted through several false narratives. The most prominent claim was that 5G technology directly caused COVID-19 symptoms or the virus itself. This theory suggested that symptoms of COVID-19 were caused by electromagnetic radiation poisoning.[8] As a result, numerous mobile phone masts (including non-5G infrastructure) were targeted in arson attacks and acts of sabotage across the UK and Europe. Around 90 attacks were reported in the UK during the lockdown period by late May 2020.[9] This vividly illustrates how fear and uncertainty during a major crisis like the COVID-19 pandemic can create fertile ground for conspiracy theories.

These three episodes – the 2024 UK riots, the violent outburst in Washington, D.C., and the unrest caused by 5G mobile networks across the UK – demonstrate the formidable power of dark ideas. Such narratives are not merely baseless fabrications; they are potent stories that exploit deep-seated fears, playing upon emotional vulnerabilities and pre-existing socio-economic tensions. Their allure lies in their simplicity and clarity, offering easy answers and a single enemy to blame amid an increasingly complex world. To counter their pull, it is crucial to understand the psychological, social, and digital forces that fuel these narratives and to develop strategies to foster resilience and rebuild trust in our communities.

THE GENESIS AND SPREAD OF DARK IDEAS

Dark ideas flourish in times of crisis and uncertainty. When factual information is scarce or overly complex, simplistic explanations – even if entirely false – offer immediate relief and a sense of order. The 2024 riots across Britain illustrate this process vividly. In communities already weakened by economic stress and social fragmentation, the rumour surrounding the murdered girls in Southport seemed to provide a convenient scapegoat. Citizens, desperate for an explanation amid mounting anxiety, were quick to embrace a narrative that identified a clear villain.

'Dark ideas' refer to concepts, narratives, or ideologies that operate on the margins of mainstream discourse, often gaining traction through fear, uncertainty, or the manipulation of information. These ideas are not simply negative or controversial but derive influence from their ability to exploit cognitive biases, social

anxieties, and gaps in collective knowledge. They frequently manifest as a result of conspiracy theories and misinformation, shaping
public perception in ways that are often subtle yet significant. The
persistence of dark ideas could be attributed to their psychological
appeal, which reinforces pre-existing beliefs and fosters a sense of
certainty in an otherwise complex and ambiguous world. Understanding dark ideas requires an examination of the psychological,
technological, and social factors that lead to them, which is what
will be done in this chapter.

Digital Platforms as Accelerators

Digital platforms have played an instrumental role in the rapid
spread of misinformation. In today's hyper-connected environment, social media algorithms are designed to prioritise content
that provokes strong emotional reactions. In Southport – where
the false news first emerged – the 'echo chamber' effect was
immediate.[10] The rapid, unchecked circulation of misinformation
created a self-reinforcing feedback loop, entrenching the false narrative and inciting public anger before any official correction could
reach the masses. Such digital momentum allowed the false story to
spark real-world violence almost instantaneously.

The Evolution of Conspiracy Theories

In Washington, D.C., the enduring Pizzagate conspiracy offers
a stark example of how digital myths can evolve into catalysts
for violence. Over a period of years, disparate pieces of unverified information, manipulated images, and pseudo-documentaries
slowly coalesced into a comprehensive, though entirely unfounded,
theory. This narrative was carefully crafted to tap into deep-seated
distrust of institutions and to stoke fears about the abuse of power.
When a lone gunman, radicalised by prolonged exposure to this
dark idea, violently invaded a local pizzeria, it underscored the
dangerous potential of such ideologies. This act was not an isolated
incident, but the tragic culmination of a gradual process of radicalisation fostered by online echo chambers.[11]

PSYCHOLOGICAL UNDERPINNINGS: WHY DARK IDEAS RESONATE

At the heart of these events lie powerful psychological forces that predispose individuals to embrace dark ideas. When modern life seems chaotic and unpredictable, many people long for the comfort of clear, simple narratives – even if these are built on falsehoods.

The Comfort of Confirmation Bias

One key mechanism is confirmation bias, the tendency to favour information that aligns with pre-existing beliefs. In times of uncertainty, this bias acts as a psychological shield against the discomfort of doubt. The false rumour about who murdered the young girls in Southport resonated particularly with some communities already suspicious of official institutions and the role that immigrants play in their societies. Embracing the 'migrant' rumour offered certain groups a fleeting sense of validation and control, as it would confirm their worst suspicions about the current system they are living in. Research in cognitive psychology consistently demonstrates that individuals are more likely to remember and accept information that supports their views, making it difficult for corrective evidence to gain traction once a narrative has taken hold.[12]

Cognitive Dissonance and Resistance to Correction

Another significant factor is cognitive dissonance – the mental discomfort experienced when new information conflicts with long-held beliefs. To alleviate this discomfort, individuals often double down on their original views, dismissing contradictory evidence as part of a broader conspiracy. When official debunkings emerged – whether refuting the Southport rumours or the Pizzagate claims – it seems that many found it psychologically easier to cling to the original narrative than to confront the possibility of having been misled. Empirical studies have shown that attempts to correct misinformation can sometimes reinforce the initial belief, as individuals seek to resolve the dissonance between their preconceptions and the new facts.[13]

The Primacy of Emotion: Fear and Anger

Emotion is a potent driver of human behaviour, and dark ideas thrive on evoking strong emotional responses. The fabricated story about the murdered girls struck a particularly raw nerve, inciting visceral reactions of fear, anger, and grief. In an age of instantaneous digital communication, emotionally charged content spreads far more rapidly than measured, factual reporting. Research has shown that emotionally arousing narratives are more likely to be shared and internalised, enabling false narratives to penetrate deeply into public consciousness before rational thought can intervene.[14]

SOCIAL AND ENVIRONMENTAL AMPLIFIERS

While individual psychology provides a foundation for the acceptance of dark ideas, broader social and environmental factors further amplify their spread and impact.

Digital Echo Chambers and Algorithmic Bias

Digital media has revolutionised the dissemination of information but has also introduced new vulnerabilities. Social media algorithms – designed to maximise user engagement – tend to promote content that elicits strong emotional reactions. This design also results in echo chambers, digital spaces where users are repeatedly exposed to the same ideas, thus reinforcing their pre-existing beliefs.[15] Across the UK, repeated exposure to sensational claims about the Southport incident, such as the one highlighted above, deepened public anger and cemented the false narrative in many minds. The constant repetition creates a self-sustaining cycle that is difficult to break, allowing misinformation to flourish unchecked.

The Dual Role of Traditional Media

Traditional media, while often instrumental in debunking misinformation, can inadvertently contribute to its spread. In the rush to capture audience attention, sensational stories may receive disproportionate coverage.[16] Early reports on the Southport incident, even when later corrected, seeded lasting doubt and fear. Dramatic headlines and striking images leave a profound impact, ensuring that the emotional resonance of dark ideas endures long after the factual record has been established. This phenomenon illustrates the powerful interplay between media practices and public perception.

Therefore, it is clear that in an increasingly treacherous landscape where engagement metrics drive the type of content that is presented to the audience, media outlets often prioritise sensationalism over accuracy, amplifying misleading narratives in the pursuit of clicks, viewership, and advertising revenue. The cycle of rapid news production may lead to incomplete fact-checking, reliance on unverified sources, or the framing of misinformative claims as legitimate debates. Furthermore, the media's role in platforming certain voices over others – whether through opinion pieces or interviews – can lend undue credibility to misinformation. Recognising this dynamic in the traditional media is essential to understanding how misinformation proliferates and why audiences may struggle to distinguish credible journalism from deceptive narratives.

Erosion of Trust in Public Institutions

Underlying many of these phenomena is a growing mistrust of public institutions. When people believe that authorities are concealing the truth or acting in bad faith, they become more receptive to alternative narratives, regardless of their veracity.[17] The false news that sparked the 2024 riots, the persistent Pizzagate conspiracy, and the 5G/COVID-19 rumours all exploited this mistrust. Restoring confidence in public institutions is, therefore, a critical step in countering the allure of dark ideas and rebuilding a cohesive social fabric.

RIGOROUS RESEARCH ON MISINFORMATION

The academic community has devoted considerable effort to understanding how misinformation takes hold and spreads. A wealth of empirical studies offers valuable insights into the psychological and social dynamics at work.

The Role of Confirmation Bias

Numerous experiments have demonstrated that confirmation bias plays a central role in the persistence of dark ideas. In controlled settings, participants consistently favoured information that confirmed their pre-existing beliefs – even when presented with clear, contradictory evidence.[18] This tendency was particularly evident in studies of political misinformation, where initial opinions proved remarkably resistant to correction. Such findings underscore the challenge of countering misinformation solely through fact-checking and corrective information.

Cognitive Dissonance and the Rejection of Contradictory Evidence

The theory of cognitive dissonance remains a cornerstone in understanding why individuals reject corrective evidence. When new information conflicts with deeply held beliefs, many experience significant mental discomfort, which they resolve by dismissing the new evidence altogether. Empirical research has demonstrated that interventions aimed at fostering reflective thinking and self-assessment can help mitigate this effect, though such measures require time and a willingness to engage in self-criticism – resources often in short supply during a misinformation crisis.[19]

Social Identity and Group Dynamics

Social psychology research has further elucidated the role of group identity in the acceptance of dark ideas. When individuals derive their sense of self from membership in a particular community, they are more inclined to adopt narratives that reinforce the group's worldview.[20] This dynamic was evident in terms of the 5G/COVID-19 conspiracies, where the rumours cemented a collective identity among residents, uniting them against an imagined common enemy. By the third week of the UK lockdown, Ofcom surveys found that almost half of UK adults had encountered false or misleading information about COVID-19, with theories linking 5G to the virus being the most commonly seen piece of misinformation. Studies have shown that group loyalty can significantly hinder the reception of corrective information, underscoring the need for community-based interventions when addressing misinformation.[21]

Digital Amplification and Algorithmic Effects

The structure of digital platforms has been subject to extensive study, particularly regarding how algorithms amplify emotionally charged content. Analyses of social media networks reveal that the prioritisation of engagement over accuracy creates a fertile environment for dark ideas.[22] Longitudinal studies indicate that echo chambers not only reinforce false narratives but can also shift public opinion in ways that persist even after the misinformation has been debunked.[23] These findings highlight the need for technological interventions that can disrupt these self-reinforcing feedback loops.

STRATEGIES TO COUNTER THE LURE OF DARK IDEAS

Addressing the scourge of dark ideas requires a multifaceted approach that tackles both the psychological roots and the environmental conditions that allow such narratives to flourish. Effective strategies must encompass education, digital reform, community engagement, and sustained research.

Strengthening Media Literacy and Critical Thinking

A long-term solution lies in education. By integrating media literacy and critical thinking into school curricula and public programmes, citizens can be equipped with the skills necessary to scrutinise information effectively. Educational initiatives should focus on recognising logical fallacies, understanding the psychology of bias, and deconstructing the mechanisms of digital media. Using real-world case studies – such as the 2024 riots, the Pizzagate incident, and the unrest caused by 5G networks – provides tangible examples of the severe consequences of unchecked misinformation. Tailored workshops, community lectures, and online courses can help ensure that critical thinking skills extend beyond academic settings into everyday life.

Reforming Digital Platforms

Collaboration between government regulators and technology companies is essential to redesign digital platforms that currently amplify dark ideas. Greater transparency in algorithmic processes is a critical first step. Social media companies should be required to explain how content is selected and promoted, thereby enabling users to understand and challenge the inherent biases of these systems. In addition, introducing friction into the content-sharing process – such as prompts that encourage users to verify information before posting – can slow the rapid spread of misinformation. Pilot programmes that prioritise a diversity of viewpoints over sheer engagement have shown promising results and could serve as models for wider adoption.

Supporting Rigorous Interdisciplinary Research

Ongoing research into the dynamics of misinformation is crucial for developing effective countermeasures. Interdisciplinary studies that integrate insights from psychology, sociology, computer science, and political science can shed light on the complex interplay of factors that enable dark ideas to proliferate. Funding for longitudinal research projects should be prioritised, as such studies offer invaluable data on how misinformation evolves over time and on the efficacy of various interventions. Research on 'prebunking' – the process of inoculating individuals against misinformation before they encounter it – has shown promising results.[24] Public health–style campaigns based on these findings could become transformative tools in the fight against dark ideas.

Promoting Intellectual Humility and Empathy

Central to countering dark ideas is the cultivation of intellectual humility and empathy.[25] Public campaigns that celebrate the willingness to question one's own beliefs and to listen to opposing views can encourage a cultural shift away from dogmatic thinking. Personal narratives that recount journeys from radicalised belief to reflective inquiry can inspire others to adopt a more nuanced approach to contentious issues. This transformation is not the sole responsibility of academia; popular media, social influencers, and community leaders all have roles to play in promoting a culture that values curiosity, openness, and mutual understanding. When intellectual humility and empathy become core societal values, the seductive appeal of dark ideas is significantly diminished.

COMPARATIVE ANALYSIS OF MISINFORMATION IN DEMOCRATIC AND AUTHORITARIAN SOCIETIES

A comparative analysis of misinformation in democratic and authoritarian contexts reveals key distinctions in both its dissemination and impact. In Western democracies like the UK and the USA, misinformation typically spreads through decentralised channels, including social media platforms, alternative media, and, at times, mainstream news outlets seeking engagement-driven content. While these societies have mechanisms for fact-checking and independent journalism, misinformation often thrives due to political polarisation, algorithmic amplification, and the commercial incentives of digital media, as has been explored earlier.

By contrast, in authoritarian states, misinformation is frequently state-controlled and strategically deployed as a tool of governance and international influence. Russia's long ongoing information warfare against Ukraine exemplifies this, where state-backed media and coordinated disinformation campaigns have been used to distort narratives about Ukraine to justify military actions, and sow division among Western audiences. For example, in 2014, Russia launched a media campaign claiming that the missing Malaysia Airlines flight (MH17) aircraft was hit by a Ukrainian missile fired from the ground, which was proven to be false by the Ukrainian government.[26]

Unlike the largely uncontrolled spread of misinformation in democratic societies, such as in the three instances described in this chapter, authoritarian misinformation campaigns often involve direct government oversight and the strategic use of digital propaganda. Comparing the two approaches highlights that dark ideas can also transpire as a result of misinformation which is organic, and state-driven, emphasising the need for tailored counter-strategies depending on the specific political environments.

SYNTHESIS: MOVING FROM THE SHADOWS TO A BRIGHTER FUTURE

The stark events of the 2024 UK Riots, Pizzagate, and the 5G/COVID-19 conspiracies offer valuable lessons. They reveal that dark ideas are not random aberrations but the products of a potent mix of psychological vulnerabilities, digital amplification, and socio-economic disintegration. These episodes underline the urgent need for rapid, coordinated responses to misinformation. Early intervention – whether through immediate fact-checking, swift public communication by trusted officials, or community meetings – can prevent false narratives from taking deep root.

Moreover, effective countermeasures must combine top-down policy reforms and technological innovations with grassroots initiatives that rebuild trust and foster dialogue. Addressing dark ideas also requires recognising that these narratives are symptomatic of broader societal challenges. Economic inequality, social fragmentation, and a pervasive mistrust in institutions all contribute to the fertile ground on which misinformation thrives. Tackling these underlying issues is as crucial as addressing the immediate falsehoods.

By strengthening media literacy, reforming digital platforms, engaging communities, and supporting rigorous interdisciplinary research, society can forge a path away from the simplistic and divisive allure of dark ideas. Each step – be it a classroom lesson in critical thinking, a new regulatory measure for social media, or a community forum that rebuilds trust – contributes to a future built on truth, reason, and shared understanding.

FORMIDABLE CHALLENGE AND SEEDS OF HOPE

The lure of dark ideas casts a long shadow over our contemporary society. From the violent riots across the UK in 2024 – triggered by a fabricated tale of murdered girls – to the violent incursion at a Washington pizzeria inspired by the persistent Pizzagate conspiracy, and the chaotic unrest caused by 5G networks during the first COVID-19 lockdown, fuelled by baseless rumours, these episodes demonstrate the tangible human cost of misinformation. The losses extend beyond injuries and economic damage; they erode trust in public institutions and fracture community cohesion.

Deep-rooted psychological needs – for certainty, identity, and belonging – converge with the design of digital media and the pressures of economic hardship to create the perfect storm for the spread of dark ideas. Rigorous research has demonstrated that confirmation bias, cognitive dissonance, and emotional arousal play central roles in this process. Moreover, the digital amplification mechanisms of social media, combined with sensationalist media practices, further entrench these harmful narratives.

Yet there is hope. By strengthening media literacy, reforming digital platforms, engaging communities, and fostering a culture of intellectual humility and empathy, society can begin to reclaim the light. Interdisciplinary research continues to provide the tools needed to understand and counteract misinformation, while grassroots initiatives can rebuild the bonds that hold communities together.

The challenge is formidable, but the stakes are nothing less than the future of our social fabric. The lessons drawn from the 2024 riots, Pizzagate, and the 5G/COVID-19 conspiracies compel us to act proactively against the forces that seek to divide and destabilise us. Every act of critical inquiry, every community dialogue, and every policy reform is a step away from the seductive simplicity of dark ideas and towards a future founded on shared understanding and mutual respect.

Our collective responsibility is clear. Through sustained effort, informed by rigorous research and guided by the principles of transparency, empathy, and intellectual curiosity, we can turn the tide. The journey from the shadows to the light is long and arduous, but it is a path that we must walk together.

ENDNOTES

1. Thomas, E., & Sardarizadeh, S. (2024, October 25). *How a deleted LinkedIn post was weaponised and seen by millions before the Southport riot.* BBC News. https://www.bbc.co.uk/news/articles/c99v90813j5o.
2. Thomas, E., & Sardarizadeh, S. (2024, October 25). *How a deleted LinkedIn post was weaponised and seen by millions before the Southport riot.* BBC News. https://www.bbc.co.uk/news/articles/c99v90813j5o.
3. Al Jazeera Labs. (2024, August 7). Mapping far-right riots in the UK. *Al Jazeera.* https://www.aljazeera.com/news/2024/8/7/mapping-far-right-riots-in-the-uk
4. Bleakley, P. (2023). Panic, pizza and mainstreaming the alt-right: A social media analysis of Pizzagate and the rise of the QAnon conspiracy. *Current Sociology, 71,* 510–516.
5. Kang, C., & Goldman, A. (2016, December 5). In Washington pizzeria attack, fake news brought real guns. *The New York Times.* https://www.nytimes.com/2016/12/05/business/media/comet-ping-pong-pizza-shooting-fake-news-consequences.html
6. British Medical Association. (2022, July). *The public health response by UK governments to COVID-19* (no. 4). https://www.bma.org.uk/media/5980/bma-covid-review-report-4-28-july-2022.pdf
7. British Medical Association. (2022, July). *The public health response by UK governments to COVID-19* (no. 4). https://www.bma.org.uk/media/5980/bma-covid-review-report-4-28-july-2022.pdf
8. Ahmed, W., Vidal-Alaball, J., Downing, J., & López Seguí, F. (2020). COVID-19 and the 5G conspiracy theory: Social network analysis of twitter data. *Journal of Medical Internet Research, 22,* 1–7.
9. Martin, A. (2020, May 25). *Coronavirus: 90 attacks on phone masts reported during UK's lockdown.* Sky News. https://news.sky.com/story/coronavirus-90-attacks-on-phone-masts-reported-during-uks-lockdown-11994401

10. Lazer, D., Baum, M. A., Benkler, Y., Berinsky, A. J., Greenhill, K. M., Menczer, F., Metzger, M. J., & Nyhan, B. (2018). The science of fake news. *Science, 359*(6380), 1094–1096.

11. Tufekci, Z. (2018). *Twitter and tear gas: The power and fragility of networked protest.* Yale University Press.

12. Nickerson, R. S. (1998). Confirmation bias: A ubiquitous phenomenon in many guises. *Review of General Psychology, 2,* 175–220.

13. Festinger, L. (1957). *A theory of cognitive dissonance.* Stanford University Press.

14. Kahneman, D. (2011). *Thinking, fast and slow.* Farrar, Straus and Giroux.

15. Sunstein, C. (2001). *Republic.com.* Princeton University Press.

16. Gillespie, T. (2018). *Custodians of the internet: Platforms, content moderation, and the hidden decisions that shape social media.* Yale University Press.

17. Van der Linden, S. (2024). Countering misinformation through psychological inoculation. *Advances in Experimental Social Psychology, 69,* 1–58.

18. McGrew, S. (2020). Learning to evaluate: An intervention in civic online reasoning. *Computers and Education, 145,* 103711.

19. Traberg, C. S., Harjani, T., Basol, M., Biddlestone, M., Maertens, R., Roozenbeek, J., & van der Linden, S. (2023). Prebunking against misinformation in the modern digital age. *Managing infodemics in the 21st century: Addressing new public health challenges in the information ecosystem [Internet],* no. 8, 99–107.

20. Cheng, A., Silvia, R., & Mariya, N. (2022). Individualism vs. collectivism. *The Wiley-Blackwell Encyclopedia of Personality and Individual Differences, 4,* 287–297.

21. Ofcom. (2020). *Half of UK adults exposed to false claims about coronavirus.* Ofcom.org.uk. Retrieved April 09, 2020, from https://www.ofcom.org.uk/media-use-and-attitudes/media-habits-adults/half-of-uk-adults-exposed-to-falseclaims-about-coronavirus

22. Barberá, P. (2020). Social media, echo chambers and political polarization. In N. Persily & J. A. Tucker (Eds.), *Social media and democracy* (pp. 34–55). Stanford University Press.

23. Barberá, P. (2015). *Social media and political polarisation: A cross-country study.* University of Oxford Working Paper.

24. Van der Linden, S. (2024). Countering misinformation through psychological inoculation. *Advances in Experimental Social Psychology, 69,* 1–58.

25. Porter, T., Elnakouri, A., Meyers, E. A., Shibayama, T., Jayawickreme, E., & Grossmann, I. (2022). Predictors and consequences of intellectual humility. *National Review of Psychology, 1*, 524–533.

26. Erlich, A., & Garner, C. (2023). Is pro-Kremlin disinformation effective? Evidence from Ukraine. *The International Journal of Press/*Politics, *28*(1), 5–28.

BIBLIOGRAPHY

Ahmed, W., Vidal-Alaball, J., Downing, J., & López Seguí, F. (2020). COVID-19 and the 5G conspiracy theory: Social network analysis of twitter data. *Journal of Medical Internet Research, 22*, 1–7.

Al Jazeera Labs. (2024, August 7). Mapping far-right riots in the UK. *Al Jazeera.* https://www.aljazeera.com/news/2024/8/7/mapping-far-right-riots-in-the-uk

Barberá, P. (2020). Social media, echo chambers and political polarization. In N. Persily & J. A. Tucker (Eds.), *Social media and democracy* (pp. 34–55). Stanford University Press.

Bleakley, P. (2023). Panic, pizza and mainstreaming the alt-right: A social media analysis of Pizzagate and the rise of the QAnon conspiracy. *Current Sociology, 71*, 510–516.

British Medical Association. (2022, July). *The public health response by UK governments to COVID-19* (no. 4). https://www.bma.org.uk/media/5980/bma-covid-review-report-4-28-july-2022.pdf

Cheng, A., Silvia, R., & Mariya, N. (2022). Individualism vs. collectivism. *The Wiley-Blackwell Encyclopedia of Personality and Individual Differences, 4*, 287–297.

Erlich, A., & Garner, C. (2023). Is pro-Kremlin disinformation effective? Evidence from Ukraine. *The International Journal of Press/Politics, 28*(1), 5–28.

Festinger, L. (1957). *A theory of cognitive dissonance.* Stanford University Press.

Gillespie, T. (2018). *Custodians of the internet: Platforms, content moderation, and the hidden decisions that shape social media.* Yale University Press.

Kahneman, D. (2011). *Thinking, fast and slow*. Farrar, Straus and Giroux.

Kang, C., & Goldman, A. (2016, December 5). In Washington pizzeria attack, fake news brought real guns. *The New York Times*. https://www.nytimes.com/2016/12/05/business/media/comet-ping-pong-pizza-shooting-fake-news-consequences.html

Lazer, D., Baum, M. A., Benkler, Y., Berinsky, A. J., Greenhill, K. M., Menczer, F., Metzger, M. J., & Nyhan, B. (2018). The science of fake news. *Science*, *359*(6380), 1094–1096.

Martin, A. (2020, May 25). *Coronavirus: 90 attacks on phone masts reported during UK's lockdown*. Sky News. https://news.sky.com/story/coronavirus-90-attacks-on-phone-masts-reported-during-uks-lockdown-11994401

McGrew, S. (2020). Learning to evaluate: An intervention in civic online reasoning. *Computers and Education*, *145*, 103711.

Nickerson, R. S. (1998). Confirmation bias: A ubiquitous phenomenon in many guises. *Review of General Psychology*, *2*, 175–220.

Ofcom. (2020). *Half of UK adults exposed to false claims about coronavirus*. Ofcom.org.uk. Retrieved April 09, 2020, from https://www.ofcom.org.uk/media-use-and-attitudes/media-habits-adults/half-of-uk-adults-exposed-to-falseclaims-about-coronavirus

Porter, T., Elnakouri, A., Meyers, E. A., Shibayama, T., Jayawickreme, E., & Grossmann, I. (2022). Predictors and consequences of intellectual humility. *National Review of Psychology*, *1*, 524–533.

Putnam, R. D. (2000). *Bowling alone: The collapse and revival of American community*. Simon & Schuster.

Sunstein, C. (2001). *Republic.com*. Princeton University Press.

Thomas, E., & Sardarizadeh, S. (2024, October 25). *How a deleted LinkedIn post was weaponised and seen by millions before the Southport riot*. BBC News. https://www.bbc.co.uk/news/articles/c99v90813j5o

Traberg, C. S., Harjani, T., Basol, M., Biddlestone, M., Maertens, R., Roozenbeek, J., & van der Linden, S. (2023). Prebunking against misinformation in the modern digital age. *Managing infodemics in the 21st century: Addressing new public health challenges in the information ecosystem [Internet]*, no. 8, 99–107.

Tufekci, Z. (2018). *Twitter and tear gas: The power and fragility of networked protest*. Yale University Press.

Van der Linden, S. (2024). Countering misinformation through psychological inoculation. *Advances in Experimental Social Psychology*, *69*, 1–58.

4

CAN PRO-CLIMATE ADVOCATES STEAL POPULISM'S CLOTHES?

Matthew Paterson

University of Manchester

COMPLEX AND SHIFTING DISCOURSES

In a speech to the Alliance for Responsible Citizenship, a transnational forum for right wing populists, UK Conservative Party leader Kemi Badenoch lumped together 'pronouns, diversity policies and climate activism' as the 'poison' that was destroying Western civilisation.[1] In so doing, she exemplified that after immigration and engaging in broad 'culture wars' around questions of gender, sexuality, and race, it is climate action which provides the top target of contemporary populists.

There has of course been longstanding lobbying and organising to oppose climate policy since it hit the global agenda in the late 1980s. But until recently, this has been organised very clearly through more traditional conservative concerns about fiscal prudence and hostility to government economic regulation, and driven fairly obviously by the naked defence of the interests of fossil fuel companies.[2] Such opposition has been the principal reason the world has not moved as fast as it needs to have done to respond adequately to the climate crisis.

Since the mid-2010s, however, the opposition to climate action has increasingly transformed in a populist direction. There are various key differences in this shift in rhetoric and strategy by anti-climate forces. While the older conservative discourse was nakedly about the defence of powerful economic interests, albeit occasionally claiming to do so on behalf of 'the consumer' or 'the motorist', the populist discourse decentres these interests and makes climate policy squarely a conflict between 'elites' and 'the people'. While the older discourse had explicit climate denial as an integral part of the arguments, climate populism is less interested in climate denial and more focussed on how governments are seeking to control people through climate policy. And while conservative discourse is largely silent on questions of inequality (for the obvious reasons that conservatives don't generally think inequality is a bad thing), for populists, the unequal impacts of climate policy are a central plank of their arguments. These contrasts are ideal types of course: real-world arguments are always somewhat messier. But the contrast helps us understand what is shifting in the strategies of those opposing climate actions.

What follows draws in particular on the experience of the UK since around 2021, but it reflects patterns around the world. One distinctive aspect of the UK is that climate denial has never had much purchase in the UK, and opposition to climate action has rarely invoked such arguments, and certainly never successfully. That may change of course: indeed as populism gains ground in the UK, with the breakthrough of Reform UK in the 2024 general election, and the dragging of the UK Conservative Party firmly into populist territory (as it seeks to compete with Reform), climate denial is creeping more regularly into their discourse. And that is clearly being pushed by a transnational organisation of populists led by the USA, where climate denial remains a relatively widely-held position.

ANTI-CLIMATE POPULISM IN THE UK

In the UK, right wing populism emerged focussed on two inter-twined sets of issues: the UK's membership of the European Union, and opposition (more or less explicitly racist) to immigration into the UK. The anti-EU forces festered from the early 1990s onwards (the first anti-EU party, the Referendum Party, was founded in 1994), and grew, both within and outside the Conservative Party over the next two decades, culminating in the Brexit referendum of 2016. The rhetorical success of populists in generating the pressure for that referendum, and in narrowly winning it, was based on mobilising three types of arguments: xenophobic/racist arguments about immigration, economic resentment in 'left-behind' areas, and political arguments about the EU as undemocratic.[3]

Having achieved the goal of getting the UK out of the EU, populists of course were deprived of their principal target. While immigration persisted as a target, and racist attacks increased, populist leaders looked for other ways to continue politically. There had always been some mention of climate change in UKIP's rhetoric: their 2017 manifesto stated clearly that they would repeal the 2007 Climate Change Act and 'would support a diverse energy market based on coal, nuclear, shale gas, conventional gas, oil, solar and hydro'.[4] Rhetorically, there is no attack on climate science, but rather a focus on energy security and bringing down energy prices, and a particular push to open up fracking in the UK.

But in around 2021, climate change became a much more persistent target of right-wing populists in the UK. The key moment was the formation of the Net Zero Scrutiny Group of Conservative MPs in October of that year.[5] Led by Steve Baker and Craig Mackinlay, the NZSG opened up a full-frontal attack on net zero as a policy goal. Net zero – the goal to have achieved as near to zero greenhouse gas emissions as possible, and all remaining emissions 'netted' by enhanced carbon sinks or direct CO_2 capture – had only been established as the legal target in the UK in late 2019 as Teresa May left office as Prime Minister. Over the next two years, the NZSG, along with allies outside parliament, notably in Nigel Farage and Richard Tice in Reform UK, and in the climate denier organisation the Global Warming Policy Foundation, which established 'Net Zero Watch' also in October 2021, spearheaded a series of rhetorical attacks on climate policy, drawing directly from the populist rhetoric that had succeeded in the Brexit campaign.[6]

The attacks mirrored the threefold political, cultural, and economic arguments underpinning the Brexit campaign.

CLIMATE POPULIST RHETORIC

The political attack on net zero was that it was being developed by undemocratic technocrats imposing their control on ordinary citizens. This is classic populist rhetoric where the world is divided into 'the elites' and 'the people'. They attacked the Climate Change Committee (CCC)[7] as incompetent, drastically under-estimating the costs of pursuing net zero. They argued that the policy support for heat pumps (essential to decarbonising home heating) was 'out of touch, net zero madness',[8] and made similar claims about support for electric vehicles (EVs) and low traffic neighbourhoods.

Culturally, populists have targeted net zero as attack on people's 'way of life'. These attacks have mostly been focussed on transport. The petrol and diesel ban was framed as 'dictatorship',[9] restricting people's rights to drive the vehicles they wanted, while low traffic neighbourhoods have been attacked (sometimes physically) as infringements on car drivers' freedom,[10] and the idea of 15-minute cities (discussed later) spawned a whole raft of conspiracy theories about the attempt to control citizens through net zero-oriented transport policy.[11] These arguments are clearly different to the racist arguments populists use to oppose immigration but nevertheless share a core of a sense of a 'British way of life' threatened by a threat that is framed as coming 'from outside'.

It is however in arguments mobilising economic resentment that populists have been most effective and vocal. Net zero has been framed overall as an attack on the poor, even at times specifically an 'attack on the working class'.[12] Most policies that they have focussed upon they have been associated with increasing costs with particular on low-income households. Thus, the fracking moratorium should be reversed, especially in the aftermath of the Russian invasion of Ukraine, to increase domestic natural gas supply and (so they claim) lower household gas bills. Support or mandates for heat pumps, EVs, subsidies for renewable energy, and the petrol and diesel ban, all increase costs for householders and car drivers.

The petrol and diesel ban was framed thus: 'Our politicians have made this arbitrary choice for its citizens without a political mandate and the most vulnerable and poorest in our society will never be able to afford an electric vehicle'.[13]

While the populist turn in UK climate politics started life as a small group, and many of the arguments seemed to go nowhere (notably the attack on the fracking moratorium, which has sunk without trace after its brief heyday in Liz Truss' government), it has had surprising reach. After a year or so, by late 2022 it looked to be subsiding, but in 2023, with the Conservative government under Rishi Sunak increasingly desperate about its electoral prospects as a general election loomed, it got a lease of life in the Uxbridge and South Ruislip by-election in July 2023. That constituency lay just outside the proposed expansion to London's Ultra Low Emissions Zone (ULEZ). While ULEZ had not been a key target of the populists in 2021–22, it fit the logic perfectly. The Conservatives adopted the populist tactics in Uxbridge as a pilot project, and, narrowly winning the by-election, concluded it was worth continuing. As a consequence, and especially regarding the aspects of climate policy focussed on transport, they shifted tack to framing themselves as 'on the side of motorists',[14] and Labour as the 'party of Just Stop Oil'.[15] This culture war framing co-existed with a continued commitment to net zero by the Conservatives, and subsided in practice in the run-up to the 2024 general election. But since then, and with the election of a new leader in Kemi Badenoch, the Conservatives have fully embraced a populist position opposing climate action. Badenoch describes herself explicitly as a 'net zero sceptic'[16] and shares platforms regularly (as in the quote that starts this chapter) with a broad swath of climate denier organisations.

CLIMATE, POPULISM, MISINFORMATION

Misinformation is important to the populist's attack on climate policy, but not really in the way that it is commonly understood. They have started to be bolder in the last two years in making climate denier arguments, but it remains a very difficult sell in the UK context at least. And as the impacts of the climate crisis get ever more palpable across the globe, it is ever less effective as an argument. Trump's assault on climate policy is notable that it is perhaps less about climate denial in the strict sense, and more about what Cara Daggett calls 'climate refusal', which is not passive in ignoring climate change, pretending it isn't real, but is active and angry in 'intensifying fossil fuel systems to the last moment'.[17] Trump's removal of climate change from all government websites and policy mentions isn't about pretending climate doesn't exist, but insisting that it must not be allowed to be part of the US governments' considerations.

What is more important in climate populism is misinformation about the design and implications of climate policy. There are obvious and crude examples of this, of which most egregious have been the nonsense arguments about 15-minute cities which manifestly and wilfully misrepresented a proposal to plan urban areas so everyone should have access to basic services within a 15-minute walk, transmogrifying it into a claim that people would be controlled and prevented leaving that area. But they extend into misleading claims about for example the costs of renewable energy and the drivers of the 'cost of living crisis', or whether fracking or expanded domestic oil and gas consumption would actually reduce household energy bills.

But here again we must be cautious. In the most important part of the populist attack on climate policy in the UK – the mobilisation of economic resentments about class inequality and how climate policy instruments intensify poverty – there is an important grain of truth. The upfront costs of heat pumps are considerable – noticeably more than average UK household savings. The costs of EVs are coming down, but they remain noticeable more expensive than petrol cars. The various forms of household subsidies for housing retrofits, which have ranged since the 1970s for rooftop solar water heaters, loft insulation, double glazing, cavity wall insulation, through to the Feed-in-Tariff for solar pV, high efficiency boilers, and now heat pumps, have, as a consequence, been regressive in their consequences. They have created a situation where well-off UK citizens now live in warm, relatively cheap to heat, well-insulated housing, and those on low-income housing live in poorly insulated, cold, damp, and expensive housing. They have also occurred at the same time as widening income and wealth inequalities across the UK, and where private landlording, almost eliminated by the 1970s, has re-emerged with a vengeance, often with small landlords owning one or two properties to supplement retirement income, who don't have the capital to retrofit houses. This is a context ripe for effective populist mobilising, where they don't need to rely on misinformation (even if they do so at times) but simply point out how climate policy is in fact making inequalities worse.

BUILDING THE PRO-CLIMATE POPULIST MESSAGE

If there is a single message of this chapter, it is that populism is an important sign that the old forms of political life had an important lack. Populists have been an important response to the lack of responsiveness of formally democratic institutions, which seemed increasingly detached from everyday lives. Mainstream political parties have increasingly become what political scientists call 'cartel parties' – small organisations detached from any social base they may claim to represent, competing with each other only within a very narrow ideological band. Policy has been developed within that narrow band, with cosy relationships between governments, parties, and business, with occasional input from insider non-governmental organisations. Voting for populist parties is as much as anything a rejection of this status quo.

In many Western countries, such populist mobilisation has for the most part been through a xenophobic, racist lens, where populism seeks to define 'the people' in narrow exclusionary terms. But this need not be the case.[18] Populism was originally coined as a term to characterise largely progressive, agrarian movements in the USA and Canada in the late 19th century, where the 'elites' that dominated and oppressed 'the people' were large corporate monopolies or oligopolies, and their allies in government. Populist reform meant destroying monopolies and gaining better deals for farmers and workers.

The implication of this for climate change is not then to defend the technocratic forms of climate policy and governance that have prevailed. Indeed, the success of populists in opposing specific aspects of climate policy is instructive for those promoting climate action: climate action can indeed itself be framed as a project for 'the people', and that in practice, global elites are systematically organising the world through continued fossil fuel extraction and use, to the detriment of the livelihoods and interests of the global majority. Green leaders have increasingly themselves accordingly adopted populist rhetoric – not with foreigners as the 'enemy', but rather the fossil fuel industry itself and their allies in government.[19]

Building this pro-climate populist message is crucial to furthering climate action since the consensus-oriented, technocratic governance of climate that has prevailed so far has provided ample grounds for populism to emerge, and cannot effectively defeat or undermine it. But a message that climate change itself is the product of undemocratic elites in business and politics that have destroyed the life chances of people around the world, combined with imaginative climate policy design to deliver widespread social benefits of climate action, has the potential to be powerful enough to defeat right-wing populists.

ENDNOTES

1. Quinn, B. (2025, February 17). Kemi Badenoch says 'western civilisation will be lost' if Tory party fails. *The Guardian.* https://www.theguardian.com/politics/2025/feb/17/kemi-badenoch-western-civilisation-will-be-lost-tory-party-fails.

2. Newell, P., & Paterson, M. (1998). A climate for business: Global warming, the state and capital. *Review of International Political Economy,* 5(4), 679–703.

3. Sobolewska, M., & Ford, R. (2020). *Brexitland.* Cambridge University Press.

4. UKIP. (2017). *Britain together: UKIP 2017 manifesto* (p. 56). UK Independence Party.

5. Paterson, M., Wilshire, S., & Tobin, P. (2024). The rise of anti-net zero populism in the UK: Comparing rhetorical strategies for climate policy dismantling. *Journal of Comparative Policy Analysis: Research and Practice,* 26(3–4), 332–350.

6. The account of the NZSG's rhetoric that follows in the next few paragraphs draws on Paterson et al. (2024). See also Atkins, E. (2022). 'Bigger than Brexit': Exploring right-wing populism and net-zero policies in the United Kingdom. *Energy Research & Social Science*, *90*, 102681.

7. The CCC was established under the Climate Change Act which both provides evidence and advice to government but also monitors progress under the five-year carbon budgets the Act requires governments to establish and pursue to reach net zero by 2050.

8. Tice, R. (2022, March 6). *Renewables have role to play amongst diverse energy sources & new technologies. In meantime, UK shale gas cheapest, most reliable, much less CO2 than importing gas and owned by us all!* [Tweet]. Twitter. https://twitter.com/TiceRichard/status/1500525165339455489.

9. Reeves, F. (2022, April 18). *"This is dictatorship": Drivers savage 2030 petrol and diesel car ban.* Express.Co.Uk. https://www.express.co.uk/life-style/cars/1597234/petrol-diesel-car-ban-2030-electric-vehicles-angry-drivers-reaction.

10. Elledge, J. (2022, April 22). Arson, death threats and 'eco-crazy councils': Low-traffic neighbourhoods are dividing England. *The Guardian.* https://www.theguardian.com/commentisfree/2022/apr/22/england-low-traffic-neighbourhoods-provoke-fury-local-elections

11. Partington, R. (2023, February 26). Tackling the 15-minute cities conspiracy means fixing inequality. *The Guardian.* https://www.theguardian.com/business/2023/feb/26/uk-economic-uncertainty-adds-fuel-to-fire-for-conspiracy-theorists

12. Chillingsworth, L. (2022, January 17). *Petrol and diesel car ban in 2030 is an attack 'on the working class.'* Express.Co.Uk. https://www.express.co.uk/life-style/cars/1551244/petrol-diesel-car-ban-electric-vehicle-ownership

13. Express reader, quoted in Reeves, "This is dictatorship".

14. Malnick, E. (2023, July 29). *I am on motorists' side, says Sunak as he orders review of anti-car schemes.* The Telegraph. https://www.telegraph.co.uk/politics/2023/07/29/rishi-sunak-on-motorists-side-review-anti-car-policies/; Paterson, M. (2023, September 5). *The Conservatives have seized on cars as a political wedge – it's a bet on public turning against climate action.* The Conversation. http://theconversation.com/the-conservatives-have-seized-on-cars-as-a-political-wedge-its-a-bet-on-public-turning-against-climate-action-211244

15. Thompson, A., & Mason, C. (2023, June 7). *Just Stop Oil eco-zealots writing Labour energy policy—Sunak*. BBC News. https://www.bbc.com/news/uk-politics-65839733

16. Sethi, P. (n.d.). *Kemi Badenoch's climate scepticism: A growing problem for the Conservative Party and its voters*. Grantham Research Institute on Climate Change and the Environment. Retrieved February 18, 2025, from https://www.lse.ac.uk/granthaminstitute/news/kemi-badenochs-climate-scepticism-a-growing-problem-for-the-conservative-party-and-its-voters/

17. Daggett, C. (2018). Petro-masculinity: Fossil Fuels and Authoritarian Desire. *Millennium*, 47(1), 25–44, at p.42.

18. Mudde, C., & Kaltwasser, C. R. (2017). *Populism: A very short introduction* (p. 2). Oxford University Press.

19. Lucas, C. (2025, February 7). It's time for climate populism. *New Statesman*. https://www.newstatesman.com/environment/2025/02/its-time-for-climate-populism

LIBERATION THROUGH EDUCATION

5

GETTING DOWN TO EARTH

David Lambert

UCL Institute of Education, London

TEACHERS TACKLING A NEW EPOCH

This chapter is written from the point of view of an educationist coming to terms with the enormity of what faces teachers in the times in which we are living. Teachers have always served the educational needs of their students in the context of society's changing priorities and goals. The inevitable tensions in this arrangement have also always existed, and in a sense 'crisis' has never been far away – in teacher recruitment, how teachers are trained, how education success is measured and so on. But there is something different and indeed frightening about the seeming steady slide into the dark epoch which is beginning to take shape. In geological terms, debates continue about whether the 'current epoch' can be classed as the Anthropocene – the 'human epoch' which coincides with the advent of industrialisation and urbanisation, and the rapacious appetite for burning fossil fuels. On top of this we can add the impacts of more recent technological developments resulting in the information revolution and artificial intelligence. These, to put it mildly, have changed individuals' and society's relationships, not only with each other but ultimately with the Earth.

DARKNESS LOOMING OVER THE PUBLIC SQUARE

There was an incident at a town hall meeting (24 February 2025) in Coeur d'Alene in the state of Idaho, USA, which for me symbolised a key dimension of the current epoch. From an uploaded video of the incident on Facebook and from various reports about it in the press,[1] we learned that a woman had been forcibly evicted from the meeting convened by the local Republican Central Committee to discuss President Trump's Orwellian-sounding Department of Government Efficiency (DOGE) led by Elon Musk. During the noisy kerfuffle surrounding her removal by two men, the emcee of the meeting exclaimed that 'your voice is meaningless right now … I can talk over all of you'.

The incident, which took place over seven thousand kilometres away from my desk and is in some ways somewhat innocuous, struck a chord. It seemed to sum up some of the darkness that looms over the so-called 'public square' that Musk claims to want to defend but in fact is helping destroy.[2] In this chapter I seek to analyse the state of affairs by which public debate has been so distracted and diminished[3] that even the global climate emergency, the existential threat to hundreds of millions of people around the world and which the President of the USA refers to as a 'hoax', is simply ignored. Indeed, the DOGE drive is actually undermining government capacity for monitoring and responding to the impacts of climate change.[4]

I shall also try to outline the parameters of an *educational* response to the fundamental challenge before us which in essence requires us to hold on to and teach the notion of *truthfulness* in a world of post-truth politics. In this context, Roger Waters' sad (and somewhat ludicrous) lament, 'we don't need no education' takes on new potency – for what shall we teach if, as another popular 1970s lyric goes, 'nothing really matters, anyone can see'? That surely is the darkest idea of them all.

YOUR VOICE IS MEANINGLESS?

The woman at the town hall meeting was protesting at the injustices arising from heavy handed and precipitous policy making.

She was put down by an official with a platform, microphone and loudspeaker. The official rejoiced in the power of the moment while the woman was rendered powerless. The incident was profoundly unedifying in that political and due process was reduced to name calling, bullying and physical duress.

The establishment in the USA, in real time before our very eyes, of an oligarchy controlled (for the moment) by a President who is a convicted felon and sexual predator and who has made lying his modus operandi, appears to be epochal. The impact of the Trump phenomenon extends far beyond domestic US politics and, despite the commonplace portrayal of Trump as an unsavoury and unhinged buffoon; it is deeply ideological.

Post truth politics is now with us. Denial of reason – whether this relates, for example, to anthropogenic climate change or the Russian invasion of Ukraine in 2022 – appears to have become widely acceptable (because it serves the ideological purpose). The way social media algorithms work means that the voting public tends to live more intensely in sealed echo chambers in which we only hear like-minded views and prejudices. Lies are denied, finessed and then embedded as 'common sense' truth.

Furthermore, despite Trump's evident lack of understanding of much of how the world works – its biological systems, its economics, its politics … in short its 'rules-based' systems – he has ploughed on and garnered popularity through his 'transactional' approach in which everything is reduced to a business deal. Betraying allies, taking control of the military, undermining the independent judiciary and other institutions (especially educational) and dominating communication via X and Meta are ultimately all about accumulating profit. A Trumpian world is made up solely of winners and losers. The latter are disparaged, belittled or simply ignored. As the man said in Congress (March 2025): 'make America rich again'.

In this broader context, critical voices are indeed rendered meaningless in the sense that, as in the Idaho town hall meeting, they are simply drowned out and extinguished. Part of the strategy, which includes waging astonishingly bigoted 'wars on woke' designed to provoke distraction, is to create cacophony. Such a wall of noise is in the interests of neither democracy nor education, because (to shift metaphors) it makes it so hard to see the wood for the trees.

NOTHING REALLY MATTERS?

In most educational settings teachers agree that voices are far from meaningless. Pedagogic techniques are employed deliberately to encourage student voices to be heard. In communicating ideas and information students can make meaning, express their understanding of phenomena, challenge themselves and others and thus perceive multiple perspectives. Students can learn in these ways, even when classrooms become literally, or even metaphorically, cacophonic. But surely, in educational settings, this is to set a low bar and is insufficiently ambitious.

As Gert Biesta[5] has reminded us, we can take it as read that students can learn, as can other animals and increasingly these days machines. However, the human animal is distinguished by its ability to be taught rather than merely programmed or trained. In this sense, the most profound issue in education is to assert clearly that some things really do matter and that the curriculum question (what shall we teach?) is paramount. In the current epoch one of the things that really does matter is truthfulness.

Truthfulness, as an idea and process, can be taught.[6] It also needs to be practised. But truthfulness about what exactly? In the current epoch, which has inherited the postmodern suspicion of grand narratives, the idea of truth has itself become so fluid as to become almost meaningless. We are encouraged to talk about truth as if it were something you can define solely for yourself, on your own terms and determined by your experience of the world and/or your identity. Biesta argues that the educational deficit in this scenario is '… a kind of 'loss' of the world'.[7] in which perspectives *on the* world replace knowledge and understanding *of the* world.

Biesta argues that the difficult, painstaking task of helping students 'arrive' in the world is lost behind a cloud of competing standpoints, in which truth-telling is reduced to no more than expressing opinion. And, when provided with evidence to the contrary this can simply be ignored or denied as 'fake news' (a variation of the Nazi slogan, *Lügenpresse*). This is the favoured get out clause for demagogues and bullies. Education, at least in democratic contexts, must always strive for something better.

WHAT REALLY MATTERS: CLIMATE CHANGE

As a geographer in education, I like the widely used description of the purpose of my subject – geography helps us 'make sense of the world'. In fact, this definition can probably apply to all subjects: from literature to sciences and from mathematics to the arts – all explorations of these subjects contribute in distinctive ways to 'making sense of the world'. But in geography, all of humanity, its societies and their interactions with planet Earth become the object of study. As the mass of geographical information in circulation appears to expand exponentially the question of what to teach in schools does not become any easier to address. And that is even before taking on the question of truthfulness.

The most significant phenomenon to grasp in attempting to make sense of the world in the current epoch is climate change. Bruno Latour, with ambition and self-conscious 'bluntness', introduced his remarkable book on 'geo-social politics' thus:

> *The hypothesis is that we can understand nothing about the politics of the last 50 years if we do not put the question of climate change and its denial front and center. Without the idea that we have entered into a New Climatic Regime, we cannot understand the explosion of inequalities, the scope of deregulation, the critique of globalisation, or, more importantly, the panicky desire to return to the old protections of the nation-state – a desire that is identified, quite inaccurately, with the "rise of popularism".*[8]

Latour's concern is with grand political trajectories and not with education itself. However, 'external' political sentiment clearly exerts influence on education including how the idea of education itself is understood. Neoliberal politics of the last 40 years or so have clearly shaped education policy-making globally. Thus, in the UK context, for example, Blair's famous three priorities for his 1997 government (Education, Education and Education) seemed to signify education becoming key in his economic policy making, driven by 'national strategies' and the reification of league tables and competition.

Latour's commentary confronts us with the realisation that 'progress' along normalised, neoliberal economic trajectories are leading to ecological catastrophe, signalled very well by the surpassing, in 2024, of the 1.5 degrees above pre-industrial levels average global temperature. Perhaps with this in mind, over 150 thought leaders have attempted to influence the national curriculum review in England, arguing that the curriculum response to climate change has been 'inadequate'. They go on to write: 'More comprehensive inclusion of climate and environmental sustainability in the National Curriculum will ensure that all schools are required to educate young people on these issues and to ensure that they leave school prepared for the future.'[9]

Of course, this is serious and important advice. But I believe it barely touches the sides of the problem that Latour has helped identify. In its business-as-usual manner and tone there is no recognition of the denialist Trumpian shift.

THE DANGER OF OTHERWORLDLY POLITICS

In his vision of geo-social politics in response to existential crisis in the current epoch, Latour rejects long-standing political binaries like left-right, traditional-modern and global-local. He encourages us to grasp that choosing sides in these terms is akin to fiddling while Rome burns. Thus, whether from left or right in politics, growth is still growth and it emits CO_2. Furthermore, traditional ways of life that eschew the modern cannot support life on Earth as we now know it, neither qualitatively nor quantitatively. And reverting to local knowledge and concerns for sustainable solutions without taking account of universal understandings (of earth systems, for example) is pie in the sky. The onward march of progress, driven by what Latour designates as the universalist, 'global attractor' (and which has given us the climate emergency), cannot simply be replaced by reverting to simpler, smaller scale living – Latour's 'local attractor'. Societies need insights and wisdoms from both, but guided by an entirely new alternative 'attractor'.

Meanwhile, Latour points to popular perceptions of the impotence of politics-as-usual in the current epoch. Such disaffection has become the launch pad for what he calls *otherworldly* alternative attractors. These are politics based on conspiracies and misinformation artfully exploited by some politicians wrapped up with the old populist favourites – for example, appealing to the comforting warmth of national identity and stoking fears concerning the defence of borders. The common stance of such politics is anti-immigration, frequently exploiting the racist sentiments of the Great Replacement theory.[10]

Otherworldly politics, supremely epitomised by Trump, is at its heart the expression of denial. Denialism includes acknowledging many of the processes and procedures upon which democracy depends (crucially of course the separation of judicial, legislative and executive powers). It includes turning away from the painstaking post-WW2 attempt to establish rules-based international relations. But it is the denial of anthropogenic climate change that is the core signature of otherworldly politics. Indeed, according to Latour, Trump's asinine call to 'drill baby drill' is in effect 'a declaration of war authorising the occupation of all other countries, if not with troops, at least with CO_2, which America retains the right to emit'.[11]

THE VITAL IMPORTANCE OF *DOWN TO EARTH POLITICS*

The alternative attractor (to the existing global, local or otherworldly options) proposed by Latour – providing the arc or impetus of new geo-social politics for the current epoch – is the *terrestrial*. This term is deliberately chosen to make a distinction between planetary Earth and what is termed its Critical Zone, a 'thin bio-film no thicker than a few kilometres up and down, from which we cannot escape'.[12] This zone is where we all (more than only humans) live – cells, plants, bugs, animals and people – and is where Latour argues 'down to Earth' politics should direct its attention.

Down to Earth politics obliges us to re-examine taken for granted assumptions about knowledge and ways of knowing the Critical Zone. Entire cosmologies which have in the modern era been discarded by modernists as archaic or primitive now take on new relevance as we seek from indigenous and traditional communities, both past and present, wisdom about, for example, the link between people, society and the soil. To be clear, this is not a naïve retreat from the modernist trajectories to an imagined alternative of local solutions for global problems. As Latour writes,

> *to move ahead in the effort to describe the geo-social conflicts, it is clear we cannot do without science and reason, but also that we must both broaden and limit the reach of the empirical sciences.*[13]

I think Latour's insights on the kind of political reorientation required to counter the otherworldly politics of denial have intriguing educational implications.

FUTURE 3 CURRICULUM AND PEDAGOGY

In short, Latour's call for the radical decoupling of politics (both left and right) from both modernising and traditional attractors (the global and local respectively), and to replace this with the terrestrial, links to the growing recent interest in re-imagining future school curriculum scenarios.[14] Young and Muller's fundamental distinction between Future 1 and Future 2 curriculum scenarios,[15] neither of which on its own can be considered adequate to serving the needs of high quality, responsive educational encounters in this day and age, resulted in their call for Future 3 alternatives. The concept was developed a little in Young and Lambert's 2014 collaboration,[16] but it has taken a decade to begin to see its greater potential.[17] In a similar manner to Latour, a new trajectory for school teaching can be proposed, guided by a renewed interest in the hitherto neglected idea of education itself and a critical development of enabling powerful knowledge. In this sense, powerful knowledge is the 'Critical Zone' of educational encounters.

Front and centre of Future 3 scenarios is powerful knowledge and powerful ways of knowing. The radical implications, not least in relation to how teachers are prepared (actually, how teaching itself is understood) is captured by the following list. Future 3 scenarios

- ask: 'who are we teaching?' This is to acknowledge and respect students' lived experiences, aspirations and drive.

- seek to show the 'power' of different ways of seeing and thinking (thinking geographically, historically, mathematically, etc).

- acknowledge epistemological diversity – that there are different ways of 'knowing' the world. For example: recognising that although learning through experience is legitimate, it is different from being taught to see the world as an object of study.

- seek to achieve high levels of epistemic quality, notably by demonstrating the dynamic nature of knowledge development ('how do we know what we claim to know?').

- drop the metaphor of delivery of knowledge in teaching, in favour of engagement with knowledge and in particular how we can judge its 'truthfulness'.

AND FINALLY, BACK TO IDAHO

In the disrupted town hall meeting in Idaho, the platform proclaimed 'your voice is meaningless right now'. The frustration felt by the woman was obvious to behold, not only in how those with power in the space sought to bully and silence her, but by the wider, *otherworldly* political moment.

Educationists must shape a response to the current epoch and do what they can to help society avoid the politics of denial. In this essay, I have argued that this response should rest upon a radical review of the fundamental curriculum question of what to teach.[18] At the heart of this response lie knowledge questions such as those implied by the above list, seeking to expand and finesse the notion of powerful knowledge and a core commitment to truthfulness.

ENDNOTES

1. For example, https://www.newsweek.com/protesters-republican-event-told-voice-meaningless-idaho-2035020.

2. https://www.washingtonpost.com/politics/2024/11/27/musk-twitter-bluesky-trump/

3. https://www.nytimes.com/2025/03/06/us/politics/trump-democracy.html?smid=nytcore-ios-share&referringSource=articleShare

4. https://abcnews.go.com/US/doge-now-access-noaas-systems-reviewing-dei-program/story?id=118493866

5. Biesta, G. (2024). From the point where I stand to the place where I can be found: the critique of perspectival reason as philosophy for education. *Educational Philosophy and Theory*, 1–15. https://doi.org/10.1080/00131857.2024.2435336.

6. I write *truthfulness* to distinguish this idea from teaching children and young people to tell 'the truth' and not tell lies. Honest explanations imply more than not lying. Honest accounts of the current epoch require a commitment to truth telling. Young people can be taught how to judge the truthfulness of assertions, evidence and arguments.

7. Biesta, G. (2024). From the point where I stand to the place where I can be found: the critique of perspectival reason as philosophy for education. *Educational Philosophy and Theory*, 1–15. https://doi.org/10.1080/00131857.2024.2435336.

8. Latour, B. (2018). *Down to earth: Politics in the new climatic regime* (p. 2). Polity.

9. https://www.globalactionplan.org.uk/news/open-letter-to-the-secretary-of-state-for-educationsustainability-and-climate-change-education-in-the-national-curriculum

10. https://theconversation.com/what-is-the-great-replacement-theory-a-scholar-of-race-relations-explains-224835

11. Latour, B. (2018). *Down to earth: Politics in the new climatic regime* (p. 84). Polity.

12. Latour, B. (2020). *Critical zones: The science and politics of landing on earth* (p. 6). MIT Press. http://www.bruno-latour.fr/node/838.html.

13. Latour, B. (2018). *Down to earth: Politics in the new climatic regime* (p. 78). Polity.

14. See for example, Béneker, T., Bladh, G., & Lambert, D. (2023). Exploring 'Future three' curriculum scenarios in practice: Learning from the GeoCapabilities project. *The Curriculum Journal*, 35(3), 396–411. This paper develops the idea of 'Future 3" curriculum thinking first posited by Young and Muller in 2010.

15. Young, M., & Muller, J. (2010). Three educational scenarios for the future: Lessons from the sociology of knowledge. *European Journal*

of Education, 45(1), 11–27.https://doi.org/10.1111/j.1465-3435. 2009.01413.x.

16. Young, M., & Lambert, D (with C. Roberts, and M. Roberts). (2014). *Knowledge and the future school: Curriculum and social justice.* Bloomsbury Academic.

17. See for example, McPhail, G., Pountney, R., & Wheelahan, L. (Eds.) (2024). *Emerging perspectives from social realism on knowledge and education.* Routledge.

18. Muller, J. (2022). Powerful knowledge, disciplinary knowledge, curriculum knowledge: Educational knowledge in question. *International Research in Geographical and Environmental Education, 32*(1), 20–34. https://doi.org/10.1080/10382046.2022.2058349; Deng, Z. (2025). Social realism, knowledge and curriculum: furthering the conversation. *Journal of Curriculum Studies, 57*(1), 1–13. https://doi.org/10.1080/00220272.20 25.2456954.

6

SCIENCE LITERACY BEATS MISINFORMATION

Andrew Morris

UCL Institute of Education

PUBLIC UNDERSTANDING OF SCIENCE

We didn't really need a pandemic to show how much we all need science; but it certainly helped. We were awestruck at the speed and ingenuity of medical staff and vaccine makers but, equally, were shaken by the work of mischief makers and conspiracy theorists. When a president suggests COVID-19 could be treated with disinfectant,[1] and his followers applaud, the dangers of a scientifically naïve public are all too apparent. Without some concept of the infection process, exponential growth and relative risk, it's all too easy to side with those opposing vaccination and mask wearing.

But, of course, scientific concepts have always been poorly understood across the population as a whole. Damaging foodstuffs have been gleefully consumed, ecosystems negligently treated and even the foundational concept of evolution widely denied. Ignorance of science and maths is socially acceptable, even amongst the otherwise well-educated. Young children begin life with a profound sense of curiosity (as parents know only too well), probing the natural world and testing physical structures around them. At some point in the secondary school curriculum, however, many become disenchanted with science and drop the subject as soon as possible. As a consequence, many adults lack basic concepts needed to navigate an increasingly technical world. This leaves them prey to false reasoning and simplistic ideas about cause and effect.

The reasons for the failure of science education to serve the majority have been debated for decades in countries across the world. The difficulty begins in the teenage years when large numbers begin to switch off science at school, particularly girls in physics.[2,3] A 2024 study found that girls are 60% less likely to continue studying science after 16 than boys with similar grades.[4] A 2024 analysis of data on science in UK secondary schools concludes 'that decades of policies along with well-funded and well-targeted initiatives have had little (if any) impact on uptake to studying the core science subjects'.[5] For most of the population, of course, school is but a distant memory; yet many adults, despite their negative recollections of science as a school subject, retain a genuine curiosity about scientific ideas. Surveys consistently show that attitudes to science, and a desire to engage with it, remain positive in the adult population.[6,7]

My own experience, as a teacher of teenagers, was that the problem lies, not with learners or their advisers, but with the way in which science is represented and communicated at secondary school level. It's simply not appropriate for the majority. With its emphasis on memorising factual knowledge at the expense of deeper understanding, and its lack of connection with their everyday experiences, it is not surprising that so many young people disengage. A major international study backs up this personal impression[8]: 'school science education has consistently failed to develop anything other than a naïve understanding of the nature of science .... [it] lacks sufficient exemplars that illustrate the application of science to the contemporary world'.

Today, in a world of misinformation and populist politics, the 'naive understanding' identified above, poses an ever more serious risk. Without some basic concepts – genes, cells, viruses, molecules, chemical reactions, energy, power generation, the water cycle – it's hard to make sense of the politics of today's increasingly technical challenges. Appeals to 'common sense' in place of expert knowledge become attractive.

It's with this sense of the societal consequences of poor understanding of science that I decided to look for an alternative approach to science teaching that connected more directly with people's real lives. I set up a discussion-based course for adults, outside the school system, in the humanities department of an adult education centre in London. It was to draw on the curiosity and life experiences of participants, free from exam syllabuses. This chapter draws on the experience of this initiative to illustrate ways in which scientific ideas can actively engage and inspire people, whatever their previous experience of the subject.

AN EXPERIMENTAL SCHEME

A series of sessions was organised for people who wouldn't usually be looking for a science-based course. They were invited to participate in a discussion-based introduction to scientific ideas based on their questions and observations, rather than a pre-determined syllabus. The idea worked well, running for many years, then moving out into cafés and online settings, subsequently.

Topics

The issues people raise in free discussion often start from an observation they have made or a query they have: 'why do I look a bit like my parents'; 'how do all flowers of a kind come out at the same time'; 'why should you avoid making tea with re-boiled water?'; 'why are clouds white?' for example. Sometimes they are driven by public affairs, such as legalising drugs or the onset of violent warfare; but they may also arise from pure fascination: 'gravity is amazing – holding the Moon in place without being connected'; 'all the activity inside a cell - it's so intricate, it's mind-boggling'.

By allowing people to explore scientific ideas in their own way, the paths followed differ dramatically from those in a logically planned exam syllabus. One discussion, which began with news about a close encounter with an asteroid, soon developed into an explanation of orbits, which, in turn, led on to how philosophers and scientists have understood the meaning of force over the centuries, culminating in the unexpected question: 'what is the force of a sneeze?'. Biological forces within our bodies proved as interesting as those that moved the heavens! As this example shows, approaching scientific concepts by drawing on real life experience means the rigid boundaries between academic disciplines break down. Enquiries often move comfortably between them. Colour on a TV screen once launched a discussion about pixels and wavelengths of light, but soon moved onto the role of the eye, lenses, retinae, optic nerves and the brain, ending with the philosophical question of what it means to 'see'.

Teacher and Learner

When discussion is allowed to stray across the conventional boundaries of physics, chemistry and biology, the role of the teacher is altered. Complete and precise factual knowledge is no longer a possibility. Nor is it of paramount importance in today's world, with so much available at the press of button. What science teachers have to offer, however, is much more than specialised, factual knowledge. They are familiar with the language and culture of science and have a broad sense of the landscape of major concepts – energy, forces, elements, atoms, reactions, cells and evolution. They also have an appreciation of scientific values and methods: scepticism, measurement, testing and evidence. In a more open-ended discussion format, the tutor employs this broader understanding, acting as a facilitator, helping people navigate their way through unfamiliar ideas, building-up a schema of basic concepts and ruling out obviously false ideas. The search for explanation becomes a joint enterprise drawing on external sources of information. In this dialogic way, not only is a full range of topics and discussion paths opened, but the learner develops a sense of empowerment, and the tutor ceases worrying about being caught out.

In one memorable discussion about ice floating on water, it became clear that the basic concept of density was not understood, nor were volume, weight or mass. Following an exhaustive in-depth discussion about the molecular make-up of matter, one participant summed it up in her own words 'so volume is how much space something takes up; density is how spread out the molecules are, and weight is how much all the molecules weigh'. Not a perfect statement, scientifically, but it helped develop the concept for everyone.

It is true that, in the absence of a planned syllabus, coverage of scientific issues can be rather haphazard in the short term. Over time, however, by raising motivation to stick at it, fundamental concepts recur, often arising from quite different starting points. The meaning of energy, for example may arise in photosynthesis, global warming or quantum levels. Connections begin to be made, and a map of fundamental concepts begins to emerge.

Outcomes

This approach motivates people to engage with science who had previously missed out, especially women – it is appealing. It encourages participants to engage more widely with science resources in the community: joining astronomy clubs, attending science talks, visiting exhibitions, festivals and museums. TV documentaries and radio broadcasts become more attractive and are often followed up more deeply in discussions.

Less obvious is the increasing confidence that people develop – feeling more able to join in discussions and challenge misconceptions or bluster in others. In one episode, a married woman, having raised the question 'what is electric charge?' in a discussion, was surprised later to discover that her husband's knowledge of their car battery was no better than hers, despite his confident sounding talk.

Feeling safe to explore concepts without shame, many participants remain engaged for a long time – often many years. This enables knowledge and understanding to gradually mature. Opinions about controversial issues, such as genetic engineering, hormone therapy and fossil fuels become better informed and, as a consequence, more nuanced. Concepts acquired in earlier discussions get built upon, so that later questions probe more deeply.

For example, during her chemotherapy treatment for cancer, one participant read about what was happening to her and discussed it with the group. Unsure about what lymph nodes were, the group took up the topic, exploring the role of B and T cells in fighting disease and ultimately the role of the adaptive immune system as a whole.

With increasing experience of testing out one's own preconceptions in the presence of others, attitudes also become more sophisticated. A more doubting stance, a quest for evidence and appetite for complexity develop. For example, medical and pharmaceutical interventions begin to be seen as carrying inevitable risks, to be weighed against their merits. Evolving theories about gravitation begin to erode the sense of finality about scientific knowledge; the presence of uncertainty in fundamental physics explodes preconceptions. By pushing scientific thought to its boundaries with history, sociology, philosophy and religion, discussions also bring out the limits of science: its restriction to the testable; its representation of reality through models that are provisional.

WIDER IMPLICATIONS

Better Scientific Understanding

The observations described above, from one small experiment in adult learning, are not, in themselves, a recipe for the reform of science education. However, the insights they offer into the way in which adults engage (or disengage) with scientific ideas provide clues as to how the general public might become better informed.

Clearly, many current social and political problems across the world entail misunderstandings, or even rejection, of scientific knowledge. Public perceptions, with their mix of semi-digested knowledge, misunderstandings and hearsay, were major social and psychological factors affecting the success of policy interventions during the COVID-19 pandemic. Likewise for other political and social issues: protecting biodiversity; greening energy supply; reducing sugar intake. The consequences of pushing so many young people away from science at school are serious.

Encouraging Engagement with Science

Formal science teaching often minimises exchange of thoughts and debate about conflicting ideas. As an international study of science education by the Nuffield Foundation concludes:

> Deep understanding ... *"requires space to discuss, to think critically and to consider others' views. Contemporary school science education offers little opportunity for such an approach."*

> Pedagogy in school science is ... *"dominated by a conduit metaphor, where knowledge is seen as a commodity to be transmitted."*

> The curriculum requires *"teachers to develop an understanding of ... a specialist vocabulary of words, symbols, mathematics, diagrams and graphs"* ... *creating an "intellectual edifice [that] seems profoundly authoritative and authoritarian ... when compared to other school subjects."*

The conclusion that an 'authoritarian' curriculum makes science an unattractive option for so many young people is reinforced by the sense of alienation from science at school expressed by participants in discussion groups. Most did badly, dropping the subject as soon as possible, but succeeding in other subjects and progressing into higher education. When the curriculum develops jointly, between those who are learning and the teacher, it takes a very different course. As described above, starting points usually relate to something meaningful to people, the path then taken is quite unpredictable and connections are often made across the various sciences, and in and out of the humanities and social sciences. Deductive reasoning, mathematical proof and rote learning play very little role. It is clear, that to engage people more widely with scientific ideas, not only do they need to feel safe in doing so, but topics need to chime with them, at least initially, and continuation needs to allow for connections they wish to make, as well as the logic of scientific explanation.

How It Could Be Different

Formal education in science is strongly linked to training for future science-related careers. For this purpose, the curriculum unfolds throughout schooling in an ordained way, emphasising the gradual build-up of knowledge and skill in a historically logical way. This often means dull, rudimentary concepts are laid down first, unconnected with people's interests and experiences. As the Nuffield study mentioned above concludes:

> *Rather than beginning with ... overarching questions, such as 'Why do you look like your parents?' or 'What does the universe consist of?', school science begins with foundational knowledge – what a cell consists of, the elements of the Solar System, or the laws of motion – ideas which appear ... as a miscellany of unrelated facts. The bigger picture only unfolds for those who stay the course to the end ... you know you are going somewhere but only the driver knows where.*

Experience with discussion groups bears this out forcefully. The noticeable weakness in participants' understanding is not just in long-forgotten facts, but more importantly in any kind of overarching schema or landscape linking together basic ideas. This makes it hard for them to place any new information – about viruses, greenhouse gases or addictive drugs, for example – into a pre-existing conceptual map.

Connections with questions of politics, world affairs, or social and economic matters, bring science 'into the fold' with other aspects of the complex of ideas we entertain as we interpret our experience; it doesn't have to be treated as a no-go area. This enables discussion of topics such as mental health, space exploration or carbon dioxide emissions to flow in a continuous way, often engendering a thirst for deeper understanding of fundamentals such as receptor molecules, neural circuits or gravitational fields. Motivation to learn is dramatically increased.

Given the evidence about the defects in formal science education and the positive effects of the scheme outlined in this chapter, what exactly are the options for improving scientific understanding across the population? Clearly, the increasing availability of plain language science books and broadcasts provides good opportunities for individuals to learn about science. The message of the experimental scheme described above is that we could go much further in the education of adults, by providing greater opportunities for open-ended learning for those previously switched off the subject. Currently, science courses are usually located in science departments and tend to cater for those wishing to study a particular branch: astronomy, environmental or health sciences, for example. More wide-ranging, introductory sessions, that start with issues about which people are curious could be marketed, or even take place, outside science departments. Tutors would need to step down from their usual role as specialists and become facilitators of discussion and enquiry. This approach to teaching would involve methods more familiar in the humanities and social sciences. Participants would be encouraged to reflect on their own thoughts and experiences, and to express fearlessly the concepts, misconceptions and partial understanding they already have, as the starting point for a journey into new ideas. Discussion rather than instruction would be the mode. Such approaches are occasionally used already, in informal settings, including pubs and cafés, where conviviality and topicality enable barriers to be broken down. Should we not scale-up this kind of practice in adult education, as part of the wider pushback on misinformation and false reasoning?

For future generations of adults, it's the curriculum and pedagogy in schools that need reform. The switch-off science in the teenage years has to stop; it's damaging for individuals and positively dangerous for society. Clearly, something resembling the current specialist subject approach is needed to prepare the minority who are destined for science-based careers. But for the majority, a general 'science-for-all' curriculum would engage with people's real lives and encourage exploration of concepts rather than the temporary acquisition of facts. Such an approach would entail an appreciation of the 'way of science' as well as its results. Critical thinking, scientific scepticism, uncertainty and the provisional nature of theory would be centre stage, rather than offered as after thoughts.

To introduce yet another option into crowded school timetables would, of course represent a major practical challenge; so too, would the training and re-training of teachers to facilitate such learning. But it would also help us breakout of the endless teacher shortage loop. With so few 16 year olds continuing with science, of whom only a small minority return later as teachers, there will always be a shortage. A more open-ended, science-for-all option would gradually expand the pool of teachers able to facilitate such a subject.

SCIENCE UNDERSTANDING CAN COMBAT MISINFORMATION

It's my belief that failings in the system of science education play a significant role in the increasing spread of false reasoning and poor understanding. There are, of course, inexorable push factors in the worlds of mass media and political power-seeking driving this malaise; but there are also pull factors that could be more readily tackled. Education, as a whole, is central to the development of critical skills and respect for evidence. Adult education has a key role to play in opening-up a different kind of second-chance opportunity for those who gave up at school. School education needs to offer a less authoritarian version of science, competing on equal terms with other subjects for the attention of young people. Clearly the approach to engaging with scientific ideas outlined in this chapter is very far from the norm today. With the increasingly technical nature of contemporary threats and opportunities, both for individuals and societies, an interconnected grasp of basic concepts and methods in science would help individuals and organisations counter the flood of misinformation and conspiratorial explanations. Let us be thankful for the inexhaustible curiosity people retain about the world around them; it makes a good starting point for building sound concepts, in the face of so much populist nonsense!

ENDNOTES

1. BBC News. (2020). *Coronavirus: Outcry after Trump suggests injecting disinfectant as treatment.* https://www.bbc.co.uk/news/world-us-canada-52399464

2. Institute of Physics. (2011.) *Mind the Gap Mathematics and the transition from A-levels to physics and engineering degrees.* Institute of Physics

3. Keenan, O., & Gupta, J. (2022) *There are reasons girls don't study physics – and they don't include not liking maths.* The Conversation.

4. Education Policy Institute. (2024). *Progression at age 16 of young people from underrepresented backgrounds towards careers in STEM.* Education Policy Institute.

5. Smith, E., & White, P. (2024). Science for all? School science education policy and STEM skills shortages. *British Journal of Educational Studies,* 72(4), 397–424.

6. Funk, C., & Rainie, L. (2015). *Public and scientists' views on science and society.* Pew Research Centre.

7. Department for Business, Energy and Industrial Strategy. (2019). *Public attitudes to science.* Department for Business, Energy and Industrial Strategy.

8. Osborn, J., & Dillon, J. (2008). *Science education in Europe: Critical reflections.* Nuffield Foundation. https://www.nuffieldfoundation.org/wp-content/uploads/2019/12/Sci_Ed_in_Europe_Report_Final1.pdf

7

DEFEATING MISINFORMATION THROUGH CLASSROOM DELIBERATION

Lee Jerome

Middlesex University, UK

CRTICALLY EMPOWERING YOUNG PEOPLE

Conspiracy theories in schools are widespread but teachers do not feel they have access to a range of successful strategies to deal with them.[1] Many of these issues are simultaneously sensitive, polarising, controversial, and overtly political, but the meagre evidence base suggests that challenging such views head on can be counter-productive. Frequently, beliefs of those advocating conspiracy theories are based on misinformation, but this chapter argues that simply teaching skills for media literacy seems an unlikely solution because these beliefs are also integrally bound up with a political world view and an emergent political identity.

To combat the lure of misinformation and conspiracy perspectives young people need to be helped to think critically about what constitutes a useful set of criteria for evaluating conflicting political beliefs. The chapter suggests that part of the solution is to build routines in the classroom where the whole class takes responsibility for pursuing a deliberative culture, so that students become as familiar with challenging and critiquing one another as they are with the more traditional skills of speaking and listening. By testing, exploring and evaluating arguments collaboratively in the context of building knowledge of politics and the nature of political knowledge and beliefs, students can become familiar with the epistemological foundations of political knowledge and the pragmatic refinement of political positions through democratic processes of deliberation.

CONSPIRACY THEORIES IN SCHOOL

In a recent survey in England,[2] focussing on extremism in the classroom with respondents drawn largely from social studies and humanities subject areas, almost 90% of teachers had encountered conspiracy belief from students and 21% had such encounters fairly regularly. In a subsequent online survey of 5,284 secondary school teachers across all subjects,[3] 62% of teachers said they had heard students mention conspiracy theories in the past two years, with 41% citing some variation of a global secretive elite (e.g. the Illuminati or New World Order) and 25% mentioning climate scepticism. In relation to COVID-19 conspiracies, almost a third of teachers had heard students mention that the virus may have been created in a laboratory and over 20% had heard students mention anti-vaccine sentiments.

This is not to suggest that all of these examples included students promoting these views, simply that they were being discussed in school. In response, teachers report using a wide variety of strategies (sometimes contradictory), including opening up discussion, closing it down, challenging students in class, and reporting individuals as safeguarding concerns. The wider research evidence on dealing with conspiracy theories suggests that several of these strategies are likely to be ineffective or even backfire to reinforce conspiracy thinking. Unsurprisingly, then, few teachers reported that they felt their teaching responses had been successful.

CRIPPLED EPISTEMOLOGY

In trying to understand conspiracy theories, some writers have stressed their psychological function in fuelling insider/outsider identity. Others have focussed on external factors, such as the pervasiveness of 'fake news' (i.e. the propagation of false stories that appear to be news) and about the implications of a 'post-truth' environment, in which appeals to emotion take precedence over factually and evidentially based assertions.[4] Others have focussed more on the conspiracy theories themselves, seeing in them evidence of a 'crippled epistemology' through which advocates adopt a belief without understanding how genuine knowledge is constructed.[5]

Hayward et al.[6] have argued that an appropriate educational response should address conspiracy theories recognising that they represent (flawed) knowledge claims about the way the world works; that they are likely to become connected to deeper ways in which we perceive ourselves in relation to others; and that they also have political effects, and are often related to political positions or organisations. This chapter suggests that the tradition of *deliberative democracy* offers a useful framework for addressing these epistemological, psychological and political dimensions.

A DELIBERATIVE WAY FORWARD

Steiner et al.[7] argue that there are six key elements to deliberative democracy.

First, they focus on making deliberation inclusive, by which they mean it is a public process that is open to all citizens on an equal basis. Second, participants should commit to the truthful expression of their views and not misrepresent themselves or engage in inauthentic rhetoric. Third, people should commit to provide justifications for the views they put forward, as Gutmann and Thompson put it, 'citizens owe one another justifications for the mutually binding laws and public policies they collectively make'.[8] Fourth, whilst acknowledging the importance of self-interest, participants should consider their arguments in relation to the common good, demonstrating empathy with others. This might sound like an unlikely aspiration but, as Ackerman and Fishkin[9] point out, in an election, this amounts to asking oneself the question 'what is good for the country?' rather than simply 'what is good for me?' and many citizens will have experience of this shift of perspective. Fifth, participants should be willing to listen to the views and arguments of others and to treat their views with respect. This constitutes what Annette[10] has called 'civic listening' and enables participants to understand others and build solidarity. Listening to others is also necessary if one is willing to subject one's own arguments to scrutiny. Finally, a sixth element is that participants should be willing to yield to the force of the better argument, in other words, try to keep a genuinely open mind.

But of course if deliberative democracy derives its legitimacy through the process of deliberation then it is difficult to specify in advance what the criteria would be for a 'better argument'. So, this leads to a form of pragmatism, in that decisions are always open to revision after further deliberation.[11] Such deliberations are context-bound to some extent, so that an argument might carry weight in one cultural context but not in another.[12]

Adopting a pragmatic deliberative approach also provides us with a way to address Kuhn's[13] ideas about the stages of 'epistemological development', which describe how children not only acquire factual knowledge but also deepen their understanding of knowledge. Kuhn suggests that younger students might start with an 'absolutist' epistemology, in which knowledge is fixed, generally held by experts, and proven by facts. By contrast, a 'multiplist' view of knowledge grasps that people have different points of view, but succumbs to a form of relativism about knowledge in which there is no way to judge between those diverse opinions. Finally, an 'evaluativist' perspective recognises this diversity of opinions but also understands that these can be subjected to scrutiny using methods of inquiry and rational evaluation to evaluate which judgements might be more defensible than others.[14]

Reznitskaya and Gregory[15] argue that opportunities for such talk might lead to the following kinds of learning outcomes:

i.   Discussion gives students experience of rational thinking, which they can then internalise.

ii. The cumulative experiences of such discussion help students build an 'argument schema' to build a general understanding of how arguments are built, questioned, and worked through, which fits in with the evaluativist epistemological world view.

iii. This contributes to students' more complex understanding of disciplinary knowledge, i.e. what it means to understand and apply concepts like rights.

They also make the argument that teachers can sometimes be tempted to multiplist pedagogies by simply accepting all student contributions as valid, rather than facilitating exploration, testing them and evaluating them appropriately – a 'pseudo-enquiry' according to Alexander.[16] This warning about pseudo-enquiries alerts us to the observation that just because valuable learning can derive from classroom talk, we should not assume that all classroom talk leads to valuable learning. The challenge is to ensure that classroom talk offers the chance to improve students' political understanding, rather than merely consolidating or spreading crippled epistemology.

THE DELIBERATIVE CLASSROOM

In this final section, I outline the criteria that might usefully describe a deliberative classroom, where contentious issues can be purposefully discussed in a way that might promote the kind of learning outlined above. Because deliberation is about the talk that takes place between members of a community and is characterised by a set of norms and processes it seems more productive to focus on the classroom as a whole rather than focus on the teacher or the student as an individual contributor. The teacher may well undertake to change aspects of their teaching and classroom management as a result of adopting these principles, but focussing on a description of the classroom, leaves open those pedagogic decisions for negotiation, and emphasises how important it is to develop a culture and ethos that supports deliberation between students. This could conceivably emerge through a negotiation with the class about their conduct rather than through any conscious changes from the teacher.

I adapted Steiner et al.'s[17] 'Discourse Quality Index' which was developed to measure the deliberative qualities of contributions in parliamentary debates. In devising the following criteria I aimed to produce a lesson observation proforma, that might be easily used by teachers to provide peer feedback, and which would be accessible to students, should the teacher want to discuss how well the class was doing in creating a deliberative space (see Table 7.1).[18]

Table 7.1.   Classroom Observation Tool.

Criteria and Target Outcome	1 Poor–4 Excellent
1. Participation *All members of the class are actively engaged with the discussion. They actively listen, respond and make contributions*	1. Very few participate willingly 2. Minority participate willingly 3. Majority participate willingly 4. All actively participate
2. Developing informed views *Students routinely offer justifications for their opinions that draw on reasonable interpretation of the facts and account for other perspectives*	1. This rarely happens 2. Simple assertions/justifications predominate 3. Most offer well-reasoned justifications 4. Students routinely offer justifications which reflect their own informed opinions and their knowledge of others' views
3. Respect towards people affected by the issue being considered *Students show empathy and respect for people affected by the issues being discussed. They challenge stereotypes and examples of prejudice and recognise diversity within groups of people*	1. Disrespectful comments throughout the lesson about people affected, although these may be challenged by others 2. Mostly a neutral tone adopted, but a lack of empathy / understanding for affected groups 3. Generally respectful tone towards people being discussed 4. Inclusive and positive tone throughout

Table 7.1. (Continued)

Criteria and Target Outcome	1 Poor–4 Excellent
4. Respect for the position adopted by other participants *Students listen attentively to the range of arguments and reasons offered. Participants can accept and value elements of others' contributions even if they disagree with their overall argument*	1. Some rude or belittling comments to other participants, although these may be challenged by others 2. Most responses are civil but opposing arguments are largely rejected or dismissed 3. Generally participants can at least agree to disagree 4. Most participants engage positively and respectfully with views different from their own
5. Constructive response to discussion *Participants recognise counter-arguments given during the discussion and respond to them in a constructive manner*	1. Generally people stick to their arguments / views throughout (listen but do not respond) 2. Some respond directly to others, either to explore other views or develop their own views 3. Most respond directly to others, either to explore other views or develop their own views 4. The discussion is generally open and exploratory with evaluation, review and development of ideas common
6. Search for knowledge and understanding *Students are engaged in a collective conversation to achieve clarity and understanding. They value the truth and seek to clarify misconceptions and fill gaps in knowledge*	1. Facts and relevant information are generally used selectively to justify views 2. Some in the class challenge misconceptions and incorrect / irrelevant information 3. Most students engage with the information shared during the discussion and use this to develop their views 4. Generally the discussion builds clarity and deeper understanding of the issues being considered

The purpose of the tool is primarily to enable teachers to understand what processes might define the classroom as a deliberative space and to enable colleagues to observe one another and provide feedback as part of their development of a more deliberative approach to teaching. Consultation with a group of experienced educators confirmed that the tool has face validity, that is, it resonates with their understanding of how deliberation takes place in their areas of expertise (Citizenship, English, including teaching English as an Additional Language, RE, and Debating). The tool was tested with 36 respondents who observed a filmed lesson and completed the observation tool individually. Their ratings of the lesson indicated a reasonable level of agreement between them.

This framework is designed as a general set of principles for promoting a democratic culture and sensibility, but in relation to the specific challenges of conspiracy theories and disinformation, there are some appealing features. These include:

- It encourages students to think about the variety of positions adopted by different groups for different reasons, and to scrutinise the relationship between opinions and beliefs; knowledge and sources of information; feelings and personal experiences, etc.

- By considering how issues are experienced by others, it encourages students to consider how particular views are perceived by others, and thus to consider some of the real political effects of these views.

- It encourages an evaluativist scrutiny of all sources of information, rather than singling out those perceived as succumbing to conspiracies. This might help reveal the connections between individual beliefs and broader ideological movements (i.e. noting how 'free speech' activists align themselves with racist movements).

- It encourages everyone to see their current point of view as provisional and open to change, whilst this does not automatically undo false beliefs, it models an approach that leaves space for reconsideration.

THE IMPORTANCE OF BUILDING A CULTURE OF DELIBERATION

Deliberation offers a model of democracy which starts from the reality of diversity within the polity and seeks ways to build empathy and work towards collective decisions for the common good. Deliberation also provides pedagogies for exploring controversial (and potentially divisive) issues in the classroom, including conspiracy theories. However, there is no reason to assume that introducing deliberation into the classroom will be a straightforward matter as established modes of talk tend to default to hierarchical teacher controlled exchanges, rather than open and inclusive discussion between class members. This means teachers will need to work over time to build up a culture for deliberation in the classroom.

They will also have to exercise judgement about the extent to which students can communicate their emotions, regulate their engagement with others, and develop the criteria for evaluating arguments, rather than simply accepting all opinions as equally valid. Whilst it might be tempting to adopt skills-focussed interventions (like digital literacy programmes) to address some of the threats represented by conspiracy theories, post-truth beliefs, and disinformation, I believe that a more comprehensive and concerted attempt to build a culture of deliberation is more likely to provide a robust educational response. Focussing on a pragmatic approach to deliberation provides a practical space for discussing whatever issues arise, and also promotes an approach to knowledge that embodies the principles of democracy.

ENDNOTES

1. Taylor, B., Mills, M., Elwick, A., Pillinger, C., Gronland, G., Hayward, J., Hextall, I., & Panjwani, F. (2021). *Addressing extremism through the classroom*. A research report from the Centre for Teachers & Teaching Research. UCL Institute of Education. https://discovery.ucl.ac.uk/id/eprint/10133809/.

2. ibid.

3. Jerome, L., Kisby, B., & McKay, S. (2024). Combatting conspiracies in the classroom: Teacher strategies and perceived outcome. *British Educational Research Journal, 50*, 1106–1126. https://doi.org/10.1002/berj.3955.

4. d'Ancona, M. (2017). *Post-truth: The new war on truth and how to fight back.* Ebury Press; McIntyre, L. (2018). *Post-truth.* MIT Press.

5. Sunstein, C. R., & Vermeule, A. (2009). Conspiracy theories: Causes and cures. *The Journal of Political Philosophy, 17*(2), 202–227. https://doi.org/10.1111/j.1467-9760.2008.00325.x.

6. Hayward, J., Jerome, L., Pace, J., & Parker, C. (2022). *Closing down classroom conversations: Why conspiracy theories and the age of misinformation necessitates the interruption of classroom dialogue* [Paper presentation]. College & University Faculty Assembly of the National Council for the Social Studies Annual Conference, Philadelphia, 30 November–3 December.

7. Steiner, J., Bächtiger, A., Spörndli, M., & Steenbergen, M. (2004). *Deliberative politics in action: Analysing parliamentary discourse.* Cambridge University Press.

8. Guttman, A., & Thompson, D. (2002). Deliberative democracy beyond process. *Journal of Political Philosophy, 10*(2), 153–174.

9. Ackerman, B., & Fishkin, J. (2002). Deliberation day. *Journal of Political Philosophy, 10*(2), 129–152, 143.

10. Annette, J. (2008). Community involvement, civic engagement and service learning. In J. Arthur, I. Davies, & C. Hahn (Eds.), *The Sage handbook of education for citizenship and democracy* (pp. 388–398). Sage.

11. Talisse, R. (2005). *Democracy after liberalism: Pragmatism and deliberative politics.* Routledge.

12. Steiner, J., Bächtiger, A., Spörndli, M., & Steenbergen, M. (2004). *Deliberative politics in action: Analysing parliamentary discourse.* Cambridge University Press.

13. Kuhn, D. (1991). *The skills of argument.* Cambridge University Press.

14. Reznitskaya, A., & Gregory, M. (2013). Student thought and classroom language: Examining the mechanisms of change in dialogic teaching. *Educational Psychologist, 48*(2), 114–133.

15. Reznitskaya, A., & Gregory, M. (2013). Student thought and classroom language: Examining the mechanisms of change in dialogic teaching. *Educational Psychologist, 48*(2), 114–133.

16. Alexander, R. J. (2017). *Towards dialogic teaching: Rethinking classroom talk* (5th ed.). Dialogos.

17. Steiner, J., Bächtiger, A., Spörndli, M., & Steenbergen, M. (2004). *Deliberative politics in action: Analysing parliamentary discourse*. Cambridge University Press.

18. Jerome, L., Liddle, A., & Young, H. (2020). *The deliberative classroom*. Middlesex University.

MISINFORMATION AND THE POWER OF KNOWLEDGE

8

DATA-DRIVEN MISINFORMATION

Anna E. Premo[a], Alexander Ratkovsky[b] and Martina A. Rau[a]

[a]Department of Humanities, Social, and Political Science, Federal Institute of Technology in Zurich (ETH Zurich), Zurich, Switzerland
[b]Duke University

MISINFORMATION IN THE CORPORATE WORLD

In the corporate arena – where many spend most of their waking hours – misinformation is commonplace. In particular, data are often used to produce misleading, albeit still technically data-driven, conclusions. While such misinformation is far from the dark ideas mentioned elsewhere in this book, the ways in which industry fosters data-driven misinformation makes individuals more susceptible to creating, using, and spreading misinformation in other aspects of their lives.

In this chapter, we begin with an overview of the role of data in information and misinformation. We then provide a vignette based on our experiences with (often unintentional) misinformation in industry and discuss strategies for combating misinformation. Finally, we provide a summary of key takeaways.

In order to better understand our perspective, we would like to briefly introduce ourselves. Anna is a researcher studying data use and misuse in complex change, Alexander is an experienced executive in a global technology services company, and Martina is a professor specializing in learning and instruction. Anna and Alexander draw from their shared experience working together on multi-year, multi-million dollar technology transformations, as well as from their more recent independent experiences with building a global emerging technologies and industries capability (Alexander) and researching socially motivated data creation and use (Anna). Martina joins us in discussing technology-based and human-centered strategies for combating the creation and spread of misinformation.

SHARED PILLARS OF INFORMATION AND MISINFORMATION

Misinformation, defined as false or misleading information, encompasses far more than the nefarious misinformation campaigns that often spring to mind. Using this definition, skewed information of any kind can be considered misinformation. To understand misinformation, it is therefore important to first understand key aspects of information, and what makes information true and reliable (versus false and unreliable, as misinformation).

In simple terms, information is made from data that has been ingested, processed, and enriched to become more easily used and understood. Accordingly, information is built on three pillars of data-centric methodology, specifically: data collection; data model construction; and data analysis and interpretation. Getting each component right is a key to achieving high veracity, reliability, and fidelity. However, any one of these three levers could impactfully skew the entire dataset, model, and resulting outcomes, ultimately resulting in the creation of misinformation. The impact of such misinformation can range from inconsequential (only appearing in one report that isn't used to make any decisions) to monumental (driving a decision that ends up costing the company millions of dollars, resulting in mass layoffs that harm individuals and their families for years to come).

Data Collection

Selecting statistically meaningful and reliable metrics is the first step to robust data collection. For example, in building business cases it is important to understand in which scenarios certain metrics drive model behavior (e.g., net present value (NPV) vs return on investment (ROI). Involved metrics often rely on similar but importantly different financial datasets that impact crucial decisions. Thus, it is important to understand what metrics are required prior to deciding what sources to use for data collection.

Often data sources vary in precision, historical reliability, and source traceability. Data collection processes must therefore include frequent checks and test source reliability. For example, to underwrite an asset, third-party supply chain sources, manifests, and manufacturer traceability will determine underwritten capital requirement accuracy.

Data Model Construction

When building a data model, it is critical to ensure that no data are disregarded or missed. Outliers, often thought to be "data noise," can indicate critical departures from initial hypotheses. For example, in IT projects focused on cloud benefits, data collected on technical debt due to asset depreciation are not captured. Instead, more emphasis is put on "accepted" or "expected" elements. However, accepted or expected does not equate to proven.

Model construction is fundamental in ensuring correct representation and metadata inclusion to enable effective analysis. It is also worth noting that technological advances enable easier inclusion of external data sources. Previously, including many data sources burdened models with capital- and human-intensive processes. Today, a variety of data sources are now easily integrated using data ingestion frameworks, often powered by artificial intelligence (AI) and large language models (LLMs).

Data Analysis and Interpretation

As in data collection and model construction, precision and accuracy in data analysis require domain expertise to ensure that the right data are used, models are constructed, and analyses are conducted.

In particular, domain expertise is required in interpreting analysis results. It is also important to note that convergence on a set of predicted outcomes should not be thought of as mere confirmation of a model's predicted behavior, but rather a multi-step recursive process that tests results against baseline metrics, including consideration of abnormal observations. While some may argue this is the very essence of any robust statistical approach, we postulate that tooling selections (e.g., technology frameworks, vendor-specific environments) and domain expertise is just as critical to testing model outcomes and accurately interpreting results as analytic expertise.

Continuing with our cloud transformation example, the gravity of collected data and constructed models may point to adoption recommendations based on metrics used in traditional business cases (e.g., capex assets and ROI). In cloud business cases, however, it is instead the velocity of innovation and new technology that are often the main drivers of business benefit, neither of which are captured in more traditional models. A domain expert, however, would likely flag that omission when interpreting the results.

Data analysis is the very foundation for alignment of concepts to sensitivity scenarios, recommendations, business outcomes, behavior predictions, and implementation. Recursive review and tuning that combines both analytic and domain expertise is essential. In addition, this stage should rely on inclusion and expansion of the model's impactful variables to include industry, cross-domain, and historical sources to pressure-proof model stability and predictability.

MISINFORMATION IN INDUSTRY: A VIGNETTE

The following vignette is not the story of any one client or project. Rather, it is an amalgamation of experiences from our combined 50+ years of work on 100+ client projects that we hope will bring the pillars of data-driven misinformation to life.

Vignette

ZaphodBank is a rising powerhouse in the financial services industry. It is a digital bank that has led the charge in integrating leading-edge technology throughout its operations. Above all, ZaphodBank prides itself on relentless commitment to customers, with the executive team focusing strongly on customer loyalty and retention.

Leesa Jones is a mid-career leader who recently joined ZaphodBank as head of retail banking. Known for excellence in the industry, she has clear, aggressive goals and high standards, aiming to move to an executive role swiftly. Her team is excited to work with such a driven, successful leader and is eager to showcase their initiatives.

Data Collection. Although Leesa is new to ZaphodBank, many on her team have been there for years. They understand that – as is the case anywhere – certain metrics are more favorable than others. For example, they know their customer satisfaction (CSAT) scores have recently been trending high, exceeding industry standards. As customer experience is a major priority for the bank, they recommend that Leesa collect CSAT data to support the new customer experience index that she's developing.

Data Model Construction. As is often the case, CSAT is reported through multiple metrics across multiple systems. Unfortunately, the standard post-transaction and email surveys are still showing low scores that are consistent with what ZaphodBank has seen over the last couple years. However, ZaphodBank recently implemented a new AI-powered tool to analyze customer sentiment from call transcripts. Data from this tool have reported unprecedented CSAT scores, which Leesa suspects is due to recent initiatives implemented by her predecessor. Accordingly, Leesa decides to weight the sentiment scores most heavily in her customer experience index and deemphasize traditional metrics.

Data Analysis and Interpretation. One member of Leesa's team conducts basic descriptive and linear regression analyses using the new index. Since the sentiment analysis tool is new, they're unable to calculate any historicals to understand change over time. The sentiment scores, however, appear much higher than what the tool reports as industry average, which is a positive story that Leesa is pleased to share in her monthly reporting call.

Unfortunately, there is one simple but detrimental issue: the AI-powered tool on which Leesa based her determination of customer experience was broken and reported dramatically higher sentiment than was accurate. As a result, Zaphod-Bank did not see that customer experience was in actuality worse than ever and did not act in time to prevent a mass customer exodus. As is often the case with a new tool – particularly one that is new to the market – there were still issues to be worked through, both within the tool itself and in how it was implemented at ZaphodBank. Rather than choosing the data source with the better story, it would have behooved Leesa and her team to investigate why the numbers were so different. It is easy to assume that such a difference is due to something readily explained (like the rollout of a new initiative that the other sources simply haven't caught up to yet), but such assumptions need to be tested.

STRATEGIES FOR REDUCING MISINFORMATION CREATION AND SPREAD

Technology-based Strategies

Modern-day tools make it easy to analyze and visualize data, even for users without much (or any) statistical knowledge. While progress in advanced analysis and visualization tools is desirable, however, a tool that is easy to use may obscure the complexity of underlying processes. Nevertheless, there are measures that bear promise for reducing creation and spread of misinformation. These could be incorporated into existing analysis and visualization tools, or could be offered by new tools.

First, **automatic detection** of misinformation can help. For example, misinformation may result from an analyst using a statistical method presuming that underlying data are normally distributed. In the case of the vignette, CSAT is a metric that typically does not follow a normal distribution as responses often cluster toward the upper end of the response scale. Indeed, the analyst's chosen analytic techniques for investigating the customer experience index may inadvertently create misinformation even when data accuracy issues have been resolved. If the analysis tool detects an error, the analyst can correct it before sharing the results. Ideally, such a system would draw on knowledge about common errors and types of misinformation relevant to the given context.

Second, whether based on detection or preemptively, a tool may **prompt users to reflect** on proper data use at critical decision points. For example, if a statistical method assumes normal distribution, the tool might prompt the user to check whether the data meet this assumption. Ideally, the tool would do so while providing sufficient information for the user (who may not know why normal distribution is important) to actually perform this check, and perhaps also provide instruction on why it matters.

Third, and similarly, **warnings** may help users realize imminent violations of statistical principles. Some tools, but by no means all, display error or warning messages when an assumption is being violated. For a statistics-naive user, it may be unclear whether the warning message matters, especially if expressed in cryptic jargon. However, such warnings could turn into learning moments, instructing the user about the nature of the underlying issue and ways to solve it. Simply directing users to the "help" function is not enough. Especially statistics-naive users will need more tailored help that refers to the issue they encountered. A generative-AI back-end could achieve this by tailoring error messages and warnings as well as follow-up instructions based on the user's work.

Finally, who doesn't love a **tutorial**? Ever since Clippy haunted Word users, tutorials have had a bad rap. But what goes for warnings and error messages goes for tutorials too. A good tutorial draws on a data example and walks the user through the analytic steps. Such tutorials would be even more effective if the user could provide their own data (perhaps with some constraints about how the data should be formatted to be usable within the tutorial). What's more, detection, prompts, warnings, and tutorials can be combined into one. The tool might detect an error, prompt the user to reflect, and if they proceed, offer a tutorial using the data the user was just working with.

Human-centered Strategies

In our technology-based recommendations, the envisioned tool initiated a change. But obviously, the human was part of the loop. In fact, we are convinced that people who work with data need to understand data analysis and visualization. Consequently, there is no way around education for analysts and designers of analysis/visualization tools. Education should focus not just on correct data analysis but also on why incorrect approaches result in misinformation that ultimately does harm. We recommend several "active ingredients" to make such an educational intervention most effective.

First, company employees need to **understand what data can accomplish and what it cannot.** For example, yes – data can answer questions, but it often cannot answer a question for which it was not collected. If a question arises that the data cannot answer, it is better to collect new data than to mold existing data into a framework that doesn't fit. Doing so will lead to misleading answers. In the case of the vignette, Leesa's new customer experience index relies heavily on CSAT data, but CSAT is a metric intended to measure a customer's satisfaction at a given moment in time, rather than their likelihood of churn. While CSAT can be an important signal, what the bank cares about is if their customers will stay or go, which goes beyond its intended purpose.

Second, employees need to **understand basic statistical methods relevant to their tasks.** Exactly what these methods are will depend on the questions the company uses data for. In some cases, ANOVAs may be sufficient, whereas in other cases, sophisticated multi-level models (MLMs) are in order (such as customers in different regions). Importantly, if an MLM is the appropriate type of analytic method given the structure of the data, then an ANOVA might yield misleading results. If a company offers a workshop on MLMs, it should also illustrate cases where an ANOVA produces incorrect results that might lead to revenue loss for the company.

Third, employees should **learn strategies for questioning tools that perform complex analyses that exceed their own understanding**. For example, suppose an employee does not understand how an MLM works but has at hand a sophisticated tool that automatically uses an MLM given the data and a few menu-based inputs. They've heard others on the team talk about using an MLM and are excited to try it out, but don't realize that their sample is too small for this technique to be appropriate. Can we trust the result?

Fourth, speaking of cherry-picking, this is always a bad idea. Employees dealing with data should **be aware of cherry-picking fallacies and other biases, such as survivorship or sampling bias**. In the context of the vignette, Leesa's team cherry-picked (used only data that supports a particular argument) when they selected only metrics that seemed to showcase their success. Survivorship bias (focusing on individuals or groups who have passed some sort of selection criteria) might occur when only surveying customers who have been with the bank for five years or more, while sampling bias (using a non-random sample that is not representative of the entire population) might result from only administering surveys for online customer support, neglecting the significant portion of customers who solely use phone-based customer service.

Finally, any of the above recommendations will fail if a company gives its employees the impression that data should be used as evidence for foregone conclusions rather than **querying data to find answers to open-ended questions**. It is up to the leaders to set a culture that values in-depth data analysis for reflection over cherry-picking. Of course, reflection takes time, and training employees in analysis requires resources. We believe that doing so will lead to better decisions for the company, but its leaders need to be convinced of it too. And they need to communicate this conviction to their employees.

SUMMARY: FUNDAMENTAL CONCERNS ABOUT MISINFORMATION

Data and misinformation are not mutually exclusive. In fact, often the most convincing misinformation is that which uses data. In the simplest case, using inaccurate data creates misinformation. However, accurate data can also be (mis)used to create misinformation. We have boiled down the ideas raised in this chapter to three areas of concern: misinformation creation, misinformation amplification, and misinformation inevitability.

Misinformation Creation

A rose by any other name would smell as sweet, but what of misinformation? Do "intentional framing", "curated summary", and "selective measures" conjure the same visceral negative reaction as if you were to call them misinformation? Indeed, much of what is standard practice in industry could be considered misinformation.

In the case of our vignette, there were key decisions that could be considered intentional creation of misinformation. For example, there was the decision to use data that were showing growth and outperforming industry averages (sentiment analysis) while omitting or deemphasizing data that did not tell the desired narrative (customer surveys). There was also unintentional misinformation creation. For example, everyone on the team seemed unaware of the inaccuracies of the sentiment analysis data, and any use would have therefore yielded unintentional misinformation. Further, while Leesa's directions may have driven others to intentionally propose misinformation creation, we might benevolently assume that Leesa did not know her words would have such unintended consequences.

Misinformation Amplification

Misinformation is a modern-day gremlin. Instead of water it needs attention, but give it a drop and it will multiply. Decades ago, misinformation replication was far slower, more cumbersome, and limited in the channels and sources that it moved through. How-ever, in this age of AI, multi-/hybrid-cloud, social media, quantum computing, machine learning, and other significant – almost unim-aginable – advances, the spread and subsequent effect of misinfor-mation is growing exponentially.

Perhaps most troubling of all is the unseen amplification of misinformation that reinforces systemic inequities. Many pro-cesses considered at one time to be "industry standard" are built on bias, and the financial services industry is no exception. While some have been outlawed, such as redlining, the targeting of and discrimination against marginalized communities persists. Worse, as banks use more complex tools, the logic upon which decisions are made becomes increasingly obscured, making it more challeng-ing to understand what biases might be baked in. Even if AI-based tools are designed with completely unbiased logic (which is already optimistic), they can still be trained on data that replicates histori-cal biases.

Misinformation Inevitability

Leesa's emphasis on delivering a strong story of success is not unique. How do we balance information veracity with socio-political pres-sures that typify industry – particularly at high-level roles? Even if a company implements every single technology-based and human-centered strategy in this chapter, they will still almost certainly encounter misinformation. (To be fair, they really shouldn't be bas-ing their strategy on a single book chapter anyway.) That then begs the question, what *is* the right strategy? As consultants love to say, *it depends.*

It depends on the organization's scope. What domain-specific and technical expertise is needed? It depends on the organization's structures. What roles, tools, and processes are already in place? It depends on the organization's maturity. How are their capabilities well-defined and managed? And most of all, it depends on wheth-er the leaders within an organization have cultivated a culture of humility and relentless curiosity. If not, we recommend starting there.

9

CONFRONTING MEDIA OUTRAGE AND RESTORING TRUST AND EVIDENCE-BASED DEBATE

Les Ebdon

University of Bedfordshire, UK

THE ORIGINS OF OUTRAGE

The public square has many origin stories but one of the most cogent is the emergence of coffee house culture in 18th-century London. Out of often heated debates about business and politics, pamphlets and political parties emerged. In time, these became newspapers. A great diversity of views and ideas were debated but with the emergence of a literate working class an opportunity to make money appeared. In the 19th century mass circulation newspapers made their owners very rich and powerful. The term 'press baron' was coined and in the UK at least this was literally true, as many newspaper owners were elevated to the peerage.

These press barons rapidly realised that outrage not balanced debate sells newspapers. Sensationalism and scandal were the key to improved circulation. The news of the day was selected and distorted to reinforce the views of the target audience. Gradually, the idea that truth must be one of two polar opposites, what I have called elsewhere[1] the 'legal paradigm', came to dominate. Surprisingly so, as it happened as more people were being inducted into what I termed the 'scientific paradigm', that is truth is best discerned by investigation and keeping an open mind. It was Lord Reith's vision that the BBC, of which he was the first Director General, would balance this dissonant press by presenting partisan views to the public in a balanced way. This has sadly only reinforced the view that there are alternative 'truths' and 'I can pick my truth'.

Prime Minister Stanley Baldwin recognised the immense political power of the press barons. In a speech in 1931, he said:

> *The papers conducted by Lord Rothermere and Lord Beaverbrook are .... engines of propaganda for the constantly-changing policies, desires, personal wishes, and personal likes and dislikes of two men? What the proprietorship of those papers is aiming at is power, and power without responsibility the prerogative of the harlot throughout the ages.*

Baldwin had his own reasons for such excoriating comments but clearly lived in a period when the power of the press was immense. Radio and then television began to challenge the hegemony of the press barons but it was the arrival of the internet that seemed to hold the promise of a free and open debate, in a new virtual public square.

HOW SOCIAL MEDIA MADE THINGS WORSE

Initially, it seemed the internet would become a cornerstone of democracy, providing citizens with information, analysis and a wide diversity of opinion. Perhaps it would become the means by which we could all check the veracity of data, evaluate conspiracy theories and would restore trust in the traditional media. The rise of social media has dashed all those hopes. A few mega-corporations seized control of the platforms, led by the new manifestation of the 'press baron' – the 'media mogul.' To make money from these platforms, the user has to be driven to click, view and to share.

This is still achieved by sensation and outrage, by the prioritising of attention-grabbing headlines over substantive reporting. While content creation and dissemination have seemingly been democratised, algorithms designed to maximise engagement have facilitated the spread of misinformation, fake news and divisive content. Echo chambers have been created where biases are reinforced, rather than challenged.

Frighteningly, we have provided the guidance that these algorithms need through our purchases, searches and messages. This has provided a profile of our likes and dislikes, our preferences and prejudices such that they know us better than we know ourselves. The information gathered is then used to direct us to content that we will like and agree with. The more sensational it is, the more likely we are to read it and share it with our friends. Thus begins a process which takes us to the extremes in a polarising descent into a world of misinformation and conspiracy theories.

This has led to an erosion of trust in the media which has profound implications for society. Citizens have become increasingly sceptical and hence disengaged as they turn away from traditional news media and rely on unverified information from alternative, highly partisan, platforms. The polarisation of opinion and the fragmentation of trust are undermining social cohesion. In some cases, leading to riots or socially damaging direct action and in many cases, confounding attempts to build consensus on critical issues.

Accountability suffers as well. Not long ago, investigative journalism was a powerful means of exposing corruption, law breaking and holding power to account. In an age where its motives are doubted and partisanship triumphs over reason, the impact of such exposures is lost.

HOW BAD IS IT?

Michael Gove, the former Cabinet Minister, in the campaign leading up to the British referendum on European Union membership, famously said that: 'the people of this country have had enough of experts'. This sentiment is entirely consistent with the undermining of specialist expertise by social media. Anyone can be an expert or an influencer now. There is no verification of claims, in its place is a culture of selecting the 'facts' you prefer.

The legal paradigm leads us to believe that there is always another view if we don't like the one which is presented to us. Social media does not encourage us to seek the evidence and use our reason to arrive at a conclusion which may be different from all those presented to us. This democratisation of information can have serious sometimes fatal consequences. For example, none of us enjoys injections, so the thought that vaccination programmes are a 'deep state conspiracy' has a passing appeal. The evidence is, of course, that vaccination has saved millions of lives over the years with no significant detriment. Yet persistent misinformation on the internet, eroding the trust in experts, has led to a growing and influential, politically motivated, anti-vaxxer movement. It is estimated that some 200,000 Americans died unnecessarily after refusing a Covid vaccine during the pandemic. In Britain, measles has returned as a childhood killer, as a result of misinformation about the tried and tested MMR vaccine.

In an age of greater accountability, there were actions that were politically fatal for election candidates. In an Iowa campaign stop in 2016, Donald Trump claimed his supporters would stay loyal even if he committed a capital offence: 'I could stand in the middle of Fifth Avenue and shoot somebody, and I wouldn't lose any voters, OK?' It has proved to be prescient, as when tapes have been revealed where he appeared to boast about sexually assaulting women, or lost a case in court to a woman who claims he raped her, and even when he was convicted on 34 counts of fraud, there was no visible impact upon his electability. The erosion of trust in the media means that we no longer have to challenge our beliefs when we encounter uncomfortable facts. We simply find different 'facts' more agreeable to us.

In July 2024, three young girls were fatally stabbed in a Taylor-Swift-themed dance class in Southport. Ten other girls were injured in the attack which rightly shocked the nation. Although the killer was arrested at the scene, in accordance with normal legal practice his name was not released immediately.

Very quickly, politically motivated individuals began posting and sharing misinformation on social media. Claims that the suspect was a Muslim illegal immigrant or asylum seeker rapidly spread. The day after the killings, the Southport Mosque was violently attacked, as were the police. A local corner shop was looted. In the following days rioting spread across England, over 100 police officers were injured. Proof if any is still needed, that social media and unverified internet news-aggregation sites have the power not only to change opinions but to change behaviour and significantly damage social cohesion. The fabric of our democratic society is being challenged.

WHAT CAN WE DO ABOUT IT?

Rebuild Trust in the Media

It has been noted that social media represents the biggest communication revolution since the printing press. This 15th-century innovation has been credited as the catalyst for great social change and, inadvertently, for a rise in intolerance, extremism and conspiracy theories. While the printing press undoubtedly led to a rise in literacy and democracy, it was a powerful stimulus to propaganda, division and civil war. The benefits of the printing press were only finally realised by a rise in education, a growing understanding of the importance of evidence and a weariness of strife. Could these be the keys to restoring trust and evidence-based debate in the age of social media?

Rebuilding trust in the media will require a collective effort from journalists, commentators, media organisations and the public. The decline in ethical standards across society has clearly exposed us to misinformation, as has the failure to understand the importance of evidence and evaluating it with an open mind. Our increasingly complex information landscape demands a return to transparency in reporting, the adherence to ethical standards and a commitment to factual accuracy. Education programmes are needed to empower individuals to separate fact from fiction by the critical evaluation of evidence.

Technology Companies Need to Mitigate Misinformation

Technology companies, particularly those that operate social media platforms and search engines, wield tremendous influence over how information is disseminated and consumed. Such power has to be coupled with great responsibility to mitigate the spread of misinformation, which has become so pervasive in the digital age.

One of the key strategies that technology companies can employ is to refine the algorithms they use to prioritise verified, accurate and balanced content. As we have seen, current algorithms often favour sensational or divisive posts because these drive user engagement. It is these algorithms that determine much of the content which is viewed by citizens in an age where we, knowingly or unknowingly, curate our own news content. Given the commercial advantages of algorithms driven by outrage, how can we persuade companies to recalibrate these algorithms to promote high-quality journalism and flag questionable sources?

Transparency in Internet Methodology

A first step should be transparency. Companies should openly disclose the methodologies behind their content curation and moderation processes. Allowing users to understand the basis on which certain content is promoted while other material is ignored, enhances transparency and informs customer choice. This would enable consumers to choose channels which offer balance, collaborate with independent fact-checking sites and suppress false information.

Technology Tools to Tackle Misinformation

Bad actors clearly target technology firms who must take sophisticated and proactive measures to combat the spread of misinformation. This can be achieved by developing advanced tools to identify and remove fake accounts, bots and co-ordinated disinformation campaigns. The rapid development of artificial intelligence (AI) tools and machine learning will play a key role here with specialist expertise in detecting patterns of manipulation.

By integrating into their platforms tools that empower users to critically evaluate information and providing warnings on dubious content or links to unverified sources, technology companies can assist in the rebuilding of trust.

Legally Enforced Standards

There has been much debate as to the role of governments and legislation in this area. Should states try to stop the use of algorithms that promote extremism, propagate misinformation and promote harmful content? Or does this constitute government interference in free speech. Given the harms inflicted upon society and the duty of states to protect their citizens is there not a case for a voluntary standards framework, legally enforceable in the case of egregious misconduct?

Given the enormous sums of money involved and hence the gigantic expansion of the Balfour dictum of power without responsibility, is self-policing or even state control a realistic option? Just as society learnt that the power of the press needed to be offset with a personal responsibility to evaluate evidence and in a world of probabilities to question everything, we have to relearn these essential safety mechanisms in the world of the internet and social media.

Harness AI for Fact Checking

It is here that AI can come to our aid. AI can analyse vast amounts of data and identify patterns, biases and gaps. At its best, generative AI can ensure that a diversity of viewpoints is contained in a single article. While AI is not infallible, it can readily be used to cross- check claims with credible sources of information and at a speed that enables real-time fact checking. Care must be taken that AI does not inherit common biases and stereotypes, as it has been shown to do without careful balance in the training sets. AI can, however, be a powerful ally in confronting media outrage and restoring trust and evidence-based debate.

It's time to push back against outrage.

ENDNOTE

1. Ebdon, L. (2023). The value of uncertainty and the tyranny of the closed mind. In C. Brown & G. Handscomb (Eds.), *The ideas-informed society: Why we need it and how to make it happen* (pp. 15–22). Emerald.

10

POPULISM AND ITS IMPACT ON THE RULE OF LAW

Robin Ellison

THE CLAMOUR FOR EXCESSIVE LEGISLATION

Around the world, there have been recent demands to reduce the quantity of law and regulation in order to enhance freedoms, and promote economic progress.[1] At the same time, there are frequent requests from the media and the public for more laws to redress a particular perceived high-profile wrong, often where there is no need for such law, or where there may be unintended consequences once the law is introduced.

How governments actually respond, and how they might better respond, to populist demands for any new law is the subject of this chapter. In democracies, it is understandable that those seeking votes will respond to a public clamour for a new law. Even autocrats and dictators commonly seek validation by elections; the fact that the public know and understand that the ballots have been rigged seems to do little to devalue any dishonest due process.[2] There is little merit is discussing the activities of autocracies; more useful is to explore why democracies continue to develop excessive legislation, and how they might in future respond to public demands for new law where none is actually needed to remedy a mischief.

Almost all governments resort to using law as a form of window-dressing or grandstanding, sometimes to justify sub-optimal behaviour. Russia, for example, introduced legislation to confirm the purported conquest of provinces of Ukraine. And even in otherwise secure liberal democracies justificatory legislation, or court decisions, can be used to justify populist laws. Recent episodes in the UK, for example, a jurisdiction sometimes hailed as a pre-eminent adherent to the rule of law, indicate that the rule of law can be fragile,[3] and can be diminished by intervention of the mainstream as well as the social media. And even normally thoughtful and considered parties can be caught up in public enthusiasm for a change in law which in normal circumstances they would abhor.

So, this chapter explores some recent examples in the UK of excesses in legal provisions occasioned by populism, discusses the causes of such excess, and suggests some solutions towards ameliorating the worst of the behaviours. It touches only one issue in populism, namely public pressure; it does not have the space to cover the other major issue, namely governments' and politicians' disregard for the rule of law, currently exemplified in the USA, but from which other governments have not been immune in recent years.

UNNECESSARY PROLIFERATION OF LAWS = SOME RECENT EXAMPLES

Set out below are some of the more egregious episodes in UK law making over the last few years.

Fire

In the UK, ever since the fire of London in 1666, there have been building codes designed to reduce the risk of fire to property. Nonetheless, in 2018, a fire in a London block of apartments, Grenfell Tower, led to its complete destruction, and the tragic death of 72 of its inhabitants. It was one of the worst fires in the capital's recent experience, and led to extensive press comment – and an expensive and prolonged public inquiry which blamed the equivalent of a perfect storm. This was despite a number of extensive building codes and the existence of several regulatory bodies to enforce them.[4]

The tragedy has resulted in demands from survivors, the press and the public for additional regulation to ensure it could not happen again, and for the establishment of new institutions to help guard against a recurrence, which seems inevitably, even before the conclusion of the public inquiry, to lead to the establishment of an additional regulatory body, and a change to building codes. The inquiry is likely to conclude that the tragedy was consequent on failures by the fire service, the local authority, the property management company, the architects, and the suppliers of materials. The irony is that it is possible, if not probable, that one of the proximate causes of the conflagration included the fact that there were in fact too many regulators and regulations involved, which led to no one body taking control.[5] There is no evidence that any new regulator will be able to prevent future failures given that the earlier regulators failed in their duties. It was the failure to execute, rather than inadequate regulation that led to the tragedy.

Murder

In another tragedy, a local resident and school caretaker, Ian Huntley, murdered two young girls[6] in 2002. The next year, Huntley was sentenced to two terms of life imprisonment, with the High Court later imposing a minimum term of 40 years. The case received extensive public coverage, and one consequence was a public inquiry into the intelligence-based record keeping and vetting system which had allowed Huntley to obtain employment as a school caretaker despite previous criminal complaints, which had been reported to police and social services. The later inquiry recommended a mandatory registration scheme for people working with children and vulnerable adults such as the elderly and mentally handicapped, which later led to the foundation of the Independent Safeguarding Authority.

The system initially established would have required the registration of all individuals working with children, about 11 million people; when it was disbanded (or rather merged with the criminal records office) its new system saved around £100M a year – the irony being that the scheme could not have prevented the Soham murders in the first place because the perpetrator knew the victims through his girlfriend, not his job.

By 2024, the Disclosure and Barring Service, the successor to the Independent Safeguarding Authority, employed around 1,400 people, and spent around £215M a year; in its very lengthy annual report there is no cost-benefit analysis of the worth of the system, for example, how much the number of child deaths or child abuse has been reduced by, or whether other measures could more usefully have spent the £200M.

Child Protection

In a horrific case known as that of Baby P, a young child was tortured and eventually killed by its mother and her boyfriend. Following a series of incidents, the child was under the supervision of the local authority, the police, and the hospital. The head of the Haringey protection system, Sharon Shoesmith, was blamed by a tabloid newspaper, the Sun, for the death[7]; it followed an earlier scandal in the same local authority involving a young child, Victoria Climbie, in relation to which there had been a public inquiry. The Sun newspaper has a somewhat chequered record, more recently suffering some discreditation following litigation by Prince Harry, but it then imposed pressure on the then Minister for children, who in turn blamed Ms Shoesmith for the failures and the death, and illegally sacked her. Following a complaint by Ms Shoesmith, his department was required to pay her around £600,000 in damages.

There were no immediate legal changes introduced as a consequence of the episode, although systems were reformed. However, legislation was later introduced, the Children and Social Work Act 2017, which created a new additional regulator. More damagingly, the behaviour of a government minister under pressure from the tabloid press, had led to inappropriate outcomes, with the unintended consequence of the taking into care of 20,000 children, probably unnecessarily and damagingly, from an abundance of caution. The minister involved later became famous for his involvement in a TV dance show.

Martyn's Law

In May 2017, Salman Abedi, an Islamist extremist, detonated a bomb at an Ariana Grande concert in Manchester; it killed 22 people and injured over 1,000. The mother of one of the deceased victims, Figen Murray, subsequently campaigned for a law in memory of her son, Martyn and largely as a result of her efforts eventually the UK parliament passed Martyn's law (the Terrorism (Protection of Premises) Act 2025).[8] The consequent costs for venues were estimated as being between £1.1B and £6.3B with a central estimate of £2.7B. The law requires venues with a capacity of 200 or more to take steps to secure their buildings against possible terrorist attacks. It covers around 800 village halls, 8,000 sports facilities, and 33,000 churches, and the legislation is being supervised by a regulator, the Security Industry Authority. The worst case cost/benefit scenario suggests £4.9B in costs and £8.4M in benefits, that is, 583 times as much cost as benefit. The question that arises is whether Martyn's law will in the end reduce the risk of terrorist attacks; there have been other attacks (see for example, the unsuccessful attacks on Liverpool Women's Hospital in 2021, or the attack on Glasgow airport, neither of which would have been prevented by this expenditure, but which were averted by the bravery of individuals[9]).

MPs Expenses

In 2009, a scandal emerged about MPs expenses. MPs salaries had been constrained due to political pressures, and they had been encouraged instead to enhance their claims for expenses. Some MPs applied for reimbursement of expenses that were excessive even by the new standards, and one even served a term of imprisonment as a consequence.

The law was changed to control expense claims, and a parliamentary department was established to supervise the new system. The excess expenses that had been claimed over the previous five-year period was around £2.5M, that is, about £500,000 pa; the new department to control excess expenditure involved costs of around £7M a year, and retained three press officers.

Control would have been less populist and more pragmatic if, for example, the requirement had been that MPs could spend whatever they wished, but would only be reimbursed once the claims were published on their website, or even a public website. Transparency rather than control would have been significantly more effective, and more cost-effective, but less dramatic to announce. The need to respond to the mood of the public had created a minor department, with overheads many times that than the mischief it was intended to control.

Prorogation/Brexit/Referenda and the Rule of Law

Following on the referendum for Brexit in 2016, the government of the day (in fact several governments) struggled to implement the exit on terms acceptable to Parliament. As part of the process, one administration attempted to prorogue Parliament, a move that was declared by the courts to be unconstitutional. The case brought to a head a constitutional conflict between the roles and powers of the administration and the judiciary; a minister (later prime minister for a brief period) acquiesced in criticism of the judiciary when a tabloid newspaper proclaimed them enemies of the people, a phrase redolent of Nazi Germany, and snidely remarked on one of the judge's sexual orientation. Politicians (not only in the UK) continue to struggle to understand the concept of separation of powers.

ANTIDOTES TO POPULARIST LAW MAKING

In most of these episodes, in which new legislation was introduced as a consequence of media pressure rather than any outcomes-based expectations, the costs have been significant, and there have been unintended consequences. There have been a range of far-reaching consequences deleteriously affecting everyday life. Examples include in relation to disclosure and barring, people deciding not to help in Scouts groups because of the expense and inconvenience, or additional administrative overheads in people applying for jobs which have no connection to child protection, such as in financial services, or the establishment of significant records and overheads which are supernumerary to requirements.

Ask Are Existing Laws Sufficient

One positive and helpful change would be to:

- require a minister to make a declaration, perhaps on oath, that any new legislation is actually needed, taking into account the balance of existing legislation which covers the issue;

- assure that the expenses incurred of implementing new legislation are cost-effective; and

- show that unintended consequences have been considered.

Training, Qualification, and Accountability of Lawmakers

A further strategic step to avoid unnecessary populist law making might be to require appropriate training and qualification of lawmakers. It is curious that lawmakers, unlike dentists, accountants or bus drivers, that is, people who could cause damage to the public, are not required to train or be qualified to make law – nor are they educated in how to respond to demands from their constituents or the press for changes in the law which not be required.

Nor are lawmakers personally responsible for the costs of excess lawmaking. In local government, for example, local councillors can be surcharged for their egregious errors. It would be impracticable to make central government lawmakers responsible, but egregious breaches of the law, for example, when Ed Balls, the minister in the Baby P case, having been found by the courts to have exceeded his authority, said he would do it again might in theory be subject to financial penalty.

Skilling in Anti-popularist Narratives

Thirdly, lawmakers struggle to respond to public demands for change, even where a failure has been due to poor administration rather than lack of legal provision. They might need training in crafting anti-populist narratives to calls for additional legislation, rather than standing on the bandwagon.

Requirement to Anticipate Unintended Consequences

Finally, lawmakers should be required to state what might be unintended consequences of any calls they make for new law. It is rare that there are none, and the practice of subsequent legislative reviews is rare. In particular, there should be a modest specific fine for any lawmaker who says that some event must never happen again. It will, despite any change in the law.[10]

Demagogues will always be amongst us; and their activities will resurge from time to time as new ones emerge, with exceptional skills of rhetoric, and exemplified by on occasion by psychopaths, narcissists or fantasists, often with a combination of such traits. They are not influenced by logic but by emotion, so the question arises whether the damage they do to the public realm can be ameliorated by systems of government. And so also will ordinary lawmakers, not psychopathic in nature, be buffeted by political headwinds.

CHECKS AND BALANCES

Demagogues clearly do not care much about systems of checks and balances. But whilst liberal democracies enjoy to a greater or lesser extent constitutional separation of powers, most if not all of them suffer from unprofessional lawmaking. It is curious that most activities that may affect the public adversely, such as dentistry, accounting or bus-driving, are subject to some form of professional requirements including training and qualification, others are not. Conceiving and rearing children is one obvious example. And one other is lawmaking. Members of Parliament, regulators and civil servants, have no formal training, qualification or professional standards before they impose requirements on others, and this lack of requirements may be one, if not a primary, cause of populist lawmaking. A need for rule makers to be trained may be one of the solutions.

Another control might be limits on the quantity of legislation; at present the sheer quantity of rules (not only primary, but secondary and tertiary) has few limits, and given the lack of technical constraints (emphasized since the abolition of the requirement for law in England and Wales to be written in manuscript on vellum). Legislative budgets could constrain calls for more laws.

Finally, this chapter has not covered the other main area of populism in law making, namely the disregard by the political framework for constitutional limits on power. England and Wales are unusual and different from some other jurisdictions, that no limit is placed on the nature of legislation by its constitution; whilst there are (or were) constitutional constraints, there is no formal standalone constitution. The behaviour of a former UK Prime Minister in challenging the role of judges suggests that it may be time.

It does not guarantee, as in the Weimar Republic, that politicians and others would refrain from implementing populist law, but it might constrain them in the most egregious cases. So, whilst psychopathic politicians will continue to ride roughshod over the usual proprieties, it might restrain the most extreme outbursts in social media and the MSM. As the UK's Attorney General noted:

> We have seen in recent years where, ... disregard for our constitutional rule of law heritage can lead. It is crucial that all institutional actors understand their role in government under law. When government invites Parliament to break international law, or oust the jurisdiction of the courts, it not only undermines the rule of law, but also the mutual respect that historically has been one of the great strengths of our constitution. It risks pitting one institution against another in ways that damage our reputation both inside and outside our borders as a law-abiding nation.[11]

The trend towards populist lawmaking is clearly therefore not restricted to the autocracies; the pressures on lawmakers in the liberal democracies continue to create new and unnecessary law, much of it with unfortunate outcomes. An obvious contributor to the solution of the problem is to create an expectation amongst lawmakers and regulators that they need to be familiar with the rule of law, alternatives to law making, and management of public expectations. There are now encouraging signs that in the UK, the EU, and the USA such expectations are beginning to emerge and be reflected in public policy.

ENDNOTES

1. The revolt against regulation, *The Economist*, 1 February 2025; *Rule-breakers: Eliminating unnecessary regulation is difficult but brings big rewards*, *The Economist*, 1 February 2025; Self-restraining Raj: A bureaucratic place tries to reform [India], *Economist*, 1 February 2025. In the United States, Elon Musk has been retained to establish a Department (GODE) to reduce the US budget by $2T by abolishing or reducing a number of government agencies. In the European Union in September 2024 Mario Draghi identified excessive regulation as holding back Europe (https://commission.europa.eu/topics/strengthening-european-competitiveness/eu-competitiveness-looking-ahead_en); and in the UK Sir Kier Starmer has asked UK agencies to identify regulations holding back UK productivity (see Europe needs to tackle its red tape problem, *Financial Times*, 3 January 2025; Reeves will urge watchdogs to pivot towards growth after No 11 summons, *Financial Times*, 15 January 2025).

2. See for example, *The Donbass: From recognition to annexation and beyond*, 15 May 2023, https://defactostates.ut.ee/donbass-recognition-annexation-and-beyond.

3. See Bingham, T. (2011). *The rule of law*. Allen Lane/Penguin.

4. For statements of evidence see https://www.grenfelltowerinquiry.org.uk/.

5. Building Safety Act 2022; Rankl, F. (2024, July 8). *Building regulations and safety* [Research Briefing]. House of Commons Library. See also Davies, D. (2024). *The unaccountability machine*. Profile.

6. *The Bichard inquiry (inquiry into the events surrounding the murders of Holly Wells and Jessica Chapman in Soham, Cambridgeshire, in 2001)*. Home Office, 2004. See *Disclosure and barring service annual report*, 24 January 2025; *Investigation into the disclosure and barring service*. National Audit Office, 1 February 2018.

7. See https://fullfact.org/education/are-more-children-being-taken-from-their-families/; https://www.communitycare.co.uk/2017/08/03/

ten-years-baby-p-social-works-story/; for the populist view see Seamark, M., & Shipman, T. (2013, October 20). Disgraced Shoesmith demanded £1.5million: As backlash grows over pay-out to woman at centre of Baby P tragedy, her greed is revealed. *Daily Mail*; for the alternative view, see Shoesmith, S. (2016). *Learning from Baby P: The politics of blame, fear and denial.* Jessica Kingsley Publishers; Bennett, R. (2010, March 12). Baby P: The tragedy that still haunts reformers. *Times*.

8. See https://www.gov.uk/government/publications/terrorism-protection-of-premises-bill-2024-factsheets/terrorism-protection-of-premises-bill-overarching-factsheet; O'Flynn, P. (2024, October 19). The futility of Martyn's Law, *Spectator*; Dawson J., & Keating, M. (2024, October 10). *The terrorism (protection of premises) Bill, 2024–2025* [Research Briefing]. House of Commons Library.

9. For the attack on Liverpool Women's Hospital in 2021, see *Operation Itonia: A summary of the key findings of the police investigation into the explosion outside the Liverpool Women's Hospital,* on 14 November 2021, Counter Terrorism Policing North West, 29 September 2023; for the attack on Glasgow airport in 2007, see Brocklehurst, S. (2017, June 30). *The day terror came to Glasgow Airport.* BBC News. There is a list of terrorist incidents in London, the majority of which in the last 50 years were IRA or Islamist related (see https://en.wikipedia.org/wiki/List_of_terrorist_incidents_in_London). Few if any would have been avoided by the implementation of Martyn's Law.

10. For anecdotes about populist law making, see for example, Gorsuch, N., & Nitze, J. (2024). *Over ruled; The human toll of too much law.* Harper Collins. Neil Gorsuch was appointed by Donald Trump to the US Supreme Court in 2017.

11. Lord Hermer, L. (2024, October 14). *The rule of law in an age of populism.* Bingham lecture on the rule of law; see also Hermer, L. (2024, December 6). *Attorney General's remarks to the Venice Commission*; Lacey, N. (2019, January). *Populism and the rule of law.* London School of Economics, International Inequalities Institute. These concerns are nothing new, see Baker, J. (2004). Human rights and the rule of law in renaissance England. *Northwestern Journal of International Human Rights, 2004*(2), 1–19.

11

IT'S DARWIN! AN EVOLUTIONARY LENS ON KNOWLEDGE AND TRUTH

Steven Warmoes

Independent consultant in knowledge management, Gent Belgium

A QUESTION OF SURVIVAL

In this chapter, the values of truth and the development and sharing of knowledge and ideas are examined from a Darwinian perspective: when do these contribute to survival, and when are they counterproductive? And survival of what?

This chapter draws on 35 years of experience in knowledge management consultancy. It explores how building trust enhances the development and sharing of ideas and knowledge and reduces the use of misinformation and deception that often arise in competitive environments. A framework is presented to understand how to maximize the benefits of knowledge sharing while accounting for the risks particularly of naivety.

THE MAP AND THE TERRITORY

Let's first examine knowledge and truth.

Before we explore how knowledge can be developed and shared, let's consider what makes knowledge valuable in the first place.

How do we decide what knowledge is worth sharing? One way to approach this question is through the metaphor of a map.

A map is a reproduction of the territory, the reality, and is available outside the territory: in one's head or explicitly on paper, a computer screen ....

How real or how true is a map?

A military topographic map contains a lot of details, yet using a pile of these maps to travel by car through the country would be very impractical. Moreover, if the reader does not have the required knowledge to understand the map, the knowledge remains inaccessible. A simplified map with only the main roads is far more useful for navigation. However, for military purposes – like identifying a location for a stronghold – such a simplified map would be nearly useless. So, the value of a map depends on its purpose.

Which of these maps is more truthful? For both maps, we can define what is false, for example, when important roads are missing, or do not connect at the right junctions .... But whether missing knowledge is a flaw depends on its purpose and the value it is meant to add. Knowledge is necessarily incomplete: there is always a compromise between understandability and practicality on one hand, and completeness on the other hand. It's an art and craft to make a good compromise. And if many maps compete, the one that fits best its purpose has higher chances to be used, and ultimately, survive.

THE SURVIVAL OF THE FITTEST

We've established our first key takeaway: the value of knowledge depends on how well it serves its intended purpose.

Returning to our map metaphor, this raises an important question: do we always want truthful maps? The military may be afraid that the map falls in the hand of the enemy and intentionally leave out key details, giving those details only to small highly trusted groups. It can go further and create false maps that fall in the hand of the enemy. They can even create multiple conflicting false maps to overwhelm and confuse their enemy – a strategy of 'flooding them with shit'. This strategy has become more attractive as in these days of the Internet and ubiquitous social media, and hacking, where keeping information secret is increasingly difficult.

Knowledge and Survival?

This brings us to the core question: does knowledge – and its sharing – contribute to survival? In nature, deception can be a survival strategy. Animals can hide or divert the attention of a predator from their breeding ground to create a false map in the head of the enemy that is safer for them. When the animal skin contributes to camouflage, the misleading information is even embodied.

From a Darwinian perspective, minds did not evolve for truth, but for survival. And survival can be understood in a broad sense – it's not just about life and death. It can be about the survival of a species or a group, but in modern society, it's often about the survival of a personal or group identity such as professional reputation, a career …. As the following story of a company illustrates, sometimes the way knowledge is shared – or withheld – can determine who thrives when the landscape becomes competitive:

A construction company is a knowledge paradise. People readily answer each other's questions, exchange ideas and experiences, and document their findings in an accessible way. Collaboration thrives, and knowledge and ideas flow freely.

One day, the team leader of the engineers and architects announces that he will leave his position, adding honestly 'according to our cherished values of transparency and meritocracy, we guarantee you that we will select the best candidate among you'.

And from that very moment, the knowledge paradise begins to change.

Candidates start 'polishing' their image of the potential best. Sharing of knowledge that makes the competitor shine is quietly stopped. Shortly after, there is a temptation to tell negative stories about the competitor. And if it takes a long time before the new boss is assigned, traps may be set up.

Not only the direct competitors show a changing behaviour. Others may also prefer who they want as their

next boss. Cliques start to form, alliances take shape.
Opponents may become adversaries or even enemies ....

This example shows how a situation can deteriorate, even if nobody has bad intentions at the outset. A perceived threat of an identity is enough, in this case, a professional identity. It's not even about losing the position itself – it's about losing the identity that comes with being a boss, a valued status symbol.

In situations where a highly valued resource is inherently scarce – where there is an unavoidable win/lose dynamic – finding a good balance is difficult. Without careful management, competition can easily descend into a kind of horse trading, compensating losses with a gain elsewhere, typical for political behaviour. This in turn may create a problem elsewhere and even create a malaise in the whole ecosystem.

However, competition does not always have to follow a win/ lose dynamic. In some cases, rivals can find ways to benefit together. Competing businesses, for instance, can choose to cooperate to expand a market, where a smaller share of a growing pie can be more valuable than a larger share of a shrinking one. By shifting the focus from merely outperforming others to creating new opportunities, competition can become a driver of mutual gain rather than a zero-sum game.

The Dangers of Destructive Competition

This highlights our second takeaway: to have a healthy flow of knowledge sharing, it is important to avoid negative spirals of destructive competition. The company in our story might have decided on a successor before communicating the departure of the current leader. While this might have prevented internal competition from spiralling out of control, it would come at a cost – the credibility of the company's commitment to transparency. Such a move could fuel cynicism, reinforcing the belief that management does not practice what it preaches.

After all, disillusionment is only possible to the extent that one had an illusion in the first place. And that is a hard-earned wisdom.

Even more difficult to grasp is the Buddhist or Stoic insight that, as a competitor for the new leadership position, your suffering comes not from external events, but from your attachment – to your self-image as a future boss, for example. Yet avoiding the competition altogether, simply to escape the pain of potential loss, is also a form of attachment. It's natural to have opponents in life, but it's crucial to recognize when they shift from opponents to adversaries, or even to enemies – whether in your mind or theirs. An opponent is someone you want to outperform. An adversary is someone you not only want to outperform but also want to see lose. An enemy is someone you seek to eliminate before they eliminate you. And so, the mere perception of a survival threat can become a self-fulfilling prophecy, where even victims may turn into perpetrators, all in the name of self-defence.

Opponents, at least, play by the rules. Adversaries, however, are suspected of deception from the start. In sports, a skilful feint by an attacker is admired, and it's accepted that a coach won't reveal their line-up far in advance. These distortions of the 'map' are considered part of fair competition on a levelled playfield.

But outside of structured play, distortions – or outright lies – signal something deeper. They reveal an underlying threat. But what exactly is at risk? What is so scarce that knowledge cannot be shared widely?

To answer that, let's explore a Darwinian ladder of direct and indirect survival values and see how we can use it to reduce the use of misinformation and deception.

A LADDER OF SURVIVAL AND DERIVED VALUES

1. *Primary physical values*:
   - Physical safety. Under lethal threat, any doubt or deception can be lethal, and no time must be wasted by empathy.
   - If everything is safe, search for food.
   - Then search for procreation, the survival across generations.

2. *Secondary values*:

These values create fertile conditions for the primary values.

- An undisputed territory. Shared knowledge and acceptance of the demarcations help to avoid conflicts, and the need to waste energy and means on fighting rather than feeding or breeding. Narratives can enforce the sense of ownership, such as the land of our fathers, the promised land .... Believing in those narratives gives strength to fight. A stock of the fruits of the land contributes to survival, as well as what it may be traded for, especially money.

- There is safety in numbers. Group cohesion, loyalty and solidarity are valuable properties of the group. Leadership is necessary and valued.

People can identify with their territory and possessions, their group(s) and associated narratives and strive for their growth and survival.

3. *Tertiary values*:

Humans can make tools. A special tool is language which allows for better thinking and communication. These valuable skills in turn are beneficial for the secondary values and hence the primary values. People can identify with their skills and knowledge domain typically in their profession. Some ambition is needed to persevere in acquiring those skills and knowledge, or leadership in the secondary values.

4. *Quaternary values*:

To develop knowledge, ideas, skills that are beneficiary to oneself and the groups one identifies with, values can contribute such as tolerance, and the values of intellectual humility and intellectual empathy, that is, a desire to engage with other perspectives. Truth can become an end rather than just a means. And of course, people such as probably most of the authors and readers of this book identify themselves with these values. I would not be myself anymore if I weren't an open-minded empathetic and tolerant person, with epistemological and ethical wisdom as one of the highest values.

All these values are sources of power.

DARWIN APPLIED TO MODERN SOCIETY

Obviously, this ladder is far from complete and perfect, but it illus-trates that a survival threat is not necessarily physical but can also apply to other identities. And that when push comes to shove, low-er order identities are seldomly sacrificed for higher ones. Dying for your country seems to be a notable example of an exception. But even then, the sacrifice is linked to an identification with what is considered a higher value.

When people feel threatened in one of their cherished identities, they distrust the perceived threatener and their messages, even if they offer (scientifically) valid perspectives. It's not irrational to look for lies, hidden threats or conspiracies of enemies. But it's dan-gerous to ignore facts, which can ultimately weaken one's defence. Reality claims its rights sooner or later. In the long run, higher values do contribute in a superior way to survival. Think about advances in medicine, surveillance systems .... But this requires a safety in the short term.

On the other hand, a perceived threat, or a desire to strengthen an identity of core values may result in a self-given right to distort maps.

In the scientific world, where funding and career advancement often depend on the number of papers published, researchers face intense pressure to produce. This can lead to prioritizing quantity over quality – rushing to publish incomplete findings, overstating results, or, in extreme cases, committing fraud. The consequences are far-reaching: invalid research enters the academic record, mis-leading other scientists, distorting public policy, and ultimately eroding trust in science itself. Ironically, a field that should stand for truth can become a victim of its own incentives.

This illustrates a third takeaway: when a measurement becomes the objective itself, it ceases to be an objective measure. The same holds for, for example, a factory with a strict production target. Workers might be tempted to overlook defects or lower quality standards just to meet quotas. The result? A short-term win weak-ens the system in the long run.

But this phenomenon isn't unique to business or academia. A similar dynamic plays out whenever a strong identity is at stake. When people feel their political allegiance, or cultural or religious affiliations are under threat, they instinctively distrust those who pose a threat to their identity. Even messages backed by solid scientific evidence, for example, on vaccination, become suspect if they come from a source that a group inherently distrusts.

STEPS TOWARDS SUPERIOR SURVIVAL BASED ON SUPERIOR KNOWLEDGE

From the foregoing, it follows that:

- The value of knowledge depends on how well it serves its intended purpose.
- To have a healthy flow of knowledge sharing, it is important to avoid negative spirals of destructive competition.
- When a person or group perceives other persons or groups as a threat to their values and beliefs or identities, there is distrust and a temptation to defend oneself with distorted maps and hiding information and knowledge.
- When a measurement becomes the goal itself, it ceases to be a reliable measure.
- On the other hand, correct information and knowledge are developed and shared with people with shared values and identities, where working together will strengthen these values and identities.

So, what can we do? The following outlines a series of forthright steps that can be taken – *analyse, plan,* and *act* – while also taking on board potential *risks*.

Analyse

When confronted with misinformation, one must ask two questions

1. Is there sheer ignorance?

2. Or is it caused by a perception of danger based in turn on the perception of different identities, values or goals? Which ones? And how correct is this perception?

In the latter case, can we postpone our judgement and associated tendency towards defensiveness or counterattack until we see clear?

The answer guides the necessary action to take.

Plan

In the first case, information and knowledge sharing is the way to go with all the tools of information and knowledge management: networking, training, publications ..., and ICT tools that support them such as websites and social media.

In the second case, common interest must be found or constructed in shared values and identities. Take as an example this experiment in a group of knowledge workers: one half of the group gets a bonus based on individual results, the other half on the collective results. Obviously, the second half shares more information, knowledge, and ideas.

Act

Once common values and identities are identified, the first maps to work on are stories that reflect them, carefully framing or avoiding the differences.

Risks

- Sharing working knowledge and ideas **prematurely** is like casting pearls before swine. Even worse, trustworthy knowledge that arrives before trust on the level of values and identity is contaminated with that distrust.

- And let's not be **overconfident,** where there is no common ground, hiding and distorting knowledge and ideas will still happen.

- Expecting that a person or group should be trustworthy on all levels is a **naivety**. Trust can then turn from too white to too black making one **cynical,** and that ultimately hurts the sharing of knowledge and ideas.

- **Moralizing** others can also be dangerous as this emphasizes the difference in values and beliefs. Furthermore, being considered as morally inferior can cause defensiveness and set negative spirals in motion. Trust based on common ground is the starting point to make somebody safely open to doubt about their current values and belief systems to improve them. Also from a Darwinian perspective, moral, as a set of values and the associated belief systems of a group, evolved to be at least good enough for the survival of that group given its environment and history. To change the morality, one has to make a good assessment of the changes in environment and history to assess which change in values, belief systems and identity will contribute to a valuable survival. If we don't use our brain, reality will teach the hard Darwinian way with no survival for those that don't fit reality.

- A similar risk lies in **condescension** towards people with lower education or less knowledge.

- **Perfectionism.** Map simplification is unavoidable for practical reasons. It's better to be approximately right, than precisely wrong!

- Building trust is a **continuous effort** – because trust, as the saying goes, comes on foot and leaves on horseback. It takes time to build but can disappear in an instant. That's why staying aware of these dynamics isn't just useful – it's necessary.

TRUST AND COLLABORATION – A FINAL REFLECTION

Ignorance, lies, and ambition are not accidental flaws – they are natural byproducts of our mortality and evolution and will always be part of human society. Superior survival in the long term is served by superior knowledge, wisdom and truth. Knowledge is Power, indeed. Yet superior knowledge only arises in a climate of trust, with minimal short-term threats to survival. This survival is not only physical but also and most often the survival of what humans identify with and value. Trust is not built overnight and can only be developed in domains where identities and values are sufficiently shared, and collaboration in domains of mutual interest is more fruitful than individual competition.

Ultimately, survival is the one value we all share. Or as Sting would sing back in 1985:

We share the same biology, regardless of ideology

But what might save us, me and you

Is if the Russians love their children too

DEMAGOGUES, DEMOCRACY AND POLITICAL ACTION

12

EXTREMISM IS THE POINT: HOW OUR SOCIETY AND POLITICS FOSTER DARK IDEAS

Sam Fowles

TWO-TIER POLICING CONSPIRACY THEORY

In March 2025, Robert Jenrick, the Shadow Home Secretary, stood up in the House of Commons and claimed that the Sentencing Council's new guidance showed 'a blatant bias against ... white people'.[1] The claim was false. Yet, Jenrick's misinformation was picked up and repeated, generally uncritically, across the traditional media. It quickly went viral on social media. It produced a flood of columns and think pieces claiming 'out of touch judges' were 'discriminating against white people'. The scandal was quickly folded into calls for the UK to leave the European Convention on Human Rights (which would strip British citizens of rights which are essential to a functioning democracy). Rather than push back against Jenrick's misinformation, the government meekly accepted his framing. The Secretary of State for Justice, adopting Jenrick's false claim, joined in the public attacks on judges and the justice system.[2]

The Sentencing Council is an independent body. It provides guidance to ensure that judges apply the sentencing ranges set by parliament in a consistent manner. The guidance in question was several years in the making (including a public consultation under the previous government, in which Jenrick served as a minister). It was developed in response to an independent report (commissioned under a Conservative government, in which Jenrick was also a minister) that indicated that people of colour, on average, receive harsher sentences than white people for the same crimes. This was attributed, in part, to unconscious bias on the part of judges.[3] The Sentencing Council sought to address the issue through an update to its guidance on pre-sentence reports.[4] These provide the judge with important information about the offender. Contrary to Jenrick's claim, the guidance recommended that a pre-sentence report should be obtained for all offenders facing a custodial or community sentence, unless the judge considers it unnecessary. The guidance suggested that a pre-sentence report was 'likely to be necessary' when sentencing a person from a minoritised community. It appeared to be based on the, relatively uncontroversial, proposition that, where there is a higher risk of unconscious bias, judges should ensure they obtain the maximum amount of information possible before making a decision. In ordering judges to ignore the guidance, the government thus preserved the existing systemic discrimination against minoritised communities. In other words: the racists got what they wanted.

Jenrick's misleading accusation drew on an ongoing conspiracy theory around 'two tier justice'. That theory claims white people are treated more harshly by the criminal justice system than others. It stems from the government response to the 2024 race riots, when thousands of (mainly white) people attacked those suspected of being immigrants, including by throwing petrol bombs at buildings where children were accommodated. Some of the rioters were arrested and prosecuted. Politicians, journalists, and social media influencers claimed they received harsher sentences than global majority people who had been involved in similar disturbances. In fact, the opposite was true. The race rioters received substantially milder sentences than those involved in peaceful protest on issues like climate change.[5] The (white) race rioters were uniformly charged with low-level public order offences. People of Asian origin, by contrast, have often been charged with terror offences (carrying a significantly higher sentence) for similar acts.[6]

The 'two tier policing' conspiracy theory is, itself, an offshoot of the 'great replacement' conspiracy theory as in the following.

POLITICAL DISCOURSE SHAPED TO PROMOTE DARK IDEAS

Conspiracy theories are, traditionally, dismissed as the preserve of cranks. Yet, as Jenrick's example shows, they can dominate the political discourse and force changes in government policy. The reason for this is that UK public and political discourse is, at a structural level, shaped to promote dark ideas.

This chapter will take 'dark ideas' to mean ideas which (a) run contrary to fundamental human rights, (b) are in some way extreme, and are (c) based on misinformation. This is adopted as a working description and is not intended to oust other descriptions in this book. Four themes run through the UK's public and political discourse, which facilitate the promotion of dark ideas:

1. The concentration of control of the discourse in the hands of a small, oligarchic, class.

2. Structural incentives which encourage appeals to the extremes of public opinion rather than the mainstream.

3. Lack of any disincentive for deceptive statements.

4. Structural incentivisation of attention grabbing and performance over substance.

These themes will be explored across three arenas of public discourse in the UK: *Political debate, traditional media,* and *social media*. The final section will argue that these structures, and the dark ideas that they facilitate, benefit an oligarchic class.

POLITICAL DEBATE

Three key elements in the arrangement of British politics create a structural incentive to promote extreme ideas.

Performance Over Substance

The role of parliament is, as 'the legislature', to make law and hold the government (as 'the executive') to account. In practice, however, the government exercises such substantial control over parliament that much of what MPs do is mere performance of the role of legislators.[7]

The government generally controls what MPs debate, how long they debate it for, and (in most cases) the outcome. Precedence is given, for most of parliamentary time, to 'government business'. This allows the government to choose what MPs will debate and for how long. As a result of the first past the post system (see below) the majority of MPs generally belong to the party of government. Their prospects for career advancement (including ministerial and junior ministerial positions, committee assignments, even roles as trade delegates) depend entirely on the favour of the executive. Parliament, insofar as it acts as a legislature, is thus governed by a matrix of perverse incentives which ensure the majority of MPs act and vote in the manner that the government directs.[8]

Even if MPs were to show independence, they have little real power to hold government (or other powerful actors) to account. Parliament has no hard powers to summon ministers to answer questions. It has a theoretical power to summon private citizens. In practice, this is relatively meaningless because it is not backed by meaningful sanctions. A finding of 'contempt of parliament' means, in practice, almost nothing. Dominic Cummings found in contempt for refusing to give evidence to the Culture Media and Sport Committee. He was appointed to a senior role in government weeks later.[9]

In practice, the best way for MPs to gain the attention of the leadership or exercise influence is by getting public attention. Junior ministers who stay in their departments and diligently deliver on their goals are less likely to be rewarded than those who achieve little of real value but constantly pop up on television. Committee hearings, in which MPs may each question a witness for a few minutes, rarely permit the sort of time and focus required for genuinely effective cross examination. They, rather, provide an opportunity for MPs to generate 'gotcha' clips which can be posted on social media or picked up by traditional media.[10]

Pandering to the Fringes

The UK's first past the post electoral system incentivises politicians to pander to the extremes of political opinion. The system ensures that parliament is not representative of the country. In 2024, the Labour Party won just 33.7% of the popular vote, yet it was rewarded with 63% of the seats in the House of Commons.[11] The Conservative Party enjoyed a similar dominance without consent after previous elections. The last time a party held both a majority of the popular vote and a majority of seats in the Commons was 1936.

Elections in the UK don't, therefore, turn on the interests of the majority. The distribution of a party's vote is significantly more important than the size of that vote. Labour in 2024, for example, doubled their share of seats in the Commons after increasing their vote share by just 1.6%.[12] Politicians are not, therefore, incentivised to respond to the views of the majority but, rather, a tiny group of swing voters in certain seats. Their views are often out of step with the mainstream. The Labour government has, for example, embraced the anti-immigration rhetoric which (until relatively recently) was primarily associated with the extreme right. Yet, less than a third of Britons think immigration is a 'bad' or 'very bad' thing.[13] This is likely because Labour has calculated that the swing vote in a small number of strategically placed constituencies may move to Reform UK (candidates for which are on record repeating conspiracy theories[14] and which has been linked to the UK and global far-right),[15] Labour has adopted the positions of Reform UK in an attempt to retain voters. These voters, however, represent a tiny percentage of, and are out of step with, the population as a whole. The government's political positioning, therefore, is skewed by an extreme fringe.

Lying Works

Dark ideas are almost uniformly based on distortions of the facts. The genesis of the modern 'anti-vax' movement, for example, was Andrew Wakefield's (debunked) claim that the MMR vaccine caused autism.[16] The 'great replacement theory', the intellectual basis for the bulk of far-right activism in the UK, promotes the lie that a 'global elite' is plotting to replace white people with Muslims.[17]

The British political system contains few meaningful incentives for truth-telling. MPs and ministers are, in Parliament, theoretically prohibited from lying and required to correct the record if they say something inadvertently misleading. In reality, however, these rules are honoured more in the breach. Of the past two cabinets, members have made at least 46 false statements (either in Parliament or in public), of which just 11% have been corrected.

The reason for this is that there is no meaningful sanction for political lying. The parliamentary rules are enforced by political committees. This means that 'truth' and 'fiction' are determined based on political rather than evidential considerations. Despite the prevalence of political lying, Boris Johnson remains the only MP to have been sanctioned for doing so. Indeed, politicians are more likely to be sanctioned for attempting to correct political lying. Labour's Dawn Butler, for example, was suspended from the Commons after (correctly) asserting that Boris Johnson had misled the county about the effect of Covid-19 vaccines.[18] When Nadine Dorries was found to have misled the Commons by making false allegations against Channel 4, the Speaker (in a ruling that he attempted to keep secret) prevented MPs from debating any sanction and then attempted to have the SNP's John Nicolson sanctioned for telling the public about the ruling.[19]

A Perfect Storm for Dark Ideas

The above three elements create a perfect storm for the promotion of dark ideas. Our political system rewards politicians who court attention over those who do the diligent work of legislating or holding the government to account. The incentive is for politicians to become something akin to social-media influencers, courting likes and clicks without regard for grounding their arguments in fact or achieving tangible results through policy. Without any disincentive for political lying, it is more politically profitable for politicians to promote attention-grabbing but facile (and often misleading) ideas than to engage in genuine debate. Meanwhile, party leaderships know that the key to winning elections lies in pandering to a tiny number of fringe voters rather than attempting to speak to the country as a whole.

TRADITIONAL MEDIA

Seventy-five per cent of print media (by readership) is, in the UK, substantially controlled by around six men.[20] All are either domiciled overseas or have significant interests in other countries. While television ownership is slightly more diverse (and the BBC, about which more below, retains a dominant position in news) three of those six have significant holdings or controlling interests in Sky, ITN, and GB News (the next largest TV news providers after the BBC).[21]

The British media is, in many respects, the oligarch's dream. It is relatively cheap to buy into and the dominance of a small number of sources means that an investor with sufficient funds can quickly capture a substantial segment of the market. Moreover, the willingness of 'mainstream' broadcasters to pick up and amplify stories from the fringes means that well-funded market entrants can have an outsized impact on national discourse. This has been demonstrated, since 2020, with the insertion of GB News[22] and Talk TV,[23] Both are loss-making businesses owned, in large part, by billionaires. Yet, they have had a significant impact on political discourse.

Talk TV and GB News also serve as a demonstration of how the oligarchic structures of UK traditional media make it vulnerable to dark ideas. Both have been accused platforming dark ideas, particularly far-right conspiracy theories and misinformation.[24] Much of GB News content, for example, seem to align with the views of its co-owner, Sir Paul Marshall (who has been accused of promoting extremist and far-right content on social media).[25]

Much of the 'traditional' media in the UK is, thus tied to a small number of oligarchs, at least some of whom appear sympathetic to dark ideas. It means that much of our public discourse is defined by little more than whether ideas find favour with (arguably extremist) oligarchs.

The BBC should stand as a bulwark against dark ideas. It is not, in theory, beholden to any oligarch or government. Yet, in practice, the BBC has done as much, if not more, to promote extremism in the UK than any other broadcaster. Much of this is to do with its promotion of the balance fallacy. This logical fallacy is baked into the structure of the BBC.[26] Broadcasters like the BBC, rather than genuinely interrogate ideas, will present an issue simply by platforming two people who disagree.

This is, supposedly, justified by the traditionally liberal proposition that the 'truth' will out through debate. In practice, however, it doesn't work like that. First, it treats all ideas as equal regardless of their factual basis or analytical consistency. Climate change denial, for example, often finds its proponents platformed in the same manner as genuine experts. Second, it privileges nonsense ideas. Under normal debate, as Christopher Hitchens put it, 'what can be asserted without evidence can be dismissed without evidence'. When the proponents of nonsense ideas are given the same platform as genuine experts, the burden of proof is, in effect, reversed. The proponents of dark ideas are permitted to dominate debates and simply by challenging their opponents to prove them wrong. Third, it legitimises the proponents of dark ideas by portraying them as equal to or the equivalent of genuine experts.[27]

The BBC's regular platforming of the proponents of dark ideas, particularly right-wing conspiracy theorists, has given fringe ideas (which would not, under normal stances, have likely progressed much further than the weirder fringes of the internet or the dodgy pub) a national audience, and presented them as deserving equal respect as genuine expertise.

SOCIAL MEDIA

Social media is, perhaps more than any other public forum, structurally programmed to promote dark ideas. Platforms make money by attracting and retaining users. Their algorithms are, consequently, designed to identify users' preferences and recommend content accordingly. Except it doesn't quite work like this. Social media algorithms work on the assumption that people are more likely to engage with content that confirms their existing views. Algorithms do not, therefore, send us content on the basis that we are likely to find it interesting or challenging. Rather, algorithms are designed to send us content that confirms our biases. In other words, social media is designed to condition users not to think. This is the perfect seeding ground for radicalisation. If a user engages with one piece of far-right content (for example), the algorithm feeds them more and more of the same. A passing interest can thus lead to a user being bombarded with extremist material.[28]

Control of social media is, like traditional media, substantially concentrated in the hands of a small number of oligarchs. This means that the 'global public square', the arena in which many ordinary people both receive their political and social news and engage in public discourse, is controlled by a tiny and unaccountable clique. So, this gives social media oligarchs a level of unaccountable power that is almost unprecedented in modern times. It is also essentially unregulated. Unlike traditional media (which is at least subject to theoretical requirements for balance), social media is not required to be politically neutral. Social media oligarchs like Elon Musk are accused of changing the algorithms that govern the sites to promote their own views.[29] This distorts the public discourse and means that users are bombarded with propaganda for a particular perspective. If they engage with or even look at the content dictated by Musk then the algorithm, as set out above, is likely to recommend ever more content along the same lines.

Other platforms have restructured their platforms to benefit dark ideas. Meta, for example, reduced the role of independent fact checkers. This enables dark ideas to spread more easily.

DARK IDEAS ARE IN THE INTERESTS OF OLIGARCHS

The structures described above are in place because they benefit a small group of economic and political oligarchs. They give these individuals a high degree of unaccountable influence over public and political discourse. This is, of course, inherently anti-democratic. When public discourse is based on evidence and expertise then anyone can, in theory, succeed in that discourse. It is, after all, open to anyone to obtain evidence and develop expertise. When public discourse is disconnected from evidence and success is based primarily on the ability to grab attention and reach audiences, then (in practice) political discourse becomes based on the approval of the oligarchs who control social and traditional media.

Dark ideas themselves, especially those promoted by the far right, benefit the oligarchic class. Right wing and far-right 'populists' generally claim to represent 'the man on the street' or 'what ordinary people are really thinking'. Once in power, however, the primary beneficiaries of their policies are the oligarchic class. Donald Trump (USA),[30] Victor Orban (Hungary),[31] Vladimir Putin (Russia),[32] Jarosław Kaczyński (Poland),[33] Javier Milei (Argentina),[34] and Liz Truss (UK) (and, to a lesser extent, Benjamin Netanyahu in Israel)[35] all sought to remove power from democratic and accountable institutions, such as courts, parliament, and regulators, and concentrate it in the hands of a small group of unaccountable individuals. They also tend to favour significant tax cuts (often coupled with increased government subsidies) for the oligarchic class.

At the same time, dark ideas protect the position of the oligarchic class. When, as set out above, government privileges the interests of a small oligarchic class ahead of the majority, that class and the government it controls risk becoming the focus of public anger. Even in minimally functioning democracies, anger focussed at the oligarchic class can promote left wing populists (such as Jeremy Corbyn in the UK, Bernie Sanders in the USA, and Jean-Luc Melanchon in France). Dark ideas help focus public anger away from oligarchs by creating 'public enemies' from marginalised groups. This also suits politicians because it is much easier to campaign by making vague promises to persecute hated groups than it is to grapple with real but complex economic and social issues. The 'great replacement' conspiracy theory, for example, casts refugees and those seeking a better life as an 'invasion' masterminded by a shadowy 'globalist elite'. Adherents, who are often victims of government and oligarchic decisions to de-industrialise, remove employment and union rights, and cut public services, blame refugees for their plight.

Dark ideas thus proliferate because their proliferation is in the interests of the powerful.

A CHANGE MUST COME

If we are to genuinely challenge dark ideas we must change the way we do politics. The solution is, quite simply, democratisation. Reforming our voting system so that parliament reflects the real will of the electorate will remove the incentive to pander to extremists. Giving MPs (rather than the government) control over parliament and real powers to hold ministers to account (such as compelling them to answer questions) will allow parliament to act like a real legislature rather than a group of performers in hoc to their government masters. Introducing genuine punishments for politicians who lie (enforced by independent courts, rather than their political allies) would push back against the perverse incentives that make 'politicians' and 'liars' too often synonymous.

Enforcing genuine competition rules in traditional and social media would break up the monopolies that currently dominate the sector and erode the power of the oligarchs. Genuine regulation of the media, requiring swift corrections with equal prominence, sanctions for misinformation, and presentation of issues based on principles of best evidence rather than crude 'balance' between extremes, and proper publication and scrutiny of algorithms would all put us on the road away from the current dominance of dark ideas.

None of these proposals are particularly new. The stumbling block is not a lack of policy solutions but, rather, a lack of political courage. Whether politicians fear a politics in which they are held to genuine account, or a discourse in which they cannot hide behind misinformation, or simply to act contrary to the interests of the oligarchic class is not clear. What is clear, however, is that those in power have all the tools to push back against dark ideas. They simply choose not to use them.

ENDNOTES

1. https://news.sky.com/story/anger-over-two-tier-sentencing-as-justice-secretary-shabana-mahmood-rejects-new-guidelines-13322444
2. https://www.theguardian.com/law/2025/mar/06/shabana-mahmood-sentencing-council-powers

3. https://assets.publishing.service.gov.uk/
media/5a82009040f0b62305b91f49/lammy-review-final-report.pdf

4. https://www.sentencingcouncil.org.uk/overarching-guides/magistrates-
court/item/imposition-of-community-and-custodial-sentences-overarching-
guideline/

5. https://www.theguardian.com/commentisfree/article/2024/aug/14/
peaceful-protest-punished-britain-racist-rioting-real-two-tier-justice

6. https://link.springer.com/book/10.1007/978-3-030-21962-8

7. See generally, Fowles, S. (2022). *Overruled: Confronting our vanishing democracy in eight cases* (Ch. 3). Oneworld.

8. Fowles, S. (2022). *Overruled: Confronting our vanishing democracy in eight cases* (pp. 52–57). Oneworld.

9. Fowles, S. (2022). *Overruled: Confronting our vanishing democracy in eight cases* (p. 57). Oneworld.

10. Hardman, I. (2019). *Why we get the wrong politicians*. Atlantic.

11. https://researchbriefings.files.parliament.uk/documents/CBP-10009/
CBP-10009.pdf

12. Miori, M., & Green, J. The most disproportionate UK election: How the Labour Party doubled its seat share with a 1.6-point increase in vote share in 2024. *Political Quarterly*, 96, 37–64.

13. https://migrationobservatory.ox.ac.uk/resources/briefings/uk-public-
opinion-toward-immigration-overall-attitudes-and-level-of-concern/

14. https://www.theguardian.com/politics/2024/may/01/reform-uk-backs-
candidates-who-promoted-online-conspiracy-theories

15. https://hopenothate.org.uk/2024/09/24/reform-uk-are-far-right-heres-
why/

16. https://pmc.ncbi.nlm.nih.gov/articles/PMC3136032/

17. https://www.theguardian.com/world/2022/jun/08/a-deadly-ideology-
how-the-great-replacement-theory-went-mainstream

18. This was on the strength of an archaic rule which prohibits MPs from calling another MP a liar; https://www.theguardian.com/politics/2021/jul/22/dawn-butler-ejected-
from-commons-for-saying-johnson-has-lied-repeatedly.

19. Fowles, S. (2024). *A model for political honesty*. ICDR. https://www.
icdr.co.uk/news/icdr-sets-out-blueprint-for-senedd-political-honesty-law.

20. Fowles, S. (2022). *Overruled: Confronting our vanishing democracy in eight cases* (p. 139). Oneworld.

21. Fowles, S. (2022). *Overruled: Confronting our vanishing democracy in eight cases* (p. 139). Oneworld.

22. https://www.cityam.com/gb-news-huge-losses-continue-despite-sales-and-audience-surge/

23. https://www.theguardian.com/media/2024/apr/29/gb-news-won-battle-talktv-both-uncertain-future

24. https://www.theguardian.com/commentisfree/2024/feb/13/gb-news-turbo-cancer-conspiracy-theories-ofcom-bias-anti-vaxxer; https://www.theguardian.com/media/2023/feb/08/jewish-groups-urge-gb-news-to-stop-indulging-conspiracy-theories; https://www.middleeasteye.net/opinion/uk-media-rife-anti-muslim-conspiracy-theories-why

25. See https://www.theguardian.com/commentisfree/2024/dec/11/gb-news-britain-muslims-ofcom-report and https://hopenothate.org.uk/2024/02/22/revealed-the-shocking-tweets-of-gb-news-co-owner-sir-paul-marshall/.

26. https://www.bbc.co.uk/editorialguidelines/guidelines/impartiality/

27. See generally https://theconversation.com/the-problem-of-false-balance-when-reporting-on-science-29077.

28. See generally, Howard, P. N. (2020). *Lie machines: How to save democracy from troll armies, deceitful robots, junk news operations, and political operatives.* Yale University Press.

29. https://www.theguardian.com/technology/2023/feb/15/elon-musk-changes-twitter-algorithm-super-bowl-slump-report

30. https://www.theguardian.com/us-news/2025/mar/24/trump-judges-impeachment-law-doge; https://www.cityam.com/trumps-victory-why-americans-chose-the-man-who-impoverished-them/

31. https://www.americanprogress.org/article/hungarys-democratic-backsliding-threatens-the-trans-atlantic-security-order/; https://www.ft.com/content/ecf6fb4e-d900-11e7-a039-c64b1c09b482

32. Miller, C. (2024). Why Russia's democracy broke. In A. Fung et al. (Eds.), *When democracy breaks* (pp. 277–298). OUP; https://www.chathamhouse.org/2023/10/putin-using-de-privatization-create-new-generation-loyal-oligarchs;

33. https://www.americanprogress.org/article/polands-democratic-resurgence-from-backsliding-to-beacon/; https://www.aljazeera.com/news/2005/9/26/centre-right-sweeps-polish-polls

34. https://odi.org/en/insights/100-days-of-president-milei-argentine-democratic-resilience-under-threat/; https://apnews.com/article/argentina-economy-crisis-javier-milei-president-peronist-crisis-8a8ac450fa5f-7942f61ab092fdd4ed15; https://www.businessinsider.com/argentina-president-milei-inspiring-musk-doge-trump-plans-slash-taxes-2024-12

35. Osnat, A. (2025). Democratic backsliding and the constitutional blitz. *European Politics and Society*, 26, 94–115; https://www.forbes.com/sites/taxanalysts/2015/11/13/netanyahus-economic-reforms-and-the-laffer-curve/.

13

PRESERVING AND SUSTAINING DEMOCRACY IN AN AGE OF DISINFORMATION

Gopal Subramanium

Supreme Court of India; Somerville College, University of Oxford

DISCONTENT AND THE SPREAD OF DARK IDEAS

Misinformed Electorates

2024 was the year of the elections. At least 64 nations and the European Union held elections in 2024, a number that represents approximately 49% of the world's population.[1]. This was a sight to behold, remarkable and inspiring. The grand dance of democracy was on display across the world. Billions participated, walking dutifully into polling booths with hope for a better future.

But were these billions making informed choices? Can we truly say that their decision to vote one way or another was based on an assessment of accurate information? We cannot. Perhaps more than any other electorate in history, the voters of 2024's elections had access to information that was simply untrue. It is difficult to determine how many votes this information affected. Indeed, Bateman and colleagues found that 'empirical research on how influence operations can affect people and societies – for example, by

altering beliefs, changing voting behaviour, or inspiring political
violence – is limited and scattered'.[2] What is clear, however, is that
disinformation is now a part of our lives, and the climate is ripe for
its proliferation.

Dwindling Faith in Democracy

The elections of 2024 took place in a climate of significant political turmoil and economic uncertainty, amidst wars, climate crises
and an ever-growing distrust in political institutions. Democracy
today is more fragile than ever; indeed, 'ours is an era of democratic recession and backsliding'.[3] Many nations appear to be moving
towards a form of elective despotism. Even though there is osten-
sible democracy, we find that narrowmindedness, fearfulness, and
the suppression of dissent rule. Media too has become vulnerable to
money and control. Political institutions seem incapable or unwill-
ing to address the world's problems. It's no surprise then that 64%
of adults in 34 countries surveyed by Pew Research believed that
their nation's economy was performing poorly,[4] while an aston-
ishing 54% of adults across 31 countries were dissatisfied with
their democracies.[5] Uncomfortably large numbers also believed
that their elected representatives didn't care for their views, or that
their nations would be better governed by autocrats who weren't
answerable to legislatures and courts.[6]

Demagogues and Hero Worship

People feel unheard, and unrepresented, and their faith in democracy as a force for good and upliftment is dwindling. This is fertile
ground for the spread of dark ideas. As democracies fail to deliver
people's aspirations, many search for new narratives to explain
their plight, for people to blame, and for heroes to set things right.
They find answers in dark ideas and see hope in leaders who
spread them.

These heroes are particularly influential, for it is they who often
direct people's discontent and anger. Hero worship fulfils people's
yearning for wisdom, inspiration, direction and meaning,[7] making

the bond between worshipped and worshipper hard to break. In fact, Dr B. R. Ambedkar, the architect of India's Constitution, recognised the threat hero worship could pose to societies in his final address to India's Constituent Assembly:

> *There is nothing wrong in being grateful to great men who have rendered life-long services to the country. But there are limits to gratefulness, as has been well said by the Irish Patriot Daniel O'Connell, no man can be grateful at the cost of his honour, no woman can be grateful at the cost of her chastity and no nation can be grateful at the cost of its liberty.*
>
> *This caution is far more necessary in the case of India than in the case of any other country. For in India, Bhakti or what may be called the path of devotion or hero-worship, plays a part in its politics unequalled in magnitude by the part it plays in the politics of any other country in the world. Bhakti in religion may be a road to the salvation of the soul. But in politics, Bhakti or hero- worship is a sure road to degradation and to eventual dictatorship.[8]*

And thus, at a time of pervasive uncertainty and discontent, we find people turning to conspiracy theories that offer simple but dark explanations for the world's problems. We see them threatened by immigrants, religious minorities or 'the elites', comfortable in the belief that their group is exceptional and their way of life under threat. In this chaos emerge demagogues, great saviours who, armed with solutions, claim to truly recognise the plight of the ordinary person.

THE NATURE OF THE PROBLEM

Technology Fuelling Disinformation and Dark Ideas

Dark ideas aren't new. People have spread falsehoods for centuries. Leaders have lied. Stories of conspiracy have been told and believed.[9] Technology has, however, altered the nature of the problem. As Kramer notes:

What has changed, what is enabling the current genera-
tion of disinformation peddlers to succeed as they have, is
the opportunity created by the internet and social media
platforms. New technologies may not have created the
problem, and they are not solely responsible for it, but
they have enabled it – providing a necessary (indeed, indis-
pensable) accelerant and catalyst for a change in degree so
extreme as to amount to a change in kind.[10]

Dark ideas can emerge from a variety of sources – from anar-
chists seeking to spread chaos, from politicians who desire power,
or from foreign adversaries attempting to destabilise nations. They
can create, replicate and disseminate disinformation at unimaginable speed. The information itself can be made to look authentic. It
may appear in what looks like a legitimate news article, well-writ-
ten, properly formatted, and suggestive of sophistication, learning
and accuracy. Even the informed and discerning observers may fall
for such 'fake news'. It is also possible to replicate real faces, voices
and mannerisms. AI-generated videos and 'deepfakes' are making it increasingly impossible to separate fact from fiction. Finally,
once we engage with disinformation, algorithms feed us more of
the same, ensuring that we have a steady supply.

The Grave Lasting Effect of Dark Ideas

Technology has thus given the spread of dark ideas unique power
to adversely affect our lives. It can distort reality at an unprecedented scale. As Starbird writes:

Disinformation 'works' by strategically shaping percep-
tions of reality within a targeted population. Once embed-
ded in those realities — and consequently in the histories,
social norms, and collective consciousness of a society —
it may be difficult to undo, address, or even identify the
manipulation.[11]

Once disinformation has a stronghold over a person or group, it
is almost impossible to undo its effects. We cannot simply convince
people of the falsity of their opinions through debate. As Douglas,

Sutton and Cichocka observe, people who believe falsehoods and conspiracy theories become 'resistant to falsification in that they postulate that conspirators use stealth and disinformation to cover up their actions—implying that people who try to debunk conspiracy theories may, themselves, be part of the conspiracy'.[12]

The threat, therefore, is real and grave. The spread of dark ideas has real-world consequences. We needn't look further than the attempted insurrection in the United States in January 2021, which was fuelled by the belief among 40% of the US population that the 2020 Presidential election was illegitimate.[13]

THE DIFFICULTY IN LEGALLY CHALLENGING THE SPREAD OF DARK IDEAS

An obvious solution, it might be said, is to ban dark ideas. Search engines and social media companies must be forced to identify and block all information that is untrue, misleading or hateful. This is easier said than done. As Kramer rightly acknowledges,

> *People are autonomous individuals entitled to make up their own minds; to do so they need to hear a wide range of views, including especially opinions that are unpopular; this exposure is necessary for individual self- actualization as well as responsible democratic citizenship; protecting hateful ideas may actually increase tolerance; self- government and deliberative democracy depend on a free and robust public dialogue; and so on.*[14]

Free people must thus be allowed access to all manner of ideas, including those that are hateful or untrue.

Moreover, if we are to prevent or restrict access to dark ideas, to whom do we give the power to determine whether information is in fact false, misleading or untrue? To private companies? To Governments? India's attempt at addressing the spread of disinformation offers an instructive example of the faults in this approach.

In 2023, India amended its Information Technology (Intermediary Guidelines and Digital Media Ethics Code) Rules, 2021. Following the amendment, intermediaries (including search engines and social media platforms) were to prevent the publication of any fake, false or misleading information about any activities of India's Central Government. The task of determining what constituted fake, false or misleading information was given to a fact check unit established by the same Central Government. Thus, having identified the problem of disinformation regarding its activities, the Central Government gave itself the power to decide what people were and weren't allowed to see.

Happily, in *Kunal Kamra* v. *Union of India*, 2024, the Bombay High Court struck down this amendment on account of, among other things, its violation of the freedom of speech and expression guaranteed under India's Constitution. One of the Court's judgments, delivered by Justice Gautam Patel, draws our attention to John Stuart Mill's treatise 'Utilitarianism, Liberty and Representative Government' and its warning against the dangers of curbing free expression:

> *But the peculiar evil of silencing the expression of an opinion is, that it is robbing the human race; posterity as well as the existing generation; those who dissent from the opinion, still more than those who hold it. If the opinion is right, they are deprived of the opportunity of exchanging error for truth; if wrong, they lose, what is almost as great a benefit, the clearer perception and livelier impression of truth, produced by its collision with error.*[15]

This example from India, extreme though it may be, shows us that in addressing the spread of dark ideas, the right way forward is not easily discoverable. What is clear, however, is that we cannot simply empower others to control our speech, especially in the absence of robust safeguards.

HOW TO PRESERVE AND SUSTAIN DEMOCRACY

Promote Information Literacy

Democratic systems must remain sufficiently unshackled to enable them to flourish. To this end, the free flow of ideas is essential. The means we adopt to prevent the spread of dark ideas must not prevent evolution and must instead ensure that the basic pillars of democratic government are preserved and strengthened. A delicate balance needs to be struck.

The first step we must take is to promote informational literacy. This is our best hope to create a society that is resilient to dark ideas. From a young age, people must be taught to identify credible sources of information. We must also encourage students to question information, especially content available online. Further, students must be shown the importance of approaching discussions on polarising subjects with empathy, not condescension and disdain. To promote critical thinking, programmes such as the International Baccalaureate already teach students to examine and analyse evidence and the credibility or sources. These efforts must be replicated across educational institutions. Particular effort must be made to ensure that a teacher's personal biases do not affect their instructions.

A Tenacious Action Plan

Additional measures must also be considered. Many of these focus on social media, which is increasingly becoming the people's primary source of news, while others focus on the role of governments.[16] Together, they constitute tenaciously pursuing the following action plan of measures:

(1) Disinformation spread by bots and foreign adversaries must be identified and access to it prevented. Speech protections that are available to citizens do not extend to such actors.

(2) Independent fact-checking organisations must be established and supported.

(3) Social-media platforms must be required by law to flag (as opposed to censor) content that it clearly false or poses an imminent threat of harm to individuals. We must also consider the use of labels to identify sources as state-funded, satirical, or as lacking credibility. Such labels have been shown to positively affect how information is perceived.[17]

(4) Nations must also reconsider the 'safe harbour' they currently offer internet companies such as search engines and social media platforms. Treated as mere intermediaries, these companies are currently saved from legal liability concerning unlawful content they host. It is imperative that they be held liable for any unlawful content on their platforms that they fail to remove. Such companies cannot be permitted to claim complete detachment from information they make available.

(5) Internet companies must be transparent about the nature of their algorithms. If necessary, changes to these algorithms must be enforced to ensure that people are not inundated with information of the same kind as this may result in intensifying and entrenching their beliefs.

(6) Governments must become more transparent. Their secrecy leaves room for conspiracy theories to emerge in attempt to explain governmental actions and motivations. Ensuring transparency will require long-term structural reforms, including the creating of information channels that are non-partisan. In the long-term, transparency may bridge the trust deficit that currently exists between the people and public institutions.

(7) We must hold politicians to a higher standard than other actors in the democratic process. This may be done, for instance, by forming multi-partisan bodies that include members of civil society to analyse political statements. Politicians who are found to have deliberately mislead the public or lied must be forced to issue corrections.

There is no single answer to the problem of dark ideas, no single method to prevent the threat they pose to the stability of the world order. A combination of measures must be adopted. And while much responsibility rests on the shoulders of governments and private companies, it is ultimately the people themselves who must learn to engage with information in a responsible manner, respecting each other, and respecting the value of the truth.

ENDNOTES

1. Ewe, K. (2023, December 28). *The ultimate election year: All the elections around the world in 2024.* Time. https://time.com/6550920/world-elections-2024/.

2. Bateman, J., Hickok, E., Courchesne, L., Thange, I., & Shapiro, J. N. (2021, June 28). *Measuring the effects of influence operations: Key findings and gaps from empirical research.* Carnegie Endowment for International Peace. https://carnegieendowment.org/2021/06/28/measuring-effects-of-influence-operations-key-findings-and-gaps-from-empirical-research-pub-84824.

3. Ginsburg, T. (2018). Democratic backsliding and the rule of law. *Ohio Northern University Law Review, 44,* 351–369.

4. Clancy, L., & Lippert, J. (2024, June 7). *Economic ratings across 34 countries are more negative than positive.* Pew Research Centre. https://www.pewresearch.org/short-reads/2024/06/07/economic-ratings-across-34-countries-are-more-negative-than-positive/.

5. Wike, R., & Fetterolf, J. (2024, June 18). *Satisfaction with democracy has declined in recent years in high-income nations.* Pew Research Centre. https://www.pewresearch.org/short-reads/2024/06/18/satisfaction-with-democracy-has-declined-in-recent-years-in-high-income-nations/.

6. Pew Research Centre. (2024, February 28). *Representative democracy remains a popular ideal, but people around the world are critical of how it's working.* https://www.pewresearch.org/global/wp-content/uploads/sites/2/2024/02/gap_2024.02.28_democracy-closed-end_report.pdf.

7. Allison, S. T., & Goethals, G. (2015). Hero worship: The elevation of the human spirit. *Journal of the Theory of Social Behaviour, 46*(2), 187–210.

8. Constituent Assembly Debates. (2014), Vol. XI. (14-11-1949 to 26-11-1949). Lok Sabha Secretariat, New Delhi. Parliament Digital Library. https://eparlib.nic.in/bitstream/123456789/763285/1/cad_25-11-1949.pdf.

9. van Prooijen, J.-W., & Douglas, K. M. (2017). Conspiracy theories as part of history: The role of societal crisis situations. *Memory Studies, 10*(3), 323–333.

10. Kramer, L. (2022). A deliberate leap in the opposite direction – The need to rethink free speech. In L. C. Bollinger & G. R. Stone (Eds.), *Social*

media, freedom of speech and the future of our democracy (pp. 17–39). Oxford University Press.

11. Starbird, K. (2022). Strategy and structure: Understanding online disinformation and how commitments to "free speech" complicate mitigation approaches. In L. C. Bollinger & G. R. Stone (Eds.), *Social media, freedom of speech and the future of our democracy* (pp. 213–229). Oxford University Press.

12. Douglas, K. M., Sutton, R. M., & Cichocka, A. (2017). The psychology of conspiracy theories. *Current Directions in Psychological Science, 26*(6), 538–542. https://doi.org/10.1177/0963721417718261.

13. Ecker, U., Roozenbeek, J., van der Linden, S, Tay, L. Q., Cook, J., Oreskes, N., & Lewandowsky, S. (2024, June 5). Misinformation poses a bigger threat to democracy than you might think. *Nature.* https://www.nature.com/articles/d41586-024-01587-3.

14. Kramer, L. (2022). A deliberate leap in the opposite direction – The need to rethink free speech. In L. C. Bollinger & G. R. Stone (Eds.), *Social media, freedom of speech and the future of our democracy* (pp. 17–39). Oxford University Press.

15. *Kunal Karma v. Union of India,* 2024:BHC-OS:1575-DB, p. 81.

16. Newman, N., Fletcher, R., Eddy, K., Robertson, C. T., & Nielsen, R. K. (2023). *Digital news report 2023.* Reuters Institute for the Study of Journalism. https://doi.org/10.60625/risj-p6es-hb13.

17. Pennycook, G., Bear, A., Collins, E. T., & Rand, D. G. (2020). The implied truth effect: Attaching warnings to a subset of fake news headlines increases perceived accuracy of headlines without warnings. *Management Science, 66*(11). https://doi.org/10.1287/mnsc.2019.3478.

14

LIVING WITH SHADE: AMBIGUITY DOES NOT MEAN ONLY DARKNESS IN WORLD POLITICS

Ben O'Loughlin, Alister Miskimmon

Royal Holloway University of London and Queen's University Belfast

EMBRACING AMBIGUITY

In these challenging times, in the face of a new cadre of determined global leaders, war in Europe, and greater centrifugal forces in world politics, it is easy to feel overwhelmed by a lack of certainty. But we argue that ambiguity is, and always has been, a feature of world politics we need to live with. Such ambiguity is an established condition which states and institutions have always faced. We need to learn to work with it and create new shared understandings with partners which underpin cooperation on the issues facing us. Nowhere is this clearer in what appears to be a wholesale rejection, in some quarters, of a liberal world order we had become accustomed to after the end of the Cold War.

There is uncertainty about how things will evolve. The situation we find ourselves in is fundamentally ambiguous, and this makes it unsettling, particularly in the face of pressing global challenges such as climate change. Yet the fact that there is nothing new about ambiguity in world politics means there are familiar paths to navigate it. It will not all be demagogues, populism and misinformation. Instead, as Groucho Marx quipped, 'Politics is the art of looking for trouble, finding it everywhere, diagnosing it incorrectly, and applying the wrong remedies.' It is therefore incumbent on our leaders to work towards common ground. In this short piece, we will survey ambiguity as a condition and ambiguity as a tool, before setting out how we can manage ambiguity in the most useful ways.

AMBIGUITY IS A BASIC CONDITION OF WORLD POLITICS

Overlapping Governance

International Relations scholar Stephanie Hofmann[1] has pointed out that the liberal world order, to the extent it exists, has rested on a UN Charter that is highly ambiguous. That ambiguity provided a useful function in that states could sign up because the meaning of the Charter was not fixed and could evolve. Such ambiguity can, in certain circumstances, act as a spur for contestation. States advance their preferred version of world order and there is no present reason why this will end anytime soon. Global institutions have long performed the vital function of serving as public fora for debates to happen and accommodations to emerge.

We concur with Hofmann's analysis. Global governance is unclear, yet for several decades, there has been an evolving set of institutions where states and non-governmental actors have met to address shared challenges. There are overlapping institutions, both regional and global. Consider, for instance, the governance of climate, finance or aid and you will find a polycentric order – many centres, many spheres, much of which is formally structured – but there is much that is informal and contingent. Some international laws are upheld or paid lip service to, but many are not. Nation-states often join or leave treaties, and have done for centuries.

Taiwan and Palestinian Statehood

The many types of actors in international affairs are also ambiguous. Examples include divergent opinions on Taiwan and how the

People's Republic of China seeks to influence engagement with Taipei on the global level. Taiwan is not recognised as a state, but it has many state features. It cannot send diplomats to the United Nations, but Taiwanese representatives can go and meet diplomats in the UN's headquarters and other fora to seek influence. Likewise, there are ongoing debates about Palestinian statehood in the international community, which have intensified in light of Israeli military actions in Gaza and the West Bank since October 2023. Exogeneous recognition of such claims creates debates and tensions. Such dynamics are indicative of the emergence and disappearance of states over time and their consequences.[2] Czechoslovakia, Kurdistan, Taiwan, and Palestine speak to this. World politics is not simply a chess board with a managed choreography where sides take turns and pieces have clear capacities.

NATO

NATO is another example where ambiguity plays both a cohesive and discordant role.[3] NATO's post-Cold War trajectory has countered claims that alliances do not outlast the rationale for their existence. Finding a new role in regional and global security was instrumental for its continuance after 1990. The desire for Central and East-European states to join NATO was to secure their status as sovereign equals, and as a defence against a revanchist Russian Federation. In the absence of the existential threat of the Cold War, there have been debates on NATO's new role around the USA's continued role in European security, transatlantic relations and over what role NATO should have.

These debates revealed a spectrum of views within the alliance. Ambiguity helped fudge some of the more challenging strategic debates within NATO, but as we have seen in recent debates over Russia's war on Ukraine, underlying debates never fully went away. Indeed, under the second Trump presidency, these have emerged with a new force. Should ambiguity become a less useful tool in containing divergent views within the alliance, institutional decay may set in. Further, within the European Union, which has long-since indicated a desire to emerge as a more important foreign and security player, we continue to witness a dominance of national strategic cultures in debates of Gaza, Ukraine and Europe's emerging role. The supportive role of ambiguity in smoothing out national preferences melts away in the white heat of crises.

Ambiguity at the Heart of International Relations

European and transatlantic relations are not the only space of strategic ambiguity. Emerging entities such as the BRICS group of Brazil, Russia, India, China, and South Africa also struggle to arrive at shared foreign policy positions on the major issues facing the globe. Where does NAFTA unity lie if the USA puts tariffs on Canada and Mexico? Member states of the African Union vary in their preference to work with the EU, China, or both, and the degree to which they will be assertive about this. Where does that leave the possibility for the EU or China to have a coherent narrative about its relations to African states? Again, ambiguity is baked into global politics to sustain areas where cooperation is possible.

It is perhaps unavoidable that other states will seem ambiguous on many aspects of global politics when viewed from national capitals. Despite intelligence services and diplomatic missions, knowledge of other states is often imperfect. The UK has tried to pivot to the Indo-Pacific but its officials' failure to listen to what countries there want, or what they expect from the UK, has hindered the UK foreign policy strategy in the region. The UK officials might reflect on what this teaches them about their own cognitive biases or 'blind spots' so that they might see more clearly.

Polyamorous Relationships

Actors also choose to appear ambiguous to others. For example, understanding the aims of others and their implications remains a vital area of foreign policy forecasting. No more is this the case than with China – what do we expect from China as great power, wielding increasing influence in international affairs? Beijing uses slogans – 'Belt and Road', 'G2 with Chinese characteristics' – without fully articulating a stance as a global player. What does Belt and Road mean? And indeed, what are Chinese characteristics and what does this mean for global order – how do these interact harmoniously or contrary to American, Indian or European characteristics?

In this era of accelerated evolution of the international system, flexibility and adaptability have become traits which are increasingly visible in interstate relations. Most states do not want to choose to trade only with the USA or China – they want a degree of trade with both. The USA and China keep trading with each other, too. In their global survey of opinion about foreign affairs in late 2024, Timothy Garton Ash and colleagues at the European Council on Foreign Relations found that 'middle' powers do not want to take sides:

> *The monogamous marriages of the cold war period are now history, and middle powers have embraced polyamorous relationships, favouring different partners for different issues.*[4]

Plural Identities

States offer plural identities too. Political movements within a state might advocate for different foreign policies. President Trump did not attend COP climate summits but leaders of US states and companies did, because they did care about climate change. In 2017, the 100th anniversary of Russia's 1917 revolutions, international news media noted Putin was not openly celebrating. However, there were exhibitions, plays, and films about 1917 in 2017 within Russia. What was 'Russia's' position? It appeared plural and thus ambiguous.[5] We must live with this dimension of ambiguity, about what is say-able, for whom, to whom.

The upshot of ambiguity as ongoing condition is that by avoiding simplicity, such as thinking world politics is just about nation-states, we can understand far more of the messiness and the nuance. We will return to the labour this involves, but next we ask how actors use ambiguity.

STRATEGIC AMBIGUITY AS A TOOL

Letting the Tree Bend But Not Break

Not only is ambiguity the condition of world politics. Actors use ambiguity as a strategic tool. Indeed, strategic ambiguity is their tool. State A can make its policies or intentions unclear so that others cannot predict how state A will act. European leaders may have made slow or vague public promises of help to Ukraine because exact information would offer targets for Russia.

Strategic ambiguity can be used to induce miscalculations by other actors. A state responding to another's ambiguous statement may commit resources that get used for no valid reason or make policy commitments that prove impossible. Signals are often misread. Post-Brexit UK foreign policy is an interesting example. Prime Minister Sir Keir Starmer and Foreign Secretary David Lammy are increasingly pressured to chart a defined strategic course, but in the context of fractious transatlantic relations, post-Brexit tensions with the EU over relations and a changing global order, flexibility is key. Deciding to commit to European cooperation or looking to transatlantic relations could limit the UK's foreign policy options in a period of flux. As we write in February 2025, news reported Starmer 'walking a tightrope' on his trip to Washington DC to meet Trump. Staying on the tightrope, not being buffeted from either side, means communicating sufficient ambiguity to ensure all sides feel some compromise in favour of their interests may occur. Starmer is seeking to avoid falling into an over-committed miscalculation. He is using the tool of strategic ambiguity.

A day later, and Trump and Zelensky are openly disagreeing in a scene before the cameras that is not sticking to diplomatic etiquette. How is Starmer to respond to such daily challenges while finding a long-term direction for UK foreign policy? The tone and fallout in responses to Trump–Zelensky indicate the many strongly held positions in countries around the world. The context has changed in 24 hours, but expect Starmer to present a set of points that signal support for Ukraine but not hostility to the USA. He will signal policies that are strong but not fixed. In the diplomatic storm, ambiguity lets the tree bend but not break.

The Danger of Promises and Expectations

Ambiguity is also a tool to prevent domestic publics forming explicit expectations about what policy will happen or what policy will achieve. Being hostage to promises can be avoided. Some publics may yearn for a degree of simplicity and clarity in foreign policy, but this carries risks for leaders. US presidents offer a long-standing, simple narrative that the genuine appeal of liberty means civil society will overthrow brutal regimes and create democracy. President Obama felt no need therefore to send troops into Syria to overthrow President Assad over a decade ago, despite Assad's use of chemical weapons. The USA was trapped into inaction as Syrians were tortured and killed before the country collapsed. When Assad crossed Obama's 'red line' on chemical weapons, the USA flinched. The simple narrative left Obama exposed in ways ambiguity would not have.

Ambiguity can be a tool of survival. Political scientist Lee Ann Fujii explored how Hutu and Tutsi people lived on in Rwanda following the 1994 genocide by Hutu of Tutsi.[6] She found in 2009 that people were incredibly careful in how they used language, because they were aware neighbours could report them to police or military. She found those she interviewed in 2004 who said they had committed violence, when interviewed again in 2009 told her the exact opposite, because the cost of cheap talk is your life. They used ambiguity to survive.

HOW TO CARRY THE BURDEN OF AMBIGUITY

Managing Uncertain Information

It is inconvenient to the public to have to spend time interpreting ambiguity in politics. It is a heavy workload. It means being comfortable with uncertainty. The enlightenment ideal of the informed individual using reason to understand the logic of events – that is only an ideal, and we need to live with other ideals at the same time. There exist many ideals, multiple perspectives, not universes but a pluriverse, because how the universe is looks different for everyone.

How do we respond? Conditions of ambiguity, and political actors' explicit creation of ambiguity for strategic ends, poses risks for truth, facts, and any shared, collective sense-making of events. We are all managing a situation of uncertain information.

This is why our expectations of news are varied. Most hope it provides accurate information. Some journalists know that perfect objective knowledge is impossible, but it is a benchmark to aim for. But other news organisations frame news reports according to their political ideology or partisan biases, and their audiences choose news that fits their worldview and allegiances. This is why fact-checking is just one of many tools we need. People are not just judging facts. They ignore some facts. If the side of the war they support is reported to have bombed a school or hospital just now, they will ignore it. To them it is irrelevant, secondary to their preference that their side wins the war.

The Complexity of Events

International affairs constitute a constant stream of events to which actors must respond. The sheer contingency of politics adds to an absence of clarity and certainty. We often ask where does truth stand as we seek to process how events shape our lives. Sociology professor Robin Wagner-Pacifici argues that these events create contingency.[7] We cannot know in advance what will happen. We don't have perfect information in the present. We cannot predict the decisions people will make, especially under pressure. Fate doesn't just stand still. Fate hangs in the balance.

It also creates more labour for the public: work out why a stand-off happened in the first place. We seek out causes to assign accountability. An event happened, so we work back from the effects, offer our interpretation of what caused those effects. Hamas attacks Israel: we ask why, which means working backwards in time, going back into recent history and longer histories. Dealing with complexity is difficult, as we interpret the past differently, based on different information available to us. Antagonisms are frozen and exposed to public scrutiny. And it is tied to a space – it can seem like in 'the eye of the storm', a stalled moment, and

all wait for any signal, gesture, movement, from either side. It is
hugely ambiguous.

A further step is needed ....

Ambiguity as a Positive Force

Here we return to Stephanie Hofmann's thesis. Ambiguity is part
of how we negotiate change. We can reach deals that are good
enough for all sides; even precise understanding of the deal among
all parties is never reached. It is still good enough for a degree of
agreement to occur. War crimes must be prosecuted, reparations
paid, tensions resolved to prevent further violence. Some people
in some roles must have information good enough to make those
things happen that satisfy enough of the world's societies.

Actors can get it wrong. Hofmann notes how in the post-Cold
War period, global North countries advanced what they took as
a liberal world order. However, they used extremely non-liberal
forms of warfare, or withheld finance from societies. As a result,
much of the global South witnessed a very non-liberal North and
non-liberal order.

Ambiguity is a positive force because if actors accept that there
can be no single order all humanity agree upon then they will have
to accept diversity of views. That can provide relative stability. We
live with ongoing competition to promote orders and that forces
us to take note of the forms of order on offer. We can see that
in different things it raises regions certain ordering processes that
actors enact. This requires actors to interpret each other on an
ongoing basis. But it is a condition allowing some compromise,
some cooperation.

EMBRACING AMBIGUITY – SOME KEY RECOMMENDATIONS

Ambiguity is ultimately an ongoing feature of global politics. This
is only heightened by the multiple crises, rapid technological developments and shifting dynamics of power in international order. We
do not know how the war on Ukraine will end, how the crisis in

Israel/Palestine may be addressed, or how the world will look after the second Trump administration. Added to this, developments in Artificial Intelligence look set to transform our lives in ways we do not yet fully comprehend. We suggest the following as a means to cope with what is in front of us:

- The UK government needs to do more to foster public discussion *about* rapid change in global politics and its implications on British citizens.

- The UK government should focus on forging new global partnerships to manage change to work towards building a conducive international environment for UK values and interests.

- Independent fact-checking is just one of many tools we need to ensure we retain a public sphere where political choices can be debated and agreed on.

AMBIGUITY – MESSY AND UNAVOIDABLE!

Ambiguity isn't going away. It is a tool leaders use in politics, and part of the context of life. But it must co-exist with sufficient degrees of certainty about some things, so that we can make collective decisions and morally acceptable decisions. Since it implies there no single model of world order, it involves both competition but also cooperation between some actors, some of the time. This is messy, neither all light nor all dark. It is the unavoidable condition of shade.

ENDNOTES

1. Hofmann, S. C. (2024). Dialectical order-making through ambiguity: Contestation is the norm in international peace and security maintenance. *Global Studies Quarterly*, 4(2). https://doi.org/10.1093/isagsq/ksae021.
2. Stokes, D. (2019). Political opportunities and the quest for political recognition in Tibet, Taiwan, and Palestine. *International Review of Sociology*, 29(1), 102–124.
3. Forster, A., & Wallace, W. (2001). What is NATO for?. *Survival*, 43(4), 107–122.

4. Garton Ash, T., Krastev, I., & Leonard, M. (2025). *Alone in a Trumpian world: The EU and global public opinion after the US elections* [Policy Brief]. European Council on Foreign Relations. https://ecfr.eu/publication/alone-in-a-trumpian-world-the-eu-and-global-public-opinion-after-the-us-elections/.

5. O'Loughlin, B. (2020). The October revolution as a global media event: Connective imaginaries in 2017. *European Journal of Cultural Studies, 23*(3), 374–392.

6. Fujii, L. A. (2021). *Show time: The logic and power of violent display.* Cornell University Press.

7. Wagner-Pacifici, R. (2019). *What is an event?* University of Chicago Press.

15

WHAT WOULD THE SUFFRAGETTES THINK?

Vivienne Porritt

WomenEd

THE DOMINANCE OF PATRIARCHY

The current social systems globally are generally described as patriarchal in that primary positions in government, the church, leadership and finance are held by men. We can see this in that in 2024, only 1I women were leaders of their countries.[1] This is the highest number ever which can be seen as a positive change. Yet, there has never been more than 17 countries with women in the highest positions of power in a single year. This is less than 10% of the number of men who have held these positions.

Patriarchy has been the major social system since our ancestors became attached to land, agriculture, property and greater domestication.

Sylvia Walby set out six overlapping structures that define patriarchy which take different forms in different cultures and times.[2]

1. The household: women's labour is more likely to be through housework and raising children.

2. Paid work: women are likely to be paid less and face exclusion from paid work.

3. The state: women are unlikely to have formal power and representation.

4. Violence: women are more prone to being abused.

5. Sexuality: women's sexuality is more likely to be treated negatively.

6. Culture: representation of women in different cultural contexts.

How Have Women Experienced Patriarchy?

- 1866: the concept of rape within marriage does not exist in the UK. It was repealed in 1994.[3]

- 1878: The University of London is the first university in the UK to accept women on equal terms with men.

- 1891: The right to use corporal punishment on a wife in the UK was removed.

- 1919: Married women were allowed to be teachers in Wales.[4]

- 1960: The first female world leader was elected in Sri Lanka, then known as Ceylon, when Sirimavo Bandaranaike became prime minister.[5]

- 1968: Ford Dagenham sewing machinists' strike in London, leading to the Equal Pay Act.

- 1974: Women in the United States could open a bank account without the signature of their husbands.[6]

- 1986: Statutory maternity pay was introduced in the UK.

- 1990: Independent taxation for women in the UK was introduced, and, for the first time, married women.

It seems shocking to me that some of these rights were not available to women until very recently. I was a married woman in 1990 and do not recall independent taxation being introduced. These earlier rights for women must be lauded, but sadly we are currently seeing attacks on women's rights globally and we need to be clear why this is happening.

THE HEROISM OF THE SUFFRAGETTES

We need to go back to the 1900s, when the Suffragettes railed against patriarchal social systems, in particular the representation of women to vote for their government. In the early 1900s, violence against women was common place. Women faced violence in their homes which was heightened when the Suffragettes began their campaign and faced sexual assault by the police:

'Several times constables and plain-clothes men who were in the crowds passed their arms round me from the back and clutched hold of my breasts in as public a manner as possible, and men in the crowd followed their example', described one Suffragette. 'My skirt was lifted up as high as possible… [the constable] threw me into the crowd and incited the men to treat me as they wished.'[7]

Many Suffragettes were imprisoned and force-fed for their goal to give women the vote. They changed the experience of women in the UK and globally for which we owe these women a debt of gratitude. Given what they went through, they surely envisioned a future where their sacrifices led to lasting change.

SOME CHANGE BUT LITTLE PROGRESS

There has been change to a certain extent. In 1995, United Nations Women published the Beijing Declaration and Platform for Action,[8] which stated that 'the status of women has advanced in some important respects in the past decade'. Since then, women have gained hard won rights, a place in the workforce and girls' academic outcomes are much higher than boys.

I believe the Suffragettes would be inspired by this progress especially in terms of education which should be the gateway into a more balanced and inclusive society where women can take their place as equals with men.

The Beijing Declaration also highlighted that 'progress has been uneven, inequalities between women and men have persisted and major obstacles remain, with serious consequences for the well-being of all people'.

The uneven progress highlighted has continued since and a backlash against both women's success and their right to be seen as equals is writ large.[9]

In multiple countries, rights have been rolled back in recent years with anti-feminist rhetoric and policies. According to UN Women, gender disparities are worsening. They believe it could take another 286 years to close the global gender gaps in legal protections for women and girls.

The Suffragettes legacy is tarnished by the way many women are being treated now: I will explore what is happening and what we can do to tackle this scourge. I have two main questions:

1. How many girls and women will die while we work out how to treat them as equals?

2. Why is this still happening?

VIOLENCE AGAINST WOMEN AND GIRLS

Misogyny and sexism are seen in a myriad of ways from violence against women and girls (VAWG), to overt misogyny and sexism in schools, online and in politics to highlight key examples.

VAWG is in every news report we see. In the UK, *The Guardian* reported that 80 women were allegedly killed by men in 2024. The newspaper had launched the Killed Women Count, a project highlighting the tragedy of women whose deaths led to a man being charged. It takes my breath away that such a count could be considered in the first place and the numbers are horrific.

In March 2025, the newspaper highlighted that nearly one in 10 of all women who died at the hands of men in the UK over the past 15 years were mothers killed by their sons.[10] The 2000 Women Report by The Femicide Census[11] shames us in the data shared, Thirty-seven women were killed alongside 53 children, most commonly by the father of the children (77%, no.=41 of 53 child victims). Femicide, the most extreme form of violence against women, is a horrifying reality.

United Nations Women highlighted that one in three women globally has been subjected to physical or sexual violence at least once in their life and 86% of women and girls are living in countries without robust legal protection from violence and discrimination.[12] We have all witnessed and been outraged by the violence perpetrated on women in Gaza, Afghanistan, Iran, and France. Globally, 4.4 million girls are currently at risk of female genital mutilation.[13]

The Suffragettes would be out on the streets shouting about these atrocities and demanding greater action to protect women and girls and I would join them.

So how did we get here? What is causing such violence and discrimination against women and girls? A new Ipsos UK survey sheds light on public opinion on the issue:

> *Whilst over three in five (63%) think public awareness of violence against women and girls is increasing, half (51%) think levels of violence against women and girls are also increasing. Just under half think that levels of toxic masculinity (48%) and misogyny (47%) are increasing, while four in ten (40%) think that the normalisation of violence against women and girls is on the rise.*[14]

An Ipsos and Kings Global Institute for Women's Leadership report in March 2025 explored attitudes to Gender Equality across 32 countries. 53% of women born from 1997 to 2012 (Gen Z) describe themselves as feminists compared to 32% of Gen Z men, 'the biggest gender split of any generation surveyed'.[15]

Half of all surveyed (54%) agree men are being expected to do too much to support equality (also up from 2019), and half (48%) agreed that things have gone so far in promoting women's equality that men are being discriminated against.

It saddens me that such prejudice is on the rise globally and threatens the progress made since the Suffragette movement. Equally, it is terrible that some members of the police are the perpetrators of violence. I recall the kidnap, rape and murder of Sarah Everard in the UK in 2021 with a serving Metropolitan parliamentary and diplomatic protection officer convicted. Alleged failures

by the Metropolitan police force to investigate two previous inde-
cent exposure incidents by the perpetrator were later shared. This
is only one frightening example of how the protectors of a just
society do not always protect women.

Unfortunately, the backlash against women's rights and women
as equal members of society is working and we see misogyny in a
range of different arenas including, schools, politics, and online.

MISOGYNY AND SEXISM

The Mainstreaming of Misogyny

First, we need to be clear on what misogyny is. Dictionary defini-
tions include:

- 'dislike of, contempt for, or ingrained prejudice against
  women'.[16]

- 'feelings of hating women, or the belief that men are much better than women'.[17]

This takes us back to darker times when women were fighting
for their rights to work and to be equal. UN Secretary-General
Antonio Guterres said:

> 'Globally, women's human rights are under attack.
> Instead of mainstreaming equal rights, we're seeing the
> mainstreaming of misogyny.' He added the world must
> stand firm 'in making human rights, equality and empow-
> erment a reality for all women and girls, for everyone, eve-
> rywhere'.

> One comment in this regard stands out for me: 'the les-
> son of Trump's win is the triumph of a misogynistic,
> masculine view of the world that intentionally denigrates
> women'.[18] Mike Johnson, the victorious House Speaker in
> the USA has blamed Roe v. Wade in the past for depriv-
> ing the country of 'able-bodied workers'[19] to prop up the
> American economy.

This suggests a reversion of progress and moving towards women being seen as unequal to men, and maybe worse. It is especially sad if girls are also seen this way as that would destroy the bright future we should all see for them.

After the USA election, researchers documented a stunning rise in misogynistic rhetoric and attacks including those in schools[20]:

a lot of reports ... including in our lab, from schools and universities, ... even from an elementary school, whose parent who reached out to me and said her 10-year-old daughter had heard a boy chant at her, 'Your body, my choice'. So beliefs in a hierarchy of superiority, beliefs in the inferiority of women, drive support for political violence.

Misogyny in Schools

Let's look at misogyny in schools.

In December 2024, The UK Education Secretary told teachers to look for signs of 'incel culture' in the classroom, as the education secretary warned that 'manosphere' influencers are radicalising teenage boys into 'hating women'.[21] Equally a headteacher of a London primary school shared this with me: 'There is a sense that girls are not as vocal about sexism as they should be. There is an acceptance that this is part of school life'. In a recent article on tackling misogyny in schools, teachers stated, 'that misogynistic actions often go unchallenged or inadequately addressed'.[22] Nuzhat Uthnani would strongly advocate for the need to 'educate young people on the dangers of online social media use and exposure to inappropriate content, in the same way we teach about substance misuse'.[23]

This is so very sad for young girls who may start to think this is their lot for the future.

Adults in schools are also vulnerable to sexism and misogyny. UK Feminista conducted an informal poll at a National Education Union conference with 98% of respondents witnessing or experiencing sexism in their school or college.[24]

The trade union, Unison surveyed female support staff in secondary schools with 1 in 10 having experienced sexual harassment, mainly from male pupils but also from male colleagues. 'Many reported shocking incidents of sexual harassment, for example, one female member of staff described how a male student tried to kiss her and pushed her head into his crotch.'[25]

Many marginalised women suffer badly from sexism and bullying.

Male colleagues told her she would have to 'bend over a desk to get a promotion' and had 'blowjob lips'. Incidents like these happened 'almost every day', she says.[26]

The charity WomenEd, which supports women educators and leaders, hears testimony such as this regularly, with women facing toxic cultures and additionally denied equitable pay and career success compared to male colleagues.[27]

The London Mayor wrote to every primary school in London asking schools to counter online misogyny by social media influencers such as Andrew Tate with classes and workshops intended to tackle VAWG. This could support the Labour Government's aim to reduce VAWG in a decade. However, the government has its work cut out given the data that is piling up.[28]

Misogyny and sexism in education must be countered at least and overcome at best if we are to enable educators and students to prosper and deal with the challenges these scourges bring to an equitable and safe world. This can be achieved by involving both women and men as allies to show girls and boys that equality can be a shared solution.

United Nations Women developed a group of male allies to champion and accelerate progress to gender equality. Their valuable toolkit for men and boys to achieve change would be useful in all schools.[29]

Men at Work[30] offers support for professionals in supporting the healthy personal development of boys and young men, and challenging sexism while fostering violence-free relationships and communities. The aim is to increase boys' confidence, knowledge and skills by facilitating constructive dialogues with boys and young men about being safe themselves and, crucially being safe to be around.

Innovative Enterprise develops awareness of unhelpful masculinities and sexism from the classroom, via the locker room to the board room.[31] Progressive Masculinity creates safe, nonjudgmental spaces where boys and men can explore their masculinity and its potential.[32]

UK Feminista's vision is a society in which women and girls live free from sexism and violence and to reduce the '37% of female students who have been sexually harassed at school'.[33] WomenEd collaborates with them and supports their annual awards. Life Lessons[34] have a set of evidence-based materials for schools, including primary schools, that empower educators to counter digital and sexual violence.

For school leaders who want to tackle misogyny, references for the above organisations are on their websites.

WOMEN UNDER ATTACK IN THE POLITICAL ARENA

The climate for women globally is threatening and what is happening in the political arena is a further provocation rather than tackling misogyny.

Women are still underrepresented in politics and country governance and when represented, their contribution is often belittled or savaged. I recall failing to spot women leaders at COP 28 and 29 while most of the women there were volunteers and activists trying to save the planet through volunteering. I seethed when Kamala Harris, a Vice President of the USA, was referred to as a childless woman and depicted on social media as a cat lady. Maybe I was furious as those examples represent me.[35]

The UK Chancellor of the Exchequer, Rachel Reeves, has been belittled by being called 'Rachel from Accounts' after she rejected allegations her CV had been embellished. One journalist asked her whether she thought she would be subjected to a condescending label if she were a man: sexism condoned by our media.[36]

Jess Phillips (UK Minister for Safeguarding and VAWG) experienced misogynistic attacks regarding an inquiry into historic sexual abuse cases, including from USA billionaires involved in the USA election. Misogyny seems to have no borders.

Jess Phillips was supported by women's aid against these attacks:

> *With one in four women being killed every week by a current or former partner, now is the time that we need to come together and stand up against VAWG.*[37]

Now is certainly the time as women are being attacked on all levels, and non-more so than online.

ASSAULT IN THE ONLINE WORLD

In March 2025, UK Feminista highlighted that 'The lawlessness of the online pornography world has been a disaster for women and girls'.[38] The exploitation of women through pornography has now spread to the online world with requests to regulate online pornography by verifying that all featured must be adults and give permission for the content. This has not happened yet which is appalling to me. Without this, girls and women are not safe and it's time to put them above the 'profits of the pornography trade'.

Equally, research suggests that girls may be more vulnerable to experiencing mental health difficulties[39] from social media use than boys, particularly in relation to sexualised pictures and self-image.

Girls and young women are subjected to negative stereotypes[40] which can limit their goals and future outcomes with the online world combined with misogyny exacerbating this. The prevalence of online sexual harassment in the lives of young people was exposed in the Ofsted report in 2021:

> *Around 9 in 10 of the girls we spoke to said that sexist name calling and being sent unwanted explicit pictures or videos happened 'a lot' or 'sometimes'. Inspectors were also told that boys talk about whose 'nudes' they have and share them among themselves like a 'collection game', typically on platforms like WhatsApp or Snapchat.*[41]

The Australian government seems convinced about online dangers, recently announcing plans to ban it entirely for young people under the age of 16.[42]

Coming up to date, a 2025 programme from Netflix, *Adolescence,* which is based on real incidents, explores the impact of the dangers of the online world on a teenage girl, a 13-year-old boy, and his family when the boy is accused of murdering a young woman.

> *We are led into a teenage world that is lived primarily online and which adults are, whatever they might think, incapable of properly monitoring or understanding.*[43]

In opening our eyes to the world of incel culture, we learn about the messages spread between boys and young men about what they are entitled to expect and to take from girls and women. The boy spent so much time in online misogyny and porn that his views of women led him to murder. It demonstrates 'what our children and young people are being exposed to online. And the normalisation and desensitisation of violence and hate'.[44]

It is vital that as a society we ask crucial questions about our development of adolescent boys. These include:

- What we are teaching boys?

- How much teachers and parents are aware of the world in which the boys live?

- How should we talk with boys and girls about sexism and misogyny?

RISING TO THE STARK RALLYING CRY

We are being taken back to when violence against women in the time of the Suffragettes was expected and we must fight against this for our partners, girls and granddaughters. This must be a rallying call for men and boys to put themselves at the fore front of this fight. In agreement with this is the prominent broadcaster, Matthew Syed, who champions this message in his stark, challenging declaration:

> *don't give me the sociological claptrap that men are merely 'reacting' to the overreach of women's rights .... The fact that women are no longer putting up with being*

underpaid, sexually harassed or (as in the case of Harvey
Weinstein, Jeffrey Epstein and their hateful ilk) raped
doesn't mean it is 'understandable' that young men feel
angry enough to choke and traduce women, as ever more
seem to do.[45]

Sir Gareth Southgate, a male figure head, especially to young boys, delivered the 2025 Richard Dimpleby Lecture and highlighted that young men are suffering. 'They're grappling with their masculinity and with their broader place in society.'[46]

Then, in the online world, girls read about Gisele Pelicot. Her experience profoundly illustrates the dark ideas of this book. Women have been raped throughout history and it is not reducing:

We've learned not to make a fuss. To fix our clothes, wipe
off the ruined mascara. Destroy the evidence and com-
partmentalise the violence done to us.[47]

For women rape is the embodiment of violence towards them and yet is often unprosecuted as if women should put up with it. To be raped by a partner and so many unknown men with no recall, as Giselle was, is a truly dark thought and a worse experience. Rape can make women feel ashamed as it makes them feel a helpless victim who couldn't stop the aggressor. And then Giselle changed the rules for women. She faced her rapists publicly and told women that 'it's not for us to have shame – it's for them'… and 'demonstrated to the world how to reject shame'.

In reaction to Giselle's experience, Bernie Bernard emphasises how men can help to make shame change sides. He highlights that none of the men who saw the advert from Giselle's husband reported it to the police which made them complicit. In this case it was all men. His resource of a Continuum of Harm helps men to see that they can 'influence other men's behaviour'.[48]

A NEW SUFFRAGETTE MOVEMENT

And Giselle has demonstrated how women could respond to the tsunami of misogyny we face currently. I was so proud for her that she was The New European's Person of the year 2024. In my view, she should have been Times Person of the Year also. The fact that Donald Trump, the purveyor of so much misogyny, was given this title means women, and men as our allies, must rise up to create our equivalent of the Suffragette movement.

To aid this, the European Commission and UN Women are co-leaders of the Action Coalition on Gender Based Violence.[49] ACT will begin in Africa and Latin America to end violence against women.

Until women are safe, Women's Aid offers ten ways to help end VAWG.[50] One suggestion is to promote healthy relationships with young people which is much needed to reject violence and misogyny from all our futures. We must build on this and reject the shame and discrimination women are taught to experience and reclaim our rights, voices and power.

If we can make the difference our world needs now the Suffragettes would be proud of us.

ENDNOTES

1. https://www.statista.com/statistics/1058345/countries-with-women-highest-position-executive-power-since-1960/

2. https://journals.sagepub.com/doi/10.1177/0038038589023002004

3. Chrome-extension://efaidnbmnnnibpcajpcglclefindmkaj/https://www.fawcettsociety.org.uk/Handlers/Download.ashx?IDMF=45a5a7f5-ffbd-4078-b0b7-4bfcccab159d

4. https://www.bbc.co.uk/wales/history/sites/themes/society/women_teaching.shtml

5. https://www.newsweek.com/map-shows-all-countries-have-women-leaders-1971362

6. https://www.forbes.com/advisor/banking/when-could-women-open-a-bank-account/

7. https://www.londonmuseum.org.uk/collections/london-stories/how-black-friday-changed-suffragette-struggle/

8. Chrome-chrome-extension://efaidnbmnnnibpcajpcglclefindmkaj/https://www.un.org/womenwatch/daw/beijing/pdf/BDPfA%20E.pdf

9. https://www.hrw.org/news/2023/03/07/global-backlash-against-womens-rights

10. https://www.theguardian.com/uk-news/2025/mar/05/more-than-170-mothers-killed-by-sons-15-years-uk-report?utm_term=67cbfa2d4
dac1b9dd74586a9924584a5&utm_campaign=SaturdayEdition&utm_
source=esp&utm_medium=Email&CMP=saturdayedition_email
11. Chrome-extension://efaidnbmnnnibpcajpcglclefindmkaj/https://www.
femicidecensus.org/wp-content/uploads/2025/03/2000-Women-full-
report.pdf
12. https://www.linkedin.com/posts/un-women_act-carouselpdf-
activity-7260683187125653504-SENR/?utm_source=share&utm_
medium=member_ios
13. https://womened.com/blog/violence-and-abuse-haunt-women-globally
14. https://www.ipsos.com/en-uk/awareness-violence-against-women-
high-action-lags-finds-new-ipsos-survey
15. https://www.ipsos.com/en-uk/international-womens-day-global-
opinion-remains-committed-to-gender-equality
16. https://uk.search.yahoo.com/search?fr=mcafee&type=E210GB714G9
1856&p=misogyny+definition
17. https://dictionary.cambridge.org/dictionary/english/misogyny
18. https://www.linkedin.com/feed/update/urn:li:activity:
7261465717013626881/
19. https://www.politico.com/news/2023/10/25/new-house-speaker-mike-
johnson-on-the-issues-00123627
20. https://www.pbs.org/newshour/show/researchers-report-stunning-
surge-of-misogyny-in-schools
21. https://www.thetimes.com/uk/education/article/teachers-told-to-spot-
toxic-incel-culture-in-class-to-prevent-attacks-h5k55pwt8
22. https://www.tes.com/magazine/analysis/general/how-do-we-stop-
misogyny-taking-root-in-our-schools?amp
23. https://www.tes.com/magazine/analysis/general/how-do-we-stop-
misogyny-taking-root-in-our-schools?amp
24 https://ukfeminista.org.uk/news/informal-poll-conducted-at-neu-con-
ference-98-of-teachers-experienced-sexism/
25. https://ukfeminista.org.uk/news/ukfeminista-and-unison-survey/
26. https://news.sky.com/story/flatplan-13238729
27. https://womened.com/
28. https://www.theguardian.com/society/2024/oct/13/labour-violence-
against-women-and-girls-vawg-policy

29. https://www.heforshe.org/en/heforshe-alliance-launches-male-allyship-toolkit-resource-building-inclusive-workplaces

30. https://menatworkcic.org/

31. https://innovativeenterprise.co.uk/we-want-to-help-your-organisations-people-perform-better-whether-you-are-a-school-a-business-a-college-a-charity-or-an-individual-our-aim-is-to-make-you-feel-better-motivate/

32. https://www.progressivemasculinity.co.uk/

33. https://ukfeminista.org.uk/resources-hub/

34. https://lifelessons.co.uk/violenceprevention

35. https://www.independent.co.uk/life-style/health-and-families/jd-vance-kamala-harris-childless-response-b2585324.html

36. https://www.independent.co.uk/news/uk/politics/rachel-reeves-accounts-nickname-chancellor-labour-b2686540.html

37. Chrome-extension://efaidnbmnnnibpcajpcglclefindmkaj/https://www.womensaid.org.uk/wp-content/uploads/2025/01/Joint-letter-to-Safeguarding-Minister-in-solidatory-from-Womens-Aid-and-members-10th-Jan-2025.pdf

38. https://www.linkedin.com/posts/activity-7300877283559440385-BsFD/?utm_medium=ios_app&rcm=ACoAAB977PABOH_XLzN__3sqqOa6se0lOF9OeG8&utm_source=screenshot_social_share&utm_campaign=mail

39. https://bmcwomenshealth.biomedcentral.com/articles/10.1186/s12905-022-01845-4

40. https://osf.io/preprints/psyarxiv/jwtg9_v1

41. https://www.gov.uk/government/news/ofsted-culture-change-needed-to-tackle-normalised-sexual-harassment-in-schools-and-colleges

42. https://www.bbc.co.uk/news/articles/c89vjj0lxx9o

43. https://www.msn.com/en-gb/entertainment/tv/adolescence-review-the-closest-thing-to-tv-perfection-in-decades/ar-AA1AOB1u?ocid=nl_article_link&cvid=2ce1491c4bc94a45ed252cc007013d3e&ei=36

44. https://x.com/LDNVictimsComm/status/1901237305626579307

45. https://www.thetimes.com/comment/columnists/article/kyle-clifford-andrew-tate-misogyny-violence-ggfpv6d8v

46. https://www.bbc.co.uk/iplayer/episode/m00029315/the-richard-dimbleby-lecture-sir-gareth-southgate

47. https://www.theneweuropean.co.uk/viva-gisele-pelicot-my-che-guevara/

48. How men very much CAN influence other men's behaviour.
49. The European Commission and UN women as co-leaders of the action coalition on gender based violence.
50. https://www.womensaid.org.uk/ten-ways-to-help-end-violence-against-women-and-girls/

POPULISM, FAITH AND BELIEF

16

FAITH COMMUNITIES AND NATIONAL POPULISMS: SEEKING INTEGRITY IN THE GREY AREAS

John P. Bradbury

General Secretary, the United Reformed Church.

CHRISTIAN NATIONALISMS

World-wide Phenomenon

It is increasingly easy to assume that popular nationalism and religion make natural bedfellows. The Christian Nationalist right in America has thrown its weight behind the Make America Great Again (MAGA) movement. At the Presidential inauguration, we heard prayers such as that from Franklin Graham:

> *Our Father, today, as President Donald J. Trump takes the oath of office once again, we come to say thank you, O Lord our God. Father, when Donald Trump's enemies thought he was down and out, You, and You alone, saved his life and raised him up with strength and power by Your mighty hand.*[1]

This is not simply a phenomenon from the United States. Victor Orban in Hungary is closely associated with the Reformed Church in Hungary, and is associated with the idea of a 'Christian Hungary', which informs his anti-Muslim immigration agenda. In Russia, the Russian Orthodox Church is an uncritical partner to Vladimir Putin. There are various examples one might take. The ones Iknowa best are the Protestant Christian examples and this chapter will concentrate on these, but one might point beyond Christianity to the relationship between Islam and nationalism in Turkey, or Hindu Nationalism in India.

Appropriation Verses Resistance

Viewed historically, we can see that in the face of totalitarian regimes or state level institutionalised injustices, Churches and the Christian Faith have always stood in complex relationship. In Germany in the 1930s, the so-called *German Christian Movement*, sponsored by Hitler and the National Socialist party effectively took over most of the regional churches in Germany. However, at the same time, some managed to maintain their independence, and within Church life the *Confessing Church*, maintained a strong adherence to what one might term orthodox Christian theology, and resisted appropriation to the Nazi party regime. The *Barmen Declaration*, is a confession of faith which squarely sets out the theological basis for the Church in that context. Members of the Confessing Church, most famously Dietrich Bonhoeffer, at times became involved in the political resistance to Hitler. The Confessing Church also played a foundational part in the reconstruction of Germany after the war. The Church was, in that context, both in part appropriated by Hitler for his own purposes, but also found within its foundational beliefs, the basis for resistance to a totalitarian state.

Similarly in South Africa in the time of Apartheid, the Church was appropriated to offer a theological basis for the doctrines of Apartheid, particularly in the theology of the Dutch Reformed Church, but also was a site of notable resistance to the evils of Apartheid. One only has to think of the ministry of someone like Desmond Tutu to understand the part that the Church played in shifting South African society beyond Apartheid.

So, it is today that Churches are in perpetual danger of being appropriated to forms of populist nationalism, but just as some of the elements in church life make this possible, others provide a profound ground for resistance, and the embodiment of an alternative position within contexts rife with disinformation, populism and forms of nationalism.

THE CHURCH LOCAL AND GLOBAL

Places of Worship as Antidotes to Echo Chambers

Churches, as other faith communities, operate at the local, the national and the international levels. This is both to state the obvious, but also to state something markedly significant. The contemporary world is marked by the rapid flow of information and disinformation through social media. Increasingly, in parts of the world that populist nationalism has taken hold, the so-called main-stream media, tends to come under ever greater state control. Disinformation works when people find themselves in echo chambers, where only the one message is heard. At their worst, local congregations become such an echo chamber.

They are not always at their worst, however. Particularly within main-stream denominations, congregations are frequently places where communities form that contain a variety of political opinions. This can frequently be challenging for clergy to contend with. How does one, in an act of worship focussed primarily on the worship of God, and the engagement with the foundational ideas of faith, hold together in one community those of divergent political differences? The very nature of the challenge is a good indication of one of the profound strengths of many local congregations – they precisely cannot be simple echo chambers. They are often places where divergent views meet. To contend with the reality that the person sitting next to you in worship, or at the fellowship meal, believes something very different to you – whilst you find that otherwise you get on, and may well respect one another, is a profound antidote to the formation of information echo-chambers. Equally, the content of that which is preached or taught is a moment of real person-to-person engagement in a digital world. It is perhaps harder to ignore the real person in front of you when you disagree, than the comment on a social media thread. Just as the context of teaching and preaching in worship can be co-opted for populist ends, it can also be the context where disinformation is countered, and alternative views experienced. It is not for nothing that during the COVID-19 crisis, in the UK context, the Westminster, Welsh and Scottish governments all sought, very intentionally, to increase their engagement with faith communities. They were realised to be trusted places where information could be spread, and fake news about vaccines countered.

Global Relationships Countering Populism

Church traditions, certainly of the mainstream variety, also are part of global networks. This is self-evident for the Roman Catholic Church. This provides an interesting space for the countering of false narratives. In the early days of the second Trump presidency, there was a fascinating moment that vice-President J.D. Vance (a recent convert to Catholicism) quoted a piece of Catholic teaching, the *ordo amoris*, essentially arguing a prioritisation of love to be first of one's immediate family and community, then nation, then those beyond. The Pope, in a letter to Catholic Bishops in America, set out the church's true understanding of this as being rooted in meditation on the parable of the Good Samaritan, in which it is the person from another ethnicity, from a group with a terrible reputation, who offers kindness, care and love to the injured one who'd been robbed. Whilst not directly cited in contradiction to Vance, there was a clear sense of the Pope correcting a misappropriation of Catholic teaching. This is a very high profile and visible example of a reality that often happens in more low-key ways. Christian churches do not live in isolated national bubbles, but rather as part of global families. Global relationships within different world church communions act as a brake on theological interpretations of matters being misappropriated for populist, nationalist purposes.

Whilst this is more obvious the case with the Roman Catholic tradition, the major Protestant traditions also embody this reality.

The Reformed, Lutheran, Methodist and Anglican world communions and connections all ensure that there is meaningful dialogue at
the global level, which serves, at its best, as a corrective to the local
misappropriation of a religious tradition.

THE NATIONAL CHURCH

Intertwining of National and Theological Identities

It is the interaction between Church and nation which historically
provides the context in which religion is appropriated for populist,
nationalist purposes. This is perhaps particularly so in the Protestant traditions. The European Reformation saw a movement in
which the reformation of the church, and the desire for greater
autonomy and independence of city states, monarchical territories
and early modern nations from the Holy Roman Empire, become
intertwined. Theological conviction, and the political reality that
reformation was one means of asserting the rights of local rulers
against the emperor have left behind various strands of Protestant-
ism in which church governance happens along national lines. At
times, the development of national identity and theological identity has happened hand in hand. Scotland is Reformed and Pres-
byterian, which is an important identity marker in distinction to
Anglican England. Switzerland is Reformed. Different regions of
Germany would historically have identified strongly as Lutheran or
Reformed, or from the 19th century in places, united. Scandinavia
is Lutheran.

Within the Christian scriptures, particularly the Hebrew scriptures shared with the Jewish people, the idea of the nation and the
chosen people is a strong one. This can be easily misappropriated
to ideas of a particular nation being a superior 'chosen people'.
This itself is perversion of the Christian gospel, in which the new
identity one finds in baptism into Christ and the body of Christ –
the church – supersedes and relativises any preexisting human
identity. So, St Paul speaks in his letter to the Galatians, that: 'There
is no longer Jew or Greek, there is no longer slave or free, there is
no longer male and female; for all of you are one in Christ Jesus'.[2]

National, ethnic, social even biological identities are superseded by the identity of being 'in Christ'. In this very brief example, we can see how there are both the seeds of populist nationalisms within scripture, but also the antidote to them.

LESSONS FROM HUNGARY

Historical Grievance and Identity

One example where perhaps we can see some of the dangers, and also the possibilities, of the relationship between church and populist nationalisms is in Hungary under its Prime Minister, Viktor Orban. Orban has spoken of creating an 'illiberal democracy', and a 'Christian Hungary'. He appeals to the sense of Hungarian identity as being one that has been abused historically and needs to be restored. Much of this is rooted in the treatment of Hungary at the end of the First World War when in the treaty of Trianon in 1920, nearly a third of ethnic Hungarians found themselves minority communities in neighbouring nations, who gained Hungarian territory. There is often, under populist cries, a grievance issue which cannot simply be dismissed, and in which injustice might lie. One important thing to realise is the importance of listening carefully for what that might be. Nonetheless, Orban has sought to limit media freedoms, educational freedoms and freedom of speech, has ensured a judiciary favourable to his government and used the levers of state power to entrench his position. One aspect of that has been his use of Christian identity. Orban himself is Hungarian Reformed, and there is a close relationship between his government, and the church.

Conflating of Church and National Identity

Zoltán Balog, a bishop in the Hungarian Reformed Church, and the Presiding bishop of its Synod until 2024, was previously a government minister in Orban's government. There is no doubt that he is a strong supporter of Orban and has used his position within the church to promote the proximity of the church and Orban.

In 2024, he was forced to resign over the scandal that led to the resignation of the then President of Hungary over an inappropriate pardon issued to a child sex offender. Balog's public comments in the wake of the scandal have been commented upon as being 'Trumpian', in that he portrays himself as the victim in the scandal. It is possible to simply write off the Hungarian Reformed Church as being the church wing of Oban's party, Fidesz. There are certainly strong supporters of Fidesz within the Reformed Church in Hungary, and the other Hungarian Reformed Churches in surrounding countries. This makes many fellow Protestant Christians in Europe profoundly uneasy, and leads to complex questions about how one relates to a Church that seemingly has allied itself strongly with a form of popular nationalism. Undoubtedly, there are strong strands within the Reformed Church in Hungary that makes me extremely nervous. Any conflation of church and national identity that leads to the uncritical support of one particular political movement is profoundly concerning.

Opening Space for Debate and Dissent

When one looks at a somewhat deeper level within the life of the Reformed Church in Hungary, however, one can also perceive something else. In the wake of Balog's resignation, there was a public letter, signed by various known figures within the life of the Church, warning the church against a path of uniting the Christian gospel with one particular political manifestation, and calling on the Church to regain some of its political independence. What this reveals is that the Church is still a space within Hungarian society where open debate is possible, and alternative views are expressed. That may not always be easy for those who do so, and the cost may at times be high – but nonetheless, the church has, to some extent at least, remained a place where recourse to the foundational theological commitments of the church lead some to stand up for a greater space between the church and this one political tradition.

There is undoubtedly a complexity in international relationships with the Reformed Church in Hungary. I served as the Executive President of the Communion of Protestant Churches in Europe

(CPCE), and presided over its General Assembly in Sibiu, Romania, in 2024. The Hungarian Reformed Church formally withdraws their delegations from the Assembly. The presenting reason was a paper on gender and sexuality which they believed did not sufficiently maintain the Christian position as they understood it, which coincides with a strongly pro-traditional family values emphasis from Orbanand Fidesz, which often manifests in an anti-LGBTQI+ agenda.

It was very clear, however, that in the wake of the resignation of Balog there was something of an internal debate going on within the Hungarian Reformed Churches. There are those within it that would lessen international ties, as international church organisations are portrayed as intrinsically liberal in orientation, and standing counter to the conservative moral stance that the Hungarian Reformed Church would typically take on issues of personal morality. By no means would all within the Hungarian Reformed Churches wish to turn their backs on international Church organisations, however. It would have been possible for the CPCE to react in a number of ways, and for some it was a reason to weaken, or even sever ties with the Hungarian Reformed Churches. This, however, in its way would have strengthened the hand of those within those churches seeking a more strongly nationalist, isolationist stance. Instead, the reaction was kept low-key. Sadness but understanding was expressed at the withdrawal. Local good relationships with Hungarian Reformed congregations in the area in which the Assembly was meeting were maintained, and a Hungarian Reformed pastor and theologian was elected to the Council of the organisation that will oversee its work for the next 6 years.

Understanding Complexity

This example of the Hungarian Reformed Churches and the CPCE serves as a helpful illustration of the complexities and grey areas in which Church life operates. The Hungarian Reformed Churches can simply be held up as having fallen in line behind one populist nationalist agenda. On the other hand, the lived life of that church is far more complex than that. For example, the church continues excellent work amongst Roma people, who are often stigmatised within Hungarian society, and who have been the focus of negative attention from Orban.

Equally, the church does remain a space within which, at least to some extent, debate can be heard. The international links the church has prevent the church from becoming isolated or only networked with other highly conservative churches often funded from American. The instinctively international nature of Christian life acts as a counterpoint to nationalism in certain respects. Equally, the ongoing exchange that happens between pastors, theologians and congregations, reminds those who take a more classical liberal, Western approach, that there are counter-narratives to those that we come to assume are the norm. There are complexities to history, and elements of liberal individualism that need challenging or repairing, when they fail convincingly to respond to social, ethnic, national, linguistic identities and differences harmed and damaged in the arbitrary repositioning of borders and boundaries.

FAITH COMMUNITIES AS POSITIVE DISRUPTORS

Disinformation spreads and supports the rise of populist nationalist agendas. Disinformation flourishes in spaces which become echo chambers. There can be a tendency, from a more classical, liberal, Western perspective to wish to detach from such echo chambers. What is perhaps more important, is to take actions which prevent echo chambers from forming or to attempt to disrupt them. The lived reality of Church life (and indeed, other faith communities) is that they can serve precisely as disrupters of emerging echo chambers. The lived, human reality of community formed in local neighbourhoods between people who might be of highly divergent perspectives provides a local space for such disruption. Equally, the global nature of church communities serves as a means of keeping conversations connected beyond any echo chamber. Ultimately, the faith that churches embody is one in which God is sovereign, which automatically relativises any human claim to power or authority. Whilst Churches can be, and are at times, co-opted into populist nationalist projects, it is also not for nothing that, from the Roman

Empire onwards, some forms of church life have been oppressed and persecutive, precisely because church communities can be spaces of resistance to perverted forms of nationalist identity.

ENDNOTES

1. Franklin Graham (2025), cited in John-Bunya (2025, January 22). Rev. Franklin Graham's prayer at Trump's inauguration: A call for wisdom and protection. *Prayer Prompt*. https://www.prayerprompt.org/rev-franklin-grahams-inauguration-prayer/

2. Galatians Chapter 3 verse 23. The New Testament.

17

RESPONDING TO (CHRISTIAN) NATIONALISM

Andy Braunston

United Reformed Church's Minister for Digital Worship

THE SPECTRE OF NATIONALISM AND WHAT'S FUELLING IT

Forms of Nationalism which are expansionist, dangerous, and which use faith to legitimise themselves haunt our world like a spectre. Christian Nationalism is utilised by these movements in America, Russia, and Hungary and is also on the rise in France and Germany; so far they are on the edge of the UK's civic life, maybe due to the relative lack of religious observance here. Christian Nationalism as a movement perverts the message of the Gospel seeking to divorce it from the message and example of Jesus to bring good news to the poor, proclaim release to the captives, recovery of sight to the blind, let the oppressed go free, proclaim 'the year of the Lord's favour', and to love our neighbours as ourselves.[1] Despite Jesus' words that his Kingdom was not of this world, Christian Nationalism seeks political and social power.

Trigger issues that make a Nationalist agenda appeal seem to include fears about migration, a sense of people being left behind by elites who are the ruling classes, and a realisation that wealth generated by the superrich doesn't trickle down to the rest of us. Add into this stretched public finances where people demand Scandinavian levels of public services with American levels of taxation, and we end up with politicians forever urging us to understand their difficult choices. Riots in England and Northern Ireland in the Summer of 2024, the surge in support of the political party *Reform* and the attraction of some figures on the far right here all add to a sense of gloom about the way things are. There's a profound lack of trust in our institutions and in the outlets where we get our news from. This drives people to extreme politics and, in Europe and America, those extremes seem to be into the far right.

EXPLORING THE MANY FORMS OF NATIONALISM

Nationalism is a simple, modern, idea that the nation should be congruent with the state. Rather than vast empires made up of different peoples, each people should be able to determine their own destiny, govern themselves, and be free from outside interference. It aims to build and maintain a national identity based on shared social characteristics such as culture, geography, language, ethnicity, religion, language, and tradition. It is an idea that is held to be self-evident and, since the 20th century, something to which many peoples have aspired, and to which many continue to aspire. Sometimes different nationalisms clash – in Spain the idea of one state for all the Spanish people and the concept of Basque independence; in Turkey, Iraq, and Syria, Kurds want their own state instead of being ruled by various other countries, and, closer to home, nationalisms in Wales, Scotland, and Northern Ireland compete with a sense of British nationalism.

Nationalism can be seen as a reaction to globalisation where societies have been transformed by market-based reforms leading to the free movement of capital, a lack of regulation of the market, privatisation of once publicly owned companies, free trade, and reductions in government spending. In reaction to this people assert their national interests – sometimes positively (reactions to the importation of chlorinated chicken or hormone treated beef from America, for example) and sometimes negatively (blaming immigrants for austerity).

Nationalism takes many forms; in the post-war years anti-colonial nationalism saw many countries emerge from the British and French empires. In civic, or liberal, nationalism the nation is defined as a political, not ethnic, entity. Welsh, Irish, and Scottish Nationalism, for example, is civic and holds that the future of the country in question should be determined by those living there. Ethnic Nationalism, on the other hand, is where the nation is defined by ethnicity and where access to the nation can't be achieved by cultural assimilation. Religious Nationalism associates belonging to the nation with membership of a particular religious tradition creating a common bond amongst the peoples of a nation. Britain, for example, was created to be a Protestant nation in the face of a predominantly Catholic Europe, Ireland in fact, if not in theory, saw itself for many years as a Catholic state, Turkey sees itself as a predominantly Muslim state despite a history of secularism and the presence of religious minorities.

Christian Nationalism seeks to promote forms of Christianity to achieve prominence, or dominance, in the political and social life of the nation. This could be as simple as preserving a single state church. We see Christian Nationalism at work now in America, Hungary, and Russia with shades of it at play in France and Germany.

SOME INSTRUCTIVE EXAMPLES

Russia

The reemergence of the Russian Orthodox Church after the Communist era has been dramatic. Buildings and wealth have been returned to the Church yet, in order to survive in the Soviet era, the Church had to cede control over itself to the State and bishops were, at best, approved by the Communist Party or, at worst, agents of the KGB. Patriarch Kirill has become close to President Putin referring to Putin's leadership as 'God's miracle' and to the Ukraine war as 'current events' avoiding terms like *war* or *invasion*. Putin has used the Church for his own ends declaring 'The restoration of church unity is an important condition for rediscovering the lost unity of the Russian people.'[2] Kirill, believing Russia's 'spiritual sovereignty' was being attacked by liberal western Protestant societies, supports the secular 'Russkiy Mir' (Russian World) doctrine that holds that Russia has the right to intervene in the fate of Russians beyond its borders and wishes to control Orthodox Churches outside Russia.

> *The Anglican Church is planning to consider the idea of a gender-neutral God. What can you say! Millions of people in the West understand that they are being led to spiritual destruction. The [western] elites are going crazy and this cannot be cured it seems. But our duty is to protect our children from degradation.*[3]

In 2023, the Royal United Services Institute noted the body of ideologically committed agents supporting the invasion was the Russian Orthodox Church in Ukraine noting that their monasteries and buildings were safe houses for Russian agents.[4] The Ecumenical Patriarch has accused the Russian Orthodox Church of 'ethnophyletism' – the instrumentalization of the Russian Church for ethno-nationalist reasons: 'They shamelessly declare that they are Russians first and then Orthodox'.[5]

Kirill advocates for ultra conservative values:

> *Today there is a test for the loyalty to this new world order, a kind of pass to that 'happy' world, the world of excess consumption, the world of false 'freedom,' Do you know what this test is? The test is very simple and at the same time terrible – it is the gay pride parade.*[6]

Hungary

In Hungary, Prime Minister Viktor Orbán, who was raised in a nominally Reformed family, renounced his atheism in the 1990s and started to court religious conservative voters. His harsh anti-immigration policies were cast as a defence of Christianity. A change to the constitution notes 'the role of Christianity in preserving the nation' and an amendment in 2018 provides for the 'protection of the constitutional identity and Christian culture of Hungary'.

Orbán frequently defines himself as a defender of Christian values in the face of the EU which he claims is anti-nationalist and anti-Christian. He defines his politics as 'illiberal Christian Democracy' and advocates closer ties with both Russia and China.

Originally describing himself as an 'agnostic liberal' he was at first against the restoration of Church property after the fall of Communism, referred to Christian Democrat opponents as 'cassocks' and referred to Pope John Paul II as 'a shark'. Addressing American conservatives in 2022 he urged Christian Nationalists in the USA and Europe to join forces and has railed against Europe becoming a 'mixed race' society and opined:

> *If you separate western civilization from its Judaeo-Christian heritage, the worst things in history happen. Let's be honest, the most evil things in modern history were carried out by people who hated Christianity. Don't be afraid to call your enemies by their name. You can't play safe but they will never show mercy.*[7]

And

> *Hungarians can only survive as Christians and each new church is a bastion in the nation's struggle for freedom and greatness ....*[8]

USA

In America, Mr Trump's Make America Great Again ideology has come to dominate the Republican Party and large sections of Protestant Churches. Despite Trump's well documented, and prosecuted, moral failings large sections of the American Church have supported him over 'culture war' issues notably abortion and the rights of transgender people. In his first term, Trump appointed many conservative justices to the Federal bench and the Supreme Court ensuring that the constitutional right to abortion was rolled back. It remains to be seen what else the Supreme Court might have in store as the culture war continues. Trump's loquaciousness provides a rich stream of his sayings which are at variance with the Church that embraces him:

When people wrong you, go after those people, because it is a good feeling and because other people will see you doing it. I always get even.

Why do I have to repent, why do I have to ask for forgiveness if [I'm] not making mistakes?

I fully think apologizing is a great thing. But you have to be WRONG ... I will absolutely apologize sometime in the hopefully distant future if I'm ever wrong.

When I go to church and when I drink my little wine and have my little cracker, I guess that is a form of forgiveness. I do that as often as I can because I feel cleansed.[9]

Christian Nationalism ignores such thoughts and flatters Trump even as he re-took office. Franklin Graham prayed at his second inauguration:

[...] Father, when Donald Trump's enemies thought he was down and out, you and you alone saved his life and raised him up with strength and power by your mighty hand. We pray for President Trump, that you watch over, protect, guide, direct him, give him your wisdom from your throne on high. We ask that you bless him and that our nation also be blessed through him. We also ask that you bless and protect Melania, his first lady. We thank you for the beauty, the warmth and grace that she shows not only to this nation, but to the whole world .... Father, thank you for the protection, the bounty, the freedoms that we so enjoy. We remember to keep our eyes fixed on you and may our hearts be included to your voice. We know that America can never be great again if we turn our backs on you. We ask for your help.[10]

A day later rather braver words were addressed to Trump's by the Rt Revd Mariann Edgar Budde:

In the name of our God, I ask you to have mercy upon the people in our country who are scared now. There are gay, lesbian and transgender children in Democratic,

Republican and independent families. Some who fear for their lives. They may not be citizens or have the proper documentation, but the vast majority of immigrants are not criminals. They pay taxes and are good neighbours. They are faithful members of our churches and mosques, synagogues.[11]

Her words give us pointers on how to respond to the perversion of Christianity that is Christian Nationalism.

HOW CAN WE CHALLENGE CHRISTIAN NATIONALISM?

Our greatest resource in countering perversions of Christianity is the Bible and, in particular, various themes which speak to the state we find ourselves in.

Perfect Love Casts Out All Fear

One of the facets of modern politics in general, and of Christian Nationalism in particular is fear. There's much to fear in our contemporary world; social upheaval following deindustrialisation and a move into new areas of work which are less secure, the subsequent changes from pensions guaranteed by one's employer to those where the employee takes the risk, the dream of being able to own one's own home seems a myth to many younger people, and the lack of investment in our public infrastructure means we're susceptible when we're told to blame those who use it more. Rapid social change has led to some feeling insecure whilst, at the same time, the institutions we used to trust are now found wanting. Yet, we believe that perfect love casts out all fear. When tempted to be fearful of the world around us and its changes, it's good to be reminded of our decision to bow to God's sovereignty and accept that perfect love which calms our fears.[12]

Made in God's Image

For Christians, the ultimate revelation of God's image is Jesus. In him we see our model for life and deep truths about how we should view ourselves and others. Many forces in our contemporary world seek to divide us, sow division and hatred; as Christians we need always to remember that we are all created in God's image and that image is good. This makes siblings of us all. God's image can be marred within us and we can refuse to see God's image in others but at the heart of Christian faith is this simple truth: humanity is made in God's image. The challenge for us is to see that image even in those we find, or are told to find, unlovely.[13]

Delighting in Diversity

In various places around the world there are political moves to impose uniformity; in India Hindu nationalism seeks to marginalise other traditions and to cast, in particular, Muslims as somehow being other than Indian. In America, the debates about undocumented people (relied on, and exploited by, business) underscore an anxiety by some white people that they will soon no longer be the largest grouping in the USA and may lose their power. In much of Europe disquiet about the mass migration of people (often due to the politics and selfishness of those of us in the West) has led to political movements seeking to restrict immigration, civil rights, and opportunity. The Tower of Babel story reminds us that God rejoices in diversity and does not desire linguistic nor cultural uniformity – and neither should we.[14]

Knowing Who Is Our Neighbour

The question 'And who is my neighbour?' is one which haunts down the years. Jesus' point in his story of the Good Samaritan is not just that our neighbours are those in need (though they are) but that the neighbour is likely to be someone we are suspicious and afraid of. Jesus' parable was difficult and dangerous as the Jews despised the Samaritans. The story was designed to broaden both our understanding and our horizons in an age where these are being narrowed. Jesus reminds us that our neighbour is often someone we'd rather not know yet alone love as ourselves.[15]

Loving the Aliens as We Love Ourselves

A key tenet in the Jewish and Christian traditions is to love others as we love ourselves, and in various Old Testament passages, to love the foreigner, the stranger, the folk the Biblical authors often called aliens.[16] The Jewish people, who had known what it was to be despised slaved in Egypt were given strict laws about not mistreating the foreigners in their midst. These themes were picked up by Jesus in his own ministry who told his followers that whatever they did to the least in society they did to Jesus; a saying set in a story encouraging his followers to feed the hungry, clothe the naked, give drink to the thirsty and visit the imprisoned.[17] If we were to encapsulate these ideas liturgically we might pray:

You who shepherd the lost and comfort the afflicted,

guide our hands to touch the untouchable,

our ears to listen to the hopeless,

our eyes to see the misery of others,

and our hearts to feel the pain of prisoners.

Empower us, O Most High, to take risks,

to be channels of healing and mercy,

so that this world might be a better place. Amen.

Neither Jew nor Gentile[18]

We each have many identities – they make us who we are, and are part of creation's rich diversity and reflect the very image of God within us. We perceive the world, and our part in it, through those identities even if they involve risk or evoke hatred; many in the churches who follow a Christian Nationalism agenda see the undermining of hard-won rights as being central to their view of being faithful. The early Christian thinker St Paul, however, had a baptismal theology which puts all distinctions around social status, identity, ethnicity, or sex as secondary to the primary one of being in Christ. Paul's teaching does not minimise those other identities which find their completion and fulfilment in Christ. Our primary, Christian, identity should inform all the others – and those other identities should inform what it is for us to be Christian. Our many identities entwine in symbiotic relationships with each other and shouldn't be feared as they provide a way to discuss the richness and diversity of our world, our faith, our church and God's own self.

What Is Truth?

Famously the Roman Governor, Pontius Pilate, examined Jesus before condemning him to death. In this encounter Jesus speaks with a fair degree of assertiveness telling Pilate he stood for the truth. Pilate spat back 'What is truth?'[19] Truth telling is a hallmark of Christian faith and ethics yet can be incredibly difficult. In an age where people are wedded to conspiracy theories, it's hard to stand carefully and faithfully for the truth. In an era where institutions are trusted less than ever before, and where the Church's lies about abuse have been exposed, we may not be seen as the first port of call for truth telling. Yet, this shouldn't stop us trying. Truth telling takes many forms: reigning in preachers' stories, exploring different ways truth is made manifest in Scripture, and being honest about our own struggles and failures are amongst them. Truth telling starts in our daily lives, should be seen in our churches, and when we dare to speak to power. Truth telling leads to trust which our society needs if it is to flourish again.

Resisting Temptation

Some may look back at Constantine's adoption of Christianity as an official Roman religion and his patronage of the Church as a good thing, ensuring our survival down the centuries. Our privileged place at the heart of European civilisation means that, at least, our culture is influenced by the Gospel. Others may look at the compromises which blunted our message as ecclesiastical mouths were stuffed with imperial gold, prophets silenced, and power concentrated in the families who ended up running both Church and state. Even now we seek to try to cling on to the trappings of power and influence. The Church continues to be tempted to support politicians who use us. One suspects the Jesus revealed in the Gospels would have harsh things to say about both our political leaders and the compromises we make with them. What, I wonder, would our history have been if we'd declined Constantine's offer? What if we'd wished him well but kept on with the simple task of proclaiming the Gospel. What if we'd founded small communities which sought nothing more than to worship God through working for the greater good? What if we'd rejected power? Of course, this image of the Church as a network of small communities is where we are now – or if not quite there, approaching it at speed. The Faustian pact with the State has not given us what was dreamt of; only from the edge can we see, critique, and tend the world as Jesus does.

My Kingdom Is Not of This World[20]

Jesus' Kingdom values are complicated. We want to work for a better world, where the homeless are housed, the sick healed, the poor enriched, the outsiders and strangers welcomed. These are all political imperatives which concern God's Kingdom and the State. There's a difference, however, between taking the values and priorities of the Kingdom and yearning for political power. A growing critique of American evangelicalism – from within that movement[21] – is about how political power has become the prime goal. The offer of policies, and judges, which appeal to some Christians around abortion, immigration, and LGBT issues has trumped the moral failings of those who offer these inducements. Instead of seeing proclamation, service, and persuasion as the Church's mission, sections of the Church have become corrupt seeking to win a culture war. Yet, at the supreme moment of crisis and temptation Jesus offered Pilate hard words.[22] With some defiant self-confidence Jesus told Pilate what's what. If he had been interested in political power a mob could have been raised, angels dragooned, and the Romans defeated. Yet, for Jesus, power is seen in weakness, strength in service, faithfulness in care. Can power be those things for the Church too?

Citizens of Heaven[23]

When the Church becomes too close to the realms and regimes, ideas and ideologies of the State, corruption sets in. In Henry VIII's England, Parliament declared him 'Head of the Church' and went on to regulate worship and seize Church land against resistance that ultimately came to little. In 1930s Germany, the 'German Christians' won power in church elections and sought to accommodate Christianity with Nazism. Those who tried to stay faithful to the Gospel adopted the Barmen Declaration which proclaimed the Church's freedom in Jesus Christ who is Lord of every area of life. As God's Word, Jesus determines the Church's order, ministry, and relationship to the state; the Church was not to be a mere State agency. It was heady stuff but allowed faithful Christians to organise and avoid Nazi corruption. This declaration has inspired contemporary Orthodox theologians to condemn the 'Russian World' teaching prevalent in some sections of Russian Orthodoxy. This teaching subordinates Christian faith to national interests. Attempts to blur the boundaries between our earthly and heavenly citizenship always end badly - whether that's the upheaval of the Reformation era, Nazi attempts to subjugate the Church, or Russian attempts to baptise imperial ideology. Paul reminds us, in an age where Roman citizenship was prized and valuable, that the only citizenship we should care about is that of Heaven.[24]

AND FINALLY, TRUST IN GOD ALONE

Our distinctive contribution as Christians to the rise of Christian Nationalism is rather basic relying on some key ideas from the Bible which is, along with our Jewish sisters and brothers, the sourcebook of our faith. Again and again in the Bible the ancient poets who wrote the Psalms warn us not to put our trust in mortal rulers who will, like us, one day head for the grave.[25] Instead, we are told to trust in God.

This is the basis behind Jesus' admonition to Pilate that His Kingdom was not of this world; not that we should divorce ourselves from a world heading to Hell but that, as Pope Paul VI once wrote, every political ideology no matter how close it might be portrayed to Christian values, has within itself the seeds of its own destruction unless it is an articulation of Jesus' good news. In the Psalms those ancient poets noted God set prisoners free, gave sight to the blind, lifted the oppressed, loved the righteous, watched over strangers, and upheld the rights of those on the edge. These other worldly values are ones we might wish to see in our politicians and we can rejoice when their policies seem to come close to these things.

We always remember, however, not to place our trust in mortals 'in whom there is no help' but instead trust only in God, our rock and redeemer. Such trust is the only sure way to navigate the difficult times in which we live and reject the siren voices that tempt us to despair.

ENDNOTES

1. Luke 4: 18–19 and Mark 12: 30–31 The New Testament.
2. *The Tablet*, 10 February 2024, p. 4.
3. *The Tablet*, 10 February 2024, p. 5.
4. https://static.rusi.org/202303-SR-Unconventional-Operations-Russo-Ukrainian-War-web-final.pdf.pdf
5. *The Tablet*, 14 August 2024.
6. *The Washington Post*, 19 April 2022.
7. https://www.theguardian.com/world/2022/aug/04/viktor-orban-cpac-speech
8. https://hungarytoday.hu/pm-orban-church-greatness/
9. https://www.huffingtonpost.co.uk/entry/donal d-trump-vs-jesus-christ_n_5798e188e4b0d3568f85724a
10. https://billygraham.org/articles/franklin-graham-prays-at-trump-inauguration-blessed-is-the-nation-whose-god-is-the-lord
11. https://cathedral.org/blog/from-the-pulpit-unity-grounded-in-dignity-truth-and-humility/
12. IJohn 4: 16b–21, The New Testament.
13. Genesis 1: 26–27, The Old Testament.
14. Genesis 11: 1–9, The Old Testament.
15. StLuke 10: 15–37, The New Testament.

16. Leviticus 19: 33–34 and Exodus 22:21. The Old Testament.

17. Matthew 25: 31–46, The New Testament.

18. Galatians 3: 27–28, The New Testament.

19. John 18: 38, The New Testament.

20. StJohn 18: 28–37, The New Testament.

21. Alberta, T. (2023). *The kingdom, the power and the glory: American Evangelicalsinan age of extremism*. Harper.

22. John 18, The New Testament.

23. Philippians 3: 17–21, The New Testament.

24. Philippians 3: 20, The New Testament.

25. See Psalm 146: 3–4 for example.

18

EMBRACING UNCERTAINTY IN A CHAOTIC AGE

Beverley Clack

Farmington Institute, Harris Manchester College, Oxford;
Oxford Brookes University

As I write, the 'Pax Americana' that shaped the post-Second World War years is being shredded. US President Donald Trump has unilaterally brought Russia in from the cold, isolating Ukraine, the country subject to Russian invasion. Adding insult to injury, Trump has described Volodymyr Zelenskyy, Ukrainian President, as a 'dictator' because of the suspension of elections necessary in a state that is at war. Subsequent developments, set in motion by the ferocious verbal assault on Zelenskyy in the White House, have further sent world diplomacy reeling. As if this were not enough, Trump's 'radical' plan for the Middle East would see Gaza taken over by the USA, emptied of its people, becoming a 'Middle Eastern Riviera'. Meanwhile, Elon Musk's DOGE is taking a chainsaw – literally and figuratively[1] – to the US federal government, thousands of public servants losing their jobs. Climate change measures have been ripped up in favour of fossil fuels. 'Illegal immigrants' have been deported.

Every morning starts with a sense of peril: what will the next news cycle bring?

As we struggle to sift the real issues from the chaff 'flooding the zone',[2] we are not only faced with man-made threats: a meteor has been spotted on course for Earth, destined to arrive in 2032.[3]

LIVING WITH THE UNCERTAINTY
OF BEING HUMAN

It is tempting to seek new certainties that render stable the shifting ground beneath our feet. This desire in no small part drives the success of leaders across the world who offer simple answers to complex problems.[4] There are no shades of grey. There are no issues that require detailed and careful analysis. Experts who might help us navigate fraught areas are derided as out of touch. Is the only way to survive to ape the certainties of these 'strong' leaders who cultivate the cult of personality? Is the only answer to become similarly authoritarian in thought and action? Like Tolkien's Gandalf, we might decide that the best thing to do is to cry 'you shall not pass'. The barricades of the Culture Wars were erected on this certain ground.[5] There is no room for uncertainty, for not-knowing. There is only the battle field. Only 'us' and only 'them'.

I want to suggest that to survive these uncertain times – even to flourish – is not merely to acknowledge uncertainty but to embrace it. This does not mean that everything is up for grabs, that there are no situations in which to hold fast. Facts exist; the truth matters; not all opinions are valid. There is moral peril in not calling out the lies and half-truths uttered by populists. Climate change is real; Ukraine was invaded.

Yet the realm of absolutes and abstractions, of political noise, is far removed from the day-to-day business of our own lives, and we can miss urgent questions about how to live and to flourish in an age when the certainties of life are being ripped up.

How can we, *where we are*, contribute to the creation of a world where we meet each other as friends and neighbours not enemies and aliens? How can we learn to live with the uncertainty of being human and see its very uncertainty as enabling us to live well *together*?

BONHOEFFER AND TAKING INDIVIDUAL RESPONSIBILITY

Our times are not without precedent; would that they were. Economic upheaval; the success of demagogues who appeal to the masses and the disruptive forces of the id, whose rhetoric creates 'others' portrayed as the root of all misfortune. We have been here before, and it is difficult not to hear echoes of 1930s Europe in the events of our day. In trying to find a way through *our* troubled times, that period offers examples that should both terrify and inspire us.

An inspiring conversation partner is Dietrich Bonhoeffer (1906–1945), theologian and member of the German resistance. Bonhoeffer was acutely aware of the threat posed by populist nationalists distorting the truth. Drawn into the resistance movement by his brother-in-law, Hans von Dohnanyi who was chief counsel in the Abwehr (German military intelligence), Bonhoeffer believed that the only responsible thing to do in his dark times was to join others committed to overthrowing the Hitler regime. This involvement was eventually to claim his life following a failed attempt on Hitler's life in July 1944.[6] In April 1945, Bonhoeffer was executed at Flossenburg Concentration Camp.

The stark choice Bonhoeffer faced seems removed from the choices facing us right now, and Bonhoeffer certainly offers more than the image of heroic opposition to a murderous regime. He directs our gaze to the importance of individual responsibility, demanding that we think seriously about the kind of lives best suited to challenge the distorting politics of our age.

THE DANGER OF 'FOLLY'

As I struggle to write this piece against the turmoil of our times, I find myself turning again to something Bonhoeffer wrote in 1942: a short reflection on 10 years of Nazi rule that was to be distributed secretly to his fellow members of the resistance.[7] In it, he considers how to effectively challenge the roots of totalitarian thinking. His approach is shaped by his Christian faith, yet it has much to offer anyone concerned with how to respond to authoritarian politics and to live a good life in times of uncertainty. Bonhoeffer did not address his thoughts only to Christians: he was greatly impressed by the atheists he met in the resistance who at great personal cost were determined to reject Hitler's regime in the strongest possible way.

Bonhoeffer starts his reflections with a question: what enables authoritarianism to succeed? His focus is less on the leader's agenda, and more on what leads people to follow them. Without followers – without ordinary German men and women – the horrors of the regime could not have been enacted.[8] Why did so many go along with the Nazis? The answer for Bonhoeffer lies in the undermining of reason and independent thinking. This defines what he calls 'folly', the reckless giving up of one's will to another. Folly he holds to be more dangerous than out-and-out evil: 'One can protest against evil; it can be unmasked and, if need be, prevented by force.' But against foolishness, against thoughtlessness, 'we have no defense. Neither protests nor force can touch it; reasoning is no use; facts that contradict personal prejudices can simply be disbelieved'. Challenging the fool can even be dangerous – 'it doesn't take much to make him aggressive'.[9]

If reasoning with the fool is no use, a better approach is to consider the roots of foolishness. It cannot be reduced to psychology or academic aptitude. As Bonhoeffer says, the uneducated man can be far from a fool, while an educated man can be foolish indeed. The fool is the one seduced by a sense of the leader's power. 'They give up trying to assess the new state of affairs for themselves' and are spellbound. Their thinking is reduced to 'slogans, catchwords and the like'. What can break this enchantment? Only 'an act of liberation'.[10] Nothing else will do.

Bonhoeffer writes towards the end of the long process of warped thinking that led to a world war and the horrors of the Holocaust. What are *we* to do, standing where we are, confronted with an uncertain future busily being shaped by the promises of demagogues?

WHAT IS THE MOST EFFECTIVE FORM RESISTANCE CAN TAKE *NOW*?

Bonhoeffer is a theologian, and his solution is to ground one's life in God. This might seem to limit what he says, but let's explore what he is getting at. Grounding his response in God, and – crucially – in the life of Jesus Christ, renders in concrete terms what it means to live responsibly. Holding fast to the truth is not for Bonhoeffer a metaphysical abstraction. In the life of the man Jesus, God is found in the patterns of ordinary, daily life, not in ascribing to a list of moral absolutes.

What might this mean for how we resist the inanities and ordinary horrors perpetuated by the demagogues of our day? How can we challenge the casual cruelties of those in thrall to the demagogues?

Bonhoeffer's suggestion that we start with ordinary life dovetails neatly with Hannah Arendt's depiction of 'the banality of evil'. Arendt, reporting on the trial of the Nazi war criminal, Adolf Eichmann, for *The New Yorker Magazine*, was surprised that he presented like a librarian, an administrator, not a monster of evil. Arendt was convinced that depicting evil as something larger than life was misleading. To understand the horrors of Nazism, its source and how it was enacted, required looking at the behaviours of ordinary – sometimes quite dull – individuals.[11]

Arendt's student, Elizabeth Minnich, some 50 years later, connects the investigation of evil *and* goodness. Like Arendt, she wants to understand the motivation of those who commit evil deeds. 'What were they thinking?' she asks at the beginning of her book. What enabled people to murder their neighbours, to look the other way as their neighbours disappeared, deported to concentration camps?

The answers to her question are surprisingly and depressingly banal. They were doing their jobs; they were chasing personal advancement; they were tailoring their behaviour to that of the majority.[12]

If the roots of evil are found in such banal behaviours, the sources of goodness are, Minnich argues, just as ordinary and easy to cultivate. We need not look to heroic or extraordinary actions to combat the weasel words of the demagogue. Focussing on the heroic obscures the very ordinary patterns of behaviour we can establish in the here-and-now to ensure that injustice and cruelty cannot take hold. We can act *now* in ways that cultivate the good. We need simply to practice daily what it is to be 'a good person; to lead a decent life; to be a responsible citizen, partner, ally, parent, friend'.[13] In other words, we must start with our *character*, working on being a good human being. If Bonhoeffer's anchoring of this activity in God does not appeal, Minnich offers an ethics reflecting Aristotle's description of the practice of virtue:

> *We aim not to know what courage is but to be courageous, not to know what justice is, but to be just, just as we aim to be healthy rather than know what health is, and to be in good condition rather than to know what good condition is.*[14]

Actions speak louder than words, and the actions that enable the good life are, for Minnich, small but vital. Respect the other person: be on time, for their time is as important as your own.[15] Treat everyone – great and small – as a human being, a person like yourself.[16] Converse with the person on the checkout; have good manners: say please and thank you, hold open doors. Practice hospitality. Moreover, pay attention: to what is happening around you *and to your neighbours*:

> *Remain honestly in touch with what is really going on and acting daily, in the moment, in ways that sustain your sense of yourself, your neighbours, your values.*[17]

This is not about withdrawing from the world to the comfortable illusions of 'self-care' where the painful political world is shut out and the suffering of others ignored. This is about cultivating a world in which love is able to thrive, because we take seriously our obligations to each other.

IT IS ABOUT STARTING 'FROM WHERE WE ARE'

We start locally, with what is happening on our doorstep. Arendt was suspicious of political parties, precisely because she felt that commitment to 'the Party' warps our more fundamental obligations to each other as *human beings*.[18] Minnich is suspicious of religion for similar reasons. Arendt, Minnich, and Bonhoeffer, in their different ways, are wary of anything that encourages giving up of one's independent thought and reason. If our lives are shaped through ideological certainties – of 'Party', 'Church', or 'Religion' – it is quite possible we will fail to see those outside our ideological frame as human beings like ourselves.

A more caring future can only be built from the ground up, starting with ourselves and our behaviour. We can only do that by attending to the real, fleshy, messy world of relationship. The Virtual World, political slogans, memes, or TikTok clips are insufficient for enabling a life fit for challenging the injustices of our day. Anything that detaches us from the complex, multifaceted nature of those amongst whom we live must be resisted.

And so, to return to the question posed at the beginning:

> *How to live with uncertainty if we give up answers grounded in promises of certainty?*

SHARED HUMANITY, MORTALITY AND VULNERABILITY

Another form of uncertainty that is more fundamental offers the possibility of creativity.

To be human is to live with the uncertainty *of existence*. Psychotherapist Irvin Yalom argues that our lives are shaped by 'confrontation with the givens of existence': *death* ('we exist now, but one day we will cease to be'); *freedom* (the individual is author of their 'world, life design, choices, and actions'); *isolation* ('each of us enters existence alone and must depart alone'); and *meaninglessness* (if each is alone 'in an indifferent universe, then what meaning does life have?').[19]

Each of us, Yalom argues, has to struggle with the import of these experiences, finding ways of establishing meaning in the face of the questions each raises. Creativity comes out of this struggle. While agreeing with the general thrust of his claims, I wonder if Yalom overstates matters. We are *not* completely alone as we struggle with the human condition, for we are social animals, shaped as much by others as by ourselves.

Here is a different way of shaping our politics, but only if we start with that shared humanity, defined by mortality, and vulnerability. Samantha Harvey's *Orbital* offers a cosmic perspective that resists a politics based on division. As her astronauts move over 'this suspended jewel so shockingly bright', the smallness of human tyranny, destruction, ransacking, and squandering emerges as an insult to 'the august stage on which it all happens'.[20] Drawn from different countries and continents to man the International Space Station, the need each has of the other, and their acknowledgement that, even suspended over it, they depend on the world itself, throws into stark relief what matters and what does not.

Starting with the basic conditions of existence offers a vision that helps resist ideologies that would divide the world and each from the other.

UNITY THROUGH RESPECTING DIFFERENCE

Right Rev Mariann Edgar Budde's sermon before the newly inaugurated President Trump and members of his inner circle sent ripples through a world reeling as America set out on its new course. Budde's text echoes Bonhoeffer's thoughts on folly: the parable of the wise and foolish man. The fool builds his house on sand, so it will inevitably fall. (The slogans will be revealed for what they are: empty words.) The wise man builds his house on rock that will weather the storm. This firm foundation implies unity, but not the unity of authoritarian thinking that asserts 'we' are 'right' while 'they' are 'wrong'. The unity to which Budde directs us is

a way of being with one another that encompasses and respects differences, that teaches us to hold multiple perspectives and life experiences as valid and worthy of respect; that enables us, in our communities and in the halls of power, to genuinely care for one another even when we disagree.

In these common, social spaces, we see that 'we are more like one another than we realise, and we need each other'.[21]

Budde's delivery of this message was as powerful as her words. She did not shout or raise her voice. She simply stood in the place of those most likely to be adversely affected by Trump's policies and quietly advocated for them, out of love.

LAYING FOUNDATIONS TO
TACKLE AN UNCERTAIN FUTURE

This might not feel adequate to the task of resisting the smashing up of institutions, of lives. In so many ways it isn't, and the coming months and years will test people opposed to the totalitarian vision to their limit. But to pretend that the change does not start with ourselves, and our behaviours, would be a mistake. If we are to be capable of responding to what an uncertain future will bring, we need to ensure that we lay the groundwork for a better tomorrow in the way we live now.

ENDNOTES

1. Reuters. (2025, February 21). *Elon Musk wields chainsaw at conservative gathering, a gift from Argentina's Milei*. Retrieved February 24, 2025, from https://www.reuters.com/world/us/elon-musk-wields-chainsaw-conservative-gathering-gift-argentinas-milei-2025-02-21/

2. WUSA9. (2025, February 6). *Flooding the zone: Trump's media strategy*. https://youtu.be/IrPAMeT51f0?feature=shared

3. Pallab Ghosh. (2025, February 3). *UN monitors asteroid with a tiny chance of hitting Earth*. https://www.bbc.co.uk/news/articles/cqx9dg-px98go

4. Witness the success of the far right AfD in German elections (February 2025) where they gained enough seats to become the second largest party.

5. Not only on the right: for critique of left wing tribalism, see Nieman, S. (2023). *Left is not woke*. Polity.

6. For the connection of the July 1944 plot to Bonhoeffer's fate, see Bethge, E. (1970). *Dietrich Bonhoeffer* (pp. 714–726). Collins.

7. 'After ten years' in Bonhoeffer, D. (1971). *Letters and papers from prison* (pp. 3–17). SCM.

8. See Goldhagen, D. J. (1996). *Hitler's willing executioners*. Knopf; Browning, C. (1992). *Ordinary men*. Aaron Asher.

9. After ten years' in Bonhoeffer, D. (1971). *Letters and papers from prison* (p. 8). SCM.

10. Bonhoeffer, D. (1971). *Letters and papers from prison* (p. 9). SCM.

11. Arendt, A. (2006/1963). *Eichmann in Jerusalem*. Penguin.

12. Minnich, E. (2017). *The evil of banality* (p. 12). Rowman and Littlefield.

13. Minnich, E. (2017). *The evil of banality* (p. 126). Rowman and Littlefield.

14. Aristotle, Eudemian Ethics, 1216b22–25.

15. Minnich, E. (2017). *The evil of banality* (p. 128). Rowman and Littlefield.

16. Minnich, E. (2017). *The evil of banality* (pp. 12, 172). Rowman and Littlefield.

17. See Minnich's discussion of Le Chambon, the village that resisted Nazism, pp. 119–124.

18. Arendt, H. (1968/1948). *Origins of totalitarianism*. Harcourt.

19. Yalom, I. (1980). *Existential psychotherapy* (pp. 8–9). Basic Books.

20. Harvey, S. (2024). *Orbital* (p. 73). Vintage.

21. McCain, C. (2025). Transcript of Bishop Mariann Budde's sermon during the 2025 inaugural prayer service. *Tunanina Blog*. https://carmen-mccain.com/2025/01/22/transcript-of-bishop-mariann-budes-sermon-during-the-2025-us-inaugural-prayer-service/

PERSONALLY FACING UP TO THE DARK

19

WRITING INTO THE DARK: DEMENTIA AND THE CULTIVATION OF HUMAN(E)NESS

Lesley Saunders

I wake and feel the fell of dark, not day.

What hours, O what black hours we have spent

This night! what sights you, heart, saw; ways you went!

*– Gerard Manley Hopkins (opening lines of the
fourth of the 'terrible sonnets')*

A PERSONAL APPROACH

It feels, a quarter of the way through the 21st century, as if the world is drowning in a whirlpool of dark ideas, dark thoughts, and their consequences – not just for the social and political ecology of humans but also the habitability of the planet for all species of living beings. Can we make any difference at all to the potentially apocalyptic future that is approaching and, if so, how?

Like many other liberal-minded people, I have lost faith to some extent in the ideals – such as mass protest movements, rational arguments, everyday activism, even education[1] – of my youthful years. Instead, my chapter proposes an intimately personal approach: in effect, an invitation to encounter the darkness within ourselves in the form of illness. And specifically, because it holds such terrors for most of us, the illness we call 'dementia'.

So the chapter begins with an **introduction to notions of what the experience of illness holds for us,** and where thinking with and about illness can take us, if we can summon just a little more courage.

The second section asks **whether we can meet the dark thoughts and ideas where they originate:** I am intrigued by the power they have, and what it is they give us, as well as what they take from us: I recall that Lucifer, the light-bringer, is the dark angel. So I sketch out some of that complicated territory.

Next, I home in on writing as a mode of encounter, **wondering what happens for writers who have suffered illness, particularly mental illness.** What does 'writing into the dark' offer them that might be, not a consolation for their experience, but possibly a new relationship with their art?

Then, since we are dependent on language to contain and shape ideas as well as to communicate our thoughts and feelings, I focus on works **from two writers to peer into the ways language is formed, deformed and reformed** in the effort to express these shadowy phenomena that inhabit the edge of consciousness.

I end by daring to suggest that, with the help of circumstances (even or especially extreme ones) and a willingness to hold still and listen, **we can change minds** – if not other people's, then at least our own.

In all that follows, allow me to proceed by association, of words and images, rather than by logic – for that is the process at work ....

THINKING WITH, AND ABOUT, ILLNESS?

Sometimes what is most alien and terrifying is the thing we need most to face.

In 2021, my husband and life-partner was diagnosed with Alzheimer's disease. The disease is a bewilderment (in its fullest sense) of the mind as well as a pathology of the brain, and so the person's sense of reality and validity is often and without warning placed under threat. The shift from certainty and stability to a radical uncertainty and precariousness leaks into the mentality of the person's care partner[2] and induces a certain kind of craziness. (Dasha Kiper gives many illustrative examples of this in her troubling and insightful book.[3])

My encounter with Alzheimer's disease has consequently brought me to a place full of dark thoughts and ideas. On a daily basis, they take the form of fury, impatience, desolation, self-pity, nostalgia, hopelessness, hostility, and revulsion. And yet I also have glimpses of where this brutal mix of reactions – which has severely undermined my image of myself – comes from. It is a complicated response to the world I find myself in: a world not only of personal distress and despair but also of broken systems, disappointed political hopes and thwarted expectations. Plus, without doubt, there is a body of received ideas and unquestioned assumptions about the darkness of dementia that has crept into my ways of thinking and feeling.

So, impelled as much by desperation as by curiosity, I keep trying to impart some meaning to what often feels like an overwhelming re-alignment of reality. One result is the attempts, like this one, to integrate the confusion and conundrums into my written work. By writing into the dark, as it were, I hope to find out what it is possible to think; how to think and feel and communicate beyond the boundaries of the apparently given.

This is not a novel approach: think of Virginia Woolf's essay, 'On Being Ill',[4] in which she declares that illness – of which she suffered many kinds, physical and psychological, throughout her life – transfigures our sense of ourselves and the world. This is how the essay opens:

> *Considering how common illness is, how tremendous the spiritual change that it brings, how astonishing, when the lights of health go down, the undiscovered countries that are then disclosed, what wastes and deserts of the soul a slight attack of influenza brings to light, what precipices and lawns sprinkled with bright flowers a little rise of temperature reveals ....*

– the sentence piles on example after example of altered experience, not ending until half a page has passed in a blur of images, each more metaphysical than the last. Woolf is not only describing the effects of illness on our perceptions, she is also manifesting the way language has to try its best to accommodate them. As Deryn Rees-Jones explains[5]: '[*Woolf's illnesses*] *demanded that she formulate a new way of accounting for the experiences she had undergone ...*'.

Illness reaches into and attacks our sense of identity. Yet if we can quiet our natural fear for a whilst we might find that thinking with, and about, illness can help us transcend our normal cast of mind, our ingrained mental habits, our dark thoughts and darker ideas. The rest of this chapter is consequently a tentative exploration of how the experience of illness – crucially, illness of the brain and mind, including of someone close to us – might potentially shed some reflective light on our encounters with 'dark ideas'. **Might we, in other words, understand our culture's malaise through our own?**

Next, I need to set out, briefly, a few notions about the darkness of 'dark ideas'.

DARK THOUGHTS, DARK IDEAS

Dark Ideas in the Ascendant?

Let's turn their lives into a crazy nightmare in which they can't distinguish wild fiction from the realities of the day ....[6]

If you believe (as I do) in the legacy of the Enlightenment, the pre-eminent value of truth, the centrality of science, the primacy of reason, and the quest for pluralist decency, then the electoral success ... of a figure like [Donald] Trump is, to say the least, difficult to digest. But digest it we must.[7]

In the wake of the 2024 USA election result which put a convicted felon in the most powerful political seat in the world – not to mention Vladimir Putin's aggression against Ukraine, Benjamin Netanyahu's razing of Gaza, the rise of other despots and dictatorships in many countries and, most of all, the continuing anthropogenic destruction of global climate and environmental ecologies – it might seem that 'dark ideas' have won. We can be forgiven for having very dark thoughts about the situation we find ourselves in. But when we speak of 'dark ideas', what do we mean? Are they different in kind from 'dark thoughts'? What associations does 'dark' have for us? I know that other chapters in this book analyse the nature and provenance of dark ideas, so here is my short personal viewpoint, to provide some context.

The Binary Nature of Primordial Ideas

First and most self-evidently, dark is one half of the primordial binary pair dark/light or yin/yang, as old as human history, where dark is the absence of light; darkness renders stuff invisible, unknowable. There is the invisibility of the universe's dark matter, for example, contained within dark stars. Or, at the other end of the cosmic scale, we still do not know who the Dark Lady of Shakespeare's sonnets was, despite a mountain of scholarship. We talk about the Dark Ages, where the written record is missing. And then there is the unseen, the out-of-reach unconscious mind, as Freud hypothesised it – the hidden reservoir of our primitive animalian instincts. Furthermore, our corporeal origin is the womb, female and quintessentially dark, just as the firmament first took shape in darkness. We will need to come back to this, of course.

Then, 'dark' becomes not just the absence but also the opposite of light. Dark is anti-enlightenment, anti-science, anti-expert, irrational, fanatical, occult, Romantic, *Sturm und Drang*. For many cultures, dark is strongly associated with evil, what people get up to under cover of night, the optimal time for practising the dark arts. And now we have the dark web, which we can imagine might be manipulatively exploited using dark money by people who exhibit personality traits of the dark triad – amorality, narcissism, psychopathy. And so on.

A Heritage of Dark Ideas

Dark ideas – ideas which play to the dark sides of human nature (our secret desires and fears) – are nothing new. Plato was an advocate of selective breeding or eugenics, to be imposed on an unwitting public. Elimination of other peoples, cultures, nations, races, which we now call genocide, can be found throughout human history, starting perhaps with Yahweh's commandment to the Israelites that they should destroy the descendants of Amalek. Surveillance and control of fellow human beings were proposed by Jeremy Bentham in his design for the Panopticon, which has been the model for many prisons, as well as some factories, ever since. Modern equivalents of eugenicist ideas include so-called 'race science'; whilst 'the great replacement theory' purports to describe how the 'white' western 'races' are being demographically and culturally replaced by non-white peoples, especially Muslims. Well, there is no need (or possibility) to give an exhaustive list of misinformation, deliberate lies, hate speech, fake news, conspiracy theories and so on and on: they rampage through our culture like pathogens.

'Othering'

But, given that 'dark ideas' can mimic stories about, say, the supposed characteristics of nations and nationalities, societies, ethnicities, or the nature of human nature, we might ask to what extent 'dark' ideas differ from foundation myths and religious teachings about the history of peoples or of the cosmos itself[8] – or indeed from preposterous but benign forms of magical thinking, or theories about alien invaders and so on. I think the difference is that **'dark ideas' all have the intention of encouraging a malignant sense of 'us and them'**, fostering notions of the superior race versus inferior and/or evil beings, and promulgating the need for a strong leader to save 'us' from being swamped by 'them'. Dark ideas are essentially in the business of denouncing, scapegoating, excluding and 'othering'. They are disseminated by those with power, whether on the far right or far left, whether through bad faith or false consciousness, greed or paranoia.

And these same ideas are also spread by those without power, through frustration, anger, hurt pride, pain, a sense of being ignored and passed over. Where the powerful and the powerless meet is in the public space of social media, where both wield influence. Their appeal lies partly in offering simplistic, authoritarian, all-encompassing solutions to complex, distressing and legitimate problems in the real world; and partly in their capacity to tap into what we have learnt, after Freud, to call 'the unconscious'. So let us not suppose that the apparatus of the Enlightenment is going to be of much use here: emotions are impervious to appeals to rationality, science and pluralistic tolerance. The dark is made darker by the presence of light.

The Lure of Populist Simplicity

In our divided state, what we need is a remedy, an antidote – though perhaps it is not the darkness that needs a corrective so much as the treacherous simplicity of those ideas and ideologies. Could it be that people (we) succumb to their lure not because they (we) are freaks or evil, but rather because they (we) are forever grappling with the lack of a sense of real agency in a chaotic world[9] and a need for consolation, for faith, they (we) cannot even name? Moreover, is it possible that this is because they (we) do not possess a sufficiently rich and subtle language with which to express their (our) deepest desires and fears? That the populist discourse is not fit for their (our) human needs, even as it promises to fulfil them?

The Great Darkness of the D-word

That is certainly true of the term 'dementia' and the ideas that trail alongside. 'Dementia' is host to a great darkness in both medical and popular discourses. The linguistic register used in medical and scientific articles about neurodegenerative diseases is negative and limited/limiting. Although words like 'impairment', 'decline', 'deficits', 'dysfunction' may look descriptive, they carry value judgements, they imply that someone with such a disease[10] is less than fully human. It is therefore a language that serves, amongst other things, to distance, to keep at bay, the existential subject. Moreover, I suspect this linguistic turn both breeds and conceals a dread: the dread of what is assumed to be creeping unreason, breakdown and eventual dissolution.

And an even deeper darkness inheres in the public imaginary of dementia. Dementia means being out of one's mind. As Hannah Zeilig[11] argues, the D-word conjures up a secretive, catastrophic sickness that makes insidious incursions into the hidden core of us for decades before the tell-tale symptoms accumulate and overwhelm. Dementia is portrayed as a scourge of old age, a monstrous, ghoulish plague with almost supernatural origins; having dementia is deemed to be a fate worse than death. The D-word turns humans into zombies, crazies, enfeebled creatures, inhuman, wholly 'Other'. And the shame of it, the deep ashamedness, is transferred from the person whose body is streaked with faeces to the person who is caring for them. For the rest of us: '*One day I may be like that ... It's hardly bearable; we turn away so that we do not have to bear it*'.[12] That is why the talk of a 'cure for dementia' is so seductive. Meanwhile the term itself seems forever in retreat from a firm definition, slithers from our grasp.

So how could I, in intimate proximity to my husband's disease hour on hour, day on day, avoid being infected by such a conceptual malaise myself? And how could my thinking not be inflected by such catastrophising tropes?

The 'Dark Room' of Discovery

And yet, and yet – the dark is also a place to which we retreat, and where we sink into ourselves, surrender to our musings; drowse, convalesce. Kat Lister says the neurologist Oliver Sacks called the limbo in which one finds oneself in sickness 'the night-womb' before a new life has been created.[13] As the light thickens and the room darkens, we fall into the slumber of the daytime self. We encounter our other selves, those who hold surprises for us in the form of half-waking dreams, sudden shifts of perspective, a curtain swaying across the windowpane in the night breeze to reveal the moon in its aloofness. This is the dark room, the fecund womb, where visions are slowly developing.

So – let the light thicken ....

ILLNESS AS ENCOUNTER

You think you have mastered it, but just as you get well
underway in following, it turns a back-somersault and
there you are. It slaps you in the face, knocks you down,
and tramples upon you. it is like a bad dream.[14]

The Divided Self of Illness

Dark ideas are other-directed. Dark thoughts are carried by the black dog of melancholy,[15] they are self-directed, drawing us down into the realms of self-deprecation, self-hatred, self-harm .... The body-mind is dark to us, we cannot see inside ourselves without the help of instruments. To the thinker, her own brain is a mystery, its synapses firing tirelessly in the futile effort to interrogate the physiology that makes her thinking possible. We humans are all divided selves. The experience of illness in particular brings to the fore our self-ignorance, our self-rupture, splitting body from mind, self from other, language from meaning:

> *Too many of the best cells in my body/are itching, feeling*
> *jagged, turning raw/in this spring chill. It's two thousand*
> *and four/and I don't know a soul who doesn't feel small/*
> *among the numbers. Razor small./Look down these days*
> *to see your feet/mistrust the pavement and your blood*
> *tests/turn the doctor's expression grave.*[16]

This is the first stanza of Jo Shapcott's 'Of Mutability', both the title and the poem capturing that strange-but-familiar sense of pathogenic instability. Falling ill has the capacity to transport us elsewhere, psychically and linguistically. Sometimes that elsewhere is the corporeal, incarnated self, the body as a '*site of complication*' when we feel strangely '*othered*' by what is happening to us.[17] Shapcott's poem ends like this: '*Don't trouble, though, to head anywhere but the sky*' – which seems to echo Woolf's febrile flight of fantasy, as if illness is bound to be attended by fever, under whose influence everything that is gross and earth-bound will evaporate.

Illness is psychotropic, expanding or dissolving the boundaries of the physical body. The sick writer feels she is literally beside herself and has to find a different mode of self-representation. Think of the artist Leonora Carrington in her memoir *Down Below*, Charlotte Perkins Gillman in her short story *The Yellow Wallpaper* (quoted above), Sylvia Plath in her mature poetry as well as in her autobiographical novel *The Bell Jar*, Anne Sexton in her first poetry collection *To Bedlam and Part Way Back* and Ntozake Shange in her novels and her play *for colored girls who have considered suicide/when the rainbow Is enuf*: they are just a few of the writers finding their ill-being to be a catalyst for their writing.

For each of them, living with, and against, prevailing attitudes towards illness – especially illnesses with a mental or psychological aspect – drove their writing towards breakdown and innovation. As Rees-Jones remarks In her preface to the volume *On Being Ill* (cited above), illness '*opens a space when our guard is down*', and this is what can both impel and permit the doors of perception to be cleansed, to borrow a well-known phrase from Aldous Huxley.

Taking two examples of 'writing into the dark', I want next to show how what is cryptic, sunless, obscure, shadowy can be made to yield up its own clarifying truths under pressure of the poet's need for meaning-making. I have chosen to write about poems rather than about any of the novels or memoirs I have just mentioned, because of poetry's way with language, and with metaphor in particular. After all, we need to concern ourselves with matters of language as much as of ideas; language renders our ideas and experiences communicable.

The Incarnate Mind

All descriptions of the brain/mind are metaphorical, and the one that has become most prevalent – the brain as machine or computer – has come to be taken for reality. We have become all too familiar with phrases like 'hard-wired', 'information transmission, processing and retrieval', and 'human brains are programmed to do x, y or z'. Whilst there are some interesting discussions about this and other metaphors (e.g., endnotes [18] and [19]), one crucial difference between computers and brains/minds is the fact that brains are situated in living, moving bodies; recent research has revealed that bodies play a crucial role in how human minds work. Without needing to know the term 'embodied cognition', poetry has always been cognisant of the phenomenon – which is perhaps is why it tends to have better metaphors that enact the richness, complexity and creativity of the incarnate brain/mind – even an ill one. In his now-famous book *The Body Keeps the Score,* Bessel van der Kolk remarks:

> [...] *the self-observing, body-based self system ... speaks through sensations, tone of voice and body tensions. Being able to perceive visceral sensations is the very foundation of emotional awareness.*[20]

– which echoes something Jorie Graham, an acclaimed American poet, said in an interview:

> *I don't think you can actually be human if you don't know you have a body. You can't have compassion, which is a physical experience at its root. You can't imagine an other, let alone the point of view of an other. You can't have a moral vocabulary in other words.*[21]

WRITING INTO THE DARK: TWO EXAMPLES

So now I take a very brief look at the work of two poets, Vicki Feaver and Philip Gross, both of whom are highly acclaimed and widely published poets. Encountering the mind's intractable difficulties in later life, they infuse their poetic explorations with a sense of bodiliness.

Fugitive Speech?

Feaver was diagnosed with Parkinson's Disease in her 70s, and has begun to write poems out of that illness, which (like dementia) causes cognitive diminution. Here is 'The Woman Who Lost Words' (first published in *Poetry Review*, Summer 2021) in its entirety[22]:

> *She lost the name for a meadow flower*
>
> *like a small round amethyst brooch*
>
> *and for a hairy, green-fleshed berry.*
>
> *Sheep's-bit and kiwi returned to her.*
>
> *But the word on the tip of her tongue*
>
> *for an ugly sight – she wanted to describe*
>
> *the shining disguise of a blanket of snow –*
>
> *slipped to the back of her throat.*
>
> *She scoured the dictionary and thesaurus,*
>
> *searching as frenziedly as her dog,*
>
> *sniffing behind curtains and under chairs*
>
> *and sofa for his hidden ball.*
>
> *She'd begun to wonder if the word existed*
>
> *when a friend gave it to her: eyesore,*
>
> *a word staring her in the face*
>
> *for a sight it hurt to look at.*
>
> *Her dog's search tool was his nose.*
>
> *Hers was a faulty circuitry of a brain*
>
> *that lost words and found them*
>
> *and lost them again, as if the inside*

of her head was a shaken snow-globe

where words, mingling with the storm

of whirling flakes, settled randomly,

revealing some and burying others.

The poem hardly needs exegesis, so what I want to draw your attention to is the sharpness of the imagery even as the poet is telling us, in the third person, about the 'shaken snow-globe' in her brain. There is a delightful cleverness in the comparison she makes between the dog's 'search tool' – his sniffing nose – and the 'circuitry' of her own brain, which belies the cognitive loss she is at pains to describe as fully as possible. Snow, which smothers and disguises the visible world, occurs in the second as well as the final stanza and I think makes a more apposite metaphor for the mind's frustrating imprecision than the notion, which is almost immediately discarded, of *'faulty circuitry'*. The lack and loss of words is a catastrophe for a poet, and this poem both faces up to that and also manages to set down something remarkably lucid as a marker of the loss. It is an encounter as morally courageous as it is poetically accomplished.

Pure Voice?

In the collections *Deep Field* and *Later* (Bloodaxe, 2011 and 2013), Philip Gross is generally writing about his father rather than himself – or rather, he is writing himself and his father into the new strange relationship between them, as his father's own use of language diminishes. Thus, in the long poem 'Vocable' from *Deep Field*, Gross is concerned with exploring the physical expulsion of voiced breath, whether or not the sounds (are intended to) carry semantic significance. The poem proceeds in non-regular lineation and in line, stanza and section breaks that seem designed to make us question our expectations of continuity, consistency, certainty. One section alludes to the devotional singing of Nusrat Fateh Ali Khan as:

the shwara, the Qawwali vocables,

drunk-staggering in God's name, juggling right to the edge

of nonsense,

and connects this with his father clutching:

> *with his wrecked voice at a-*
>
> *ya ... e-na ... ah-la ... like handholds of air.*

Gross recently commented on this poem, '*Looking at it now, I like what it does – saying to him, No, you're not an aberration; you're a representative of the human race*' (Personal communication). Gross' work in both collections enacts the capacity of language to shape itself to accommodate the darkest of phenomena, loss of identity.

And so what I find compelling about both Feaver's and Gross' poems is their willingness to sit in a kind of aporia, a doubting uncertainty, where meaning is always on the brink of fracture. They are playing in the dark, playing with the dark. They discover for us as well as themselves a kind of optimism – not a false hope that things will get better and all will be well, but a radical acceptance of what is. These poems show us how to receive life's catastrophes with the creative embrace of language – language that is itself far from whole and rational and perfect.

CODA

This chapter may have given the impression that I am proposing poetry as the antidote to dark ideas. Well, there is a grain of truth in that; once again, the poet Jorie Graham has something to say that feels pertinent:

> *This fracturing of subjectivity led to experiments [in my writing] .... The attempt changes one. Radically. It changes one's size, one's sense of one's centrality as the speaker; it compels a kind of radical imagination of otherness. You try to feel your own unlikeness.*[23]

But of course we all know that '*poetry makes nothing happen*',[24] and in any case both reading and writing poetry remain minority pastimes. The broader point I have used poetry to make is that the encounter with the darkness within – for example, in the form of cognitive loss and dementia – can ultimately return us to our human(e)ness, where paradoxically we know ourselves as Other;

not resisting the darkness, but playing within its shifting, dancing, awe-inspiring shadows ....

And, ultimately, this place of personal darkness is where we may discover the deeper common truths, of uncertainty in the face of plausible public untruths and of our mysterious, shared humanity in the face of noisy hatred. It offers us an invitation to reach beyond the limitations of our assumptions and biases about what is apprehensible, comprehensible, in the human condition.

ENDNOTES

1. An interesting argument against '*reasoned engagement*' with extremist ideas appears in this article 'A little less conversation, a little more action: Schools and the prevention of violent extremism through reasoned engagement', *Theory and Research in Education*, 2 January 2025, https://journals.sagepub.com/doi/full/10.1177/14778785241309278.

2. I am indebted for this term, in preference to 'carer' or 'caregiver', to Gerrard, N. (2019). *What dementia teaches us about love* (p. 115). Allen Lane.

3. Kiper, D. (2023). *Travellers to unimaginable lands: Dementia, carers and the hidden workings of the mind*. Profile Books.

4. First published in *The New Criterion* in 1926 and republished in 1930 by the Hogarth Press.

5. 'On Being Ill', preface to the volume of essays by various authors, *On Being Ill*, Open Archive, Amsterdam 2021.

6. Dmitry Medvedev, former president of Russia, remark reported by Reuters, June 2024.

7. D'Ancona, M. (2024, November 7). Where the darkness prevails. *The New European*.

8. There's a wonderful passage in John Milton's *Paradise Lost* about how '*th' Almighty Maker [might] ordain His dark materials to create more Worlds*.

9. For examples of attempts to explain and empathise, see: https://www.theguardian.com/us-news/2024/nov/03/its-not-just-shameful-it-is-humiliating-four-celebrated-authors-on-their-hopes-and-fears-before-the-2024-us-election and https://www.theguardian.com/lifeandstyle/2024/nov/03/my-friend-has-embraced-conspiracy-theories-and-im-fed-up-with-it.

10. Alzheimer's disease is one of the neuro-degenerative diseases commonly known as 'dementias'. It is accompanied, though not

necessarily caused, by a build-up of beta-amyloid protein in the form of plaques, which interrupt the brain's neuronal networks, initially in the entorhinal cortex and hippocampus, and later in the cerebral cortex. This process is also accompanied by the detachment of tau proteins within neurons to form neurofibrillary tangles, which appear to disrupt the synaptic communication between neurons. Eventually the person's brain atrophies to the point where it cannot sustain life.

11. Zeilig, H. (2014). Dementia as a cultural metaphor. *The Gerontologist*, 54(2), 258–267.

12. Gerrard, N. (2019). *What dementia teaches us about love* (p. 111). Allen Lane.

13. Lister, K. (2024, 1 December). I felt like a bystander in my own internal recovery. *The Observer*. https://www.theguardian.com/society/2024/dec/01/i-felt-like-a-bystander-in-my-own-internal-recovery-one-womans-battle-for-health-after-a-life-changing-diagnosis.

14. Gilman, C. P. (2009). *The yellow wallpaper and selected writings* (p. 15). Virago Modern Classics.

15. The term *black dog* was coined by Samuel Johnson and popularised by Sir Winston Churchill.

16. Jo Shapcott, from the title poem, *Of Mutability*, Faber and Faber, 2010.

17. Lister, K. (2024, 1 December). I felt like a bystander in my own internal recovery. *The Observer*. https://www.theguardian.com/society/2024/dec/01/i-felt-like-a-bystander-in-my-own-internal-recovery-one-womans-battle-for-health-after-a-life-changing-diagnosis.

18. https://www.frontiersin.org/journals/computerscience/articles/10.3389/fcomp.2022.810358/full

19. http://mechanism.ucsd.edu/teaching/w12/philneuro/metaphorsand conceptionsofbrain.key.pdf

20. van der Kolk, B. (2014). *The body keeps the score* (p. 284). Penguin Books.

21. Interview with Jorie Graham, http://www.praccrit.com/poems/cryo/.

22. I am very grateful to Vicki Feaver, and to the editors of *Poetry Review*, for allowing me to quote the entire poem.

23. 'Jorie Graham takes the long view', *The New Yorker*, 1 January 2023.

24. Auden, W. H. (1940). In memory of W. B. Yeats. In *Another Time*. Random House .

20

TAKING CONTROL: BE MORE SELECTIVE IN CHOICE OF MEDIA

Lynn Wood

Every day we see negative headlines. Yet also every day, many stories about positive ideas and innovations go unnoticed. We need to be much more selective in our choice of media to be better informed in an environment where we are being swamped with negative news.

This chapter will answer three questions:

- Why is there so much negative news?

- Why should we consider a media diet?

- How can we go on a media diet?

WHY IS THERE SO MUCH NEGATIVE NEWS?

Humans Are Primed for Negative News

First, let's consider the argument that we are hard wired to be disposed towards bad news! Humanity evolved in Africa millions of years ago surrounded by a world of severe and immediate danger. To deal with this constant danger, our brains evolved the temporal lobe – the amygdala. It scans everything we see and listens for signs of danger and when it senses danger it puts us on alert.

A consequence of this is that we are more likely to read negative news as it offers us more value.

This 'fight or flight' response is an automatic physiological reaction to an event that is perceived as stressful or frightening. The perception of threat activates the sympathetic nervous system and triggers an acute stress response that prepares the body to fight or flee. The amygdala is more likely to record and store negative events than positive ones. This leads to a negativity bias, where we are more likely to focus on negative news.

Negative News Is Easier to Report

As a result of this strong human tendency to pivot towards bad news, most newsrooms operate on the principle 'if it bleeds it leads' and 'bad news is good news'. According to a 2022 British Library exhibition in London that I attended called 'Breaking the News-Reported or Distorted' these points make an event news: Crime and sensationalism; Scandal; Conflict; Disaster; Power; Suppression; Satire; Chaos; Celebrity; Celebration. There's not much to celebrate here and much journalistic output is geared to the immediate and sensational. Journalism has a built-in bias towards the negative, because bad things are sudden (a shooting rampage, a major accident, a war, an epidemic), while good things are usually more gradual and not always easy to photograph.

As well as being popular with journalists given it's easier to report, negative news is also popular with media owners because advertisers support media based on readership and more readers mean more money. Even more money can be made by publishers who bend the truth for profits. Media power can be said to be built on a 'loophole in democracy' that protects the freedom of the press without requiring ethical, moral or societal responsibility from its owners. The First Amendment to the US Constitution and similar laws in other countries support a view that liberty depends on the freedom of the press.[1]

News in a Digital World

So, given that our brains are wired to pay attention to bad news publishers are keen to feed this appetite, and it is becoming increasingly clear that the digital world is compounding the effect. Whereas previously publishers had to estimate readership for advertising support, now they use click numbers that they can count – and because we have a tendency to click negative stories they are publishing more of them. In the advent of our new digital media environment a new term has been given to spending too much time consuming negative news online – *doomscrolling*.

In a digital world, there are more opportunities to doomscroll as there are many more sources of news, including social media which has become very influential in relation to sharing as well as accessing news. Nearly 40% of Australians, for example, use social media to access news, including near 60% of Gen Z.[2]

Most social media have a hedonic (pleasure) focus. Receiving recognition and approval online, in the form of 'likes', gives people a positive feeling of elation and satisfaction.[3] Unfortunately, when we share negative news (rather than positive news) using social media we get more likes. Furthermore, when social media messages include emotional-moral terms, their spread has been found to increase substantially. Posts causing outrage and anger spread faster and reach more users than other emotions.

Researchers at Cambridge University found, for example, that political posts from accounts criticising or mocking an opposing political party or ideology received twice as many shares as posts that uplifted or celebrated their own partisan views.[4] In essence, there is more value in negative news and ideas than positive ones as we click and share more of them and media business cases are built on our clicking and sharing news. Another main driver for the increase of negative news in a digital world is we can see the news 24/7, not just mainly at set times as we did previously.

WHY SHOULD WE CONSIDER A MEDIA DIET?

Negative News Causes Harm

While negative news is popular, particularly in the digital world, there is increasing evidence to indicate that when we watch, read, or listen to negative news, it can exacerbate our tendency to worry.[5] This exposure to negative news can cause stress and affect behaviour negatively. What we let into our minds influences our thoughts, conversations, and feelings, driving fear and anxiety for many. These emotional states are associated with increased levels of cortisol, commonly known as the 'stress hormone', which can cause inflammation and reduce the immune system's efficacy.

Emerging research is indicating that 7 in 10 adults (72%) agree with the statement that the 'media blow things out of proportion', and more than half (54%) say that they want to stay informed about the news, but following it causes them stress.[6]

Differently aged groups reported different levels of stress that they attribute to the news media, with more people in their 30s and younger admitting to being upset by the news cycle.

Young People Are Particularly Affected by Negative News

AustralianWellbeing results for 2024 were a surprise in that they also revealed people aged under 35 had a much higher level of loneliness than older generations. The loneliness score for someone aged 18–24 was about double that of someone aged 75 plus. It was not expected as young people use social media more than older people and a benefit of social media is connecting people. People who are lonely are reported to have lower levels of wellbeing.[7]

Loneliness scores by age

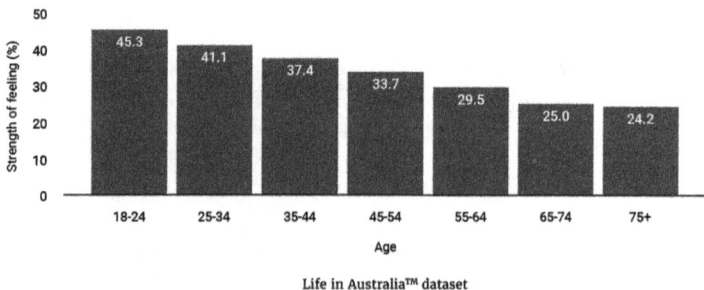

Life in Australia™ dataset

The results indicate that young people are concerned about the future given the way it is being portrayed by the media. Between climate change, the situation in the Middle East, the war in Ukraine and the threat to democracy worldwide, the geopolitical situation can be very unsettling for young people in particular.

There is now much better recognition of the harm caused by the media as a result of legal action by US states to support children. Meta, the parent company of Instagram and Facebook, is being sued by 41 US states that have accused the company of deliberately designing algorithms to cause addictive behaviour in children and of concealing its own research that proves that these products are harming young users, in particular their mental health.[8] Furthermore, TikTok is being sued by the State of Utah for putting profit and power before people to become the fastest-growing platform for children. When TikTok eventually submitted court-ordered documents, it became evident that the dangers posed by the platform to children extend beyond its addictive algorithm. Its TikTok LIVE feature includes a way for criminals to exploit users, particularly minors.[9]

International cooperation is an important feature of internet governance, given the internet doesn't recognise international boundaries. Australia is considered to have had one of the first online safety acts with the 'Enhancing Online Safety Act' passed in 2015, which also established the world's first dedicated online safety regulator, the Children's eSafety Commissioner, making it a pioneer in online safety legislation globally. There are now Online Safety Acts in the UK as well as Australia and the European Union has a Digital Services Act.

Australia also led the world with a News Media Bargaining Code in 2021 which contains powers to force tech companies to deal with media companies and pay for news shared in good faith or face fines of 10% of Australian revenue. New ways of implementing this code are being considered. Canada introduced a similar code in the Online News Act in 2023; however, Meta refused to comply and stopped sharing news resulting in an overall decrease of 43% in engagement with news in Canada.[10] While this response by Meta was not expected the Canadian Government has held its position to help ensure a healthy ecosystem for news. These actions by the Australian and Canadian governments are particularly important given the dominance Meta and Google have now achieved in online advertising at the expense of media organisations that previously depended on advertising to fund quality journalism.

Since 2024, Generative AI products such as ChatGPT are increasingly being used in the production of journalism, raising more concerns about the origin and veracity of information produced by their algorithmic programs. This is in turn leading to increasing concern about how AI is potentially fuelling misinformation. Indeed, a recent survey shows that misinformation is now a significant concern to Australians having increased from 64% in 2022 to 75% in 2024.[2] Disinformation and misinformation are now deemed more dangerous, in the short run (next two years), than violent climate events, wars and societal disintegration.[11] As a result of these concerns Australia has banned children under 16 from being on social media or opening new accounts. The law, which takes effect in 2026, holds social media companies responsible for verifying children's ages.

As he left office, President Joe Biden warned of the Tech Industrial Complex and the 'dangerous consequences' of 'power in the hands of a very few ultra-wealthy people'. He warned that a tech 'oligarchy' is emerging as Americans 'are being buried under an avalanche of misinformation and disinformation enabling the abuse of power'.[12]

Promoting Positive Opportunities

While dystopian visions of the world paint pictures of sombre possible futures, we should also imagine a future for humanity that is positive to encourage and support ideas and innovations that drive a better world. Sir Anthony Seldon said 'Without ideas, no progress can be made. With the wrong ideas, no progress can be made. But with the right ideas, at the right time, anything is possible'.[13] (Note: Anthony Seldon has also written a chapter in this book.)

There are many wonderful ideas at various stages of commercialisation happening in Australia and around the world. They are solutions to many world problems. We just need to look around and see them.

We all tend to live not noticing the positives in our environment and consequently miss perceiving some of life's riches. New positive vitas can open up through being more alert and observant in looking for the clever, the surprising, the interesting, and the humorous. Often this is easier to do when we travel to new environments. There are many benefits of being more attuned to positive news, a prime one being that we can see more opportunities in life, as well as improving our wellbeing.

The Wellbeing Dividend

Positive news can significantly enhance wellbeing by fostering positive emotions, which in turn influence psychological and physical health, leading to improved life satisfaction and reduced depression.[14] It impacts our health by triggering hormones linked to wellbeing like Dopamine, Oxytocin, Serotonin and Endorphins. They help to regulate stress hormones such as cortisol and adrenaline.

The advice to focus on the positive is already being used in health care to help settle anxious patients. It's been recommended that the news is not displayed in waiting rooms. Instead, positive media is recommended in waiting rooms like kindness and nature media. When a more relaxed patient enters the examination room better clinical outcomes can be achieved.[15] So, just as we manage our physical health with nutritional food, we should manage our mental health and wellbeing with more positive news. We are what we see as well as what we eat. A media diet means reading less negative news and looking around for the positive.

HOW CAN WE GO ON A *MEDIA DIET?*

Our Attention Is Under Our Control

To go on a media diet, we need to monitor what news we let into our minds just as we monitor what we eat to be healthy. Fortunately, we can do this because how we engage with media and consume news are within our own control. We should simply ask whether we are giving our attention to the right things. The 19th century philosopher and a founding father of positive psychology, William

James, had a powerful insight into the concept of 'attention', that is very relevant today. He wrote that 'Attention ... is the taking possession by the mind, in clear and vivid form, of one out of what seem several simultaneously possible objects or trains of thought' i.e. what we attend to shapes the experiences we have.[16]

This insight underscores the critical importance of reducing our attention to negative news particularly in the digital age, where the proliferation of social media and advancements in AI have increased the risks of misinformation and harm. By becoming more discerning in choosing the content we consume, we can shape our experiences and foster wellbeing.

It seems that already many in Australia are reducing their attention to news (68%)[2] and hopefully this is particularly the case with negative news which can foster a sense of powerlessness and fear. However, the good news is that we have agency to control attention and how we engage with media.

Look Out for Positive News

We should instead direct our attention to positive and constructive content that we believe we can trust. It's now possible to check news media for reliability and political bias – more bias means less trust – through outlets like Ad Fontes Media which uses a panel of analysts across the political spectrum to evaluate media.[17]

When we find appropriate media we can create our own positive feed by bookmarking it so we can refer to it again, and this can include articles as well as websites. It's also possible to add websites to the home screen of phones so the website looks like an app. I co-founded the open innovation platform IdeaSpies in 2016, disturbed by the growing impact of negative news on mental health. Coincidentally, while news cycle-related anxiety has probably existed for centuries, it became particularly obvious in 2016 when we launched IdeaSpies, a year packed with global events that polarised communities.[6]

Also, coincidentally Australian interest in news fell significantly from 2016. In 2016, 64% of Australians had high interest in news but in 2024 only 54% say they do. The fall in interest has been greatest among under 35s (-14pp).

INTEREST IN NEWS BY AGE 2016-2024 (% HIGH INTEREST)

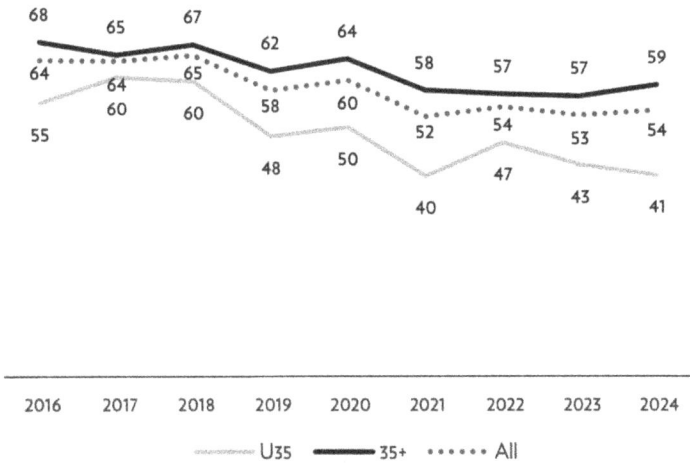

| 2016 | 2017 | 2018 | 2019 | 2020 | 2021 | 2022 | 2023 | 2024 |

⸺ U35   ▬▬ 35+   ••••• All

   IdeaSpies was developed as a platform for sharing positive ideas that are in use and new discoveries that could be easily shared. Innovation starts from ideas and every innovation is based on an idea.

   People around the world could directly post ideas and innovations they saw to the platform, explained simply. We shared more than 7,000 positive ideas between 2016 and 2024 in topics ranging from AgTech to Wellbeing, generating more than 225 million views. IdeaSpies was featured in the book about the importance of ideas in creating healthy societies.[13]

Share Positive Ideas and News

If we can't come up with ideas ourselves, we can share positive ideas and stories we see, so others can see and support them (as indeed modelled by IdeaSpies). It's easy to share ideas now by 'liking' them and sharing them to social media as well as by email. In that way, we are creating more positive content for others to see and act on. We are also creating more positive content for ourselves given media offer us more of what we click. Furthermore, sharing these positive ideas can reflect on us well as people who care about the world and are interested in helping to improve it.

Pay for News

Positive news is often hard to find because many publisher business models don't support it, instead offering mainly negative news which is free on social media. Therefore, if we recognise the value of news, we should be prepared to pay for it. Interestingly Australians, particularly younger people, are increasingly prepared to pay for news, as shown in the following chart.[2]

PAYING FOR ONLINE NEWS 2016-2024 (%) BY AGE

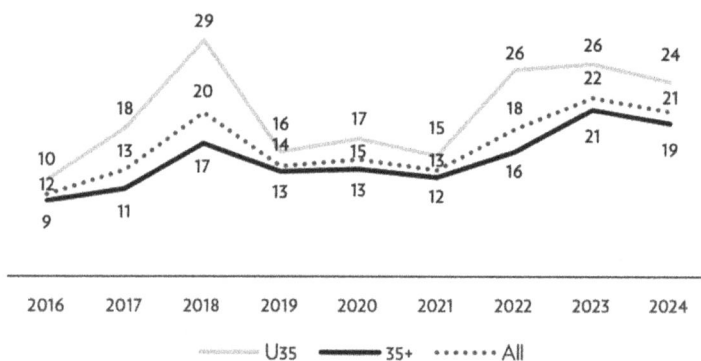

| 2016 | 2017 | 2018 | 2019 | 2020 | 2021 | 2022 | 2023 | 2024 |

‑‑‑‑‑ U35   ——— 35+   ⋯⋯ All

When we prevent ourselves from clicking negative news, which reinforces it, and focus instead on positive news that we may have to pay for, we encourage professional journalism that is public-oriented, solution-oriented, future-oriented and action-oriented, avoiding a bias towards negativity.[18] This is now called constructive journalism as it involves applying positive psychology techniques to the news process in an effort to strengthen the field and facilitate productive news stories.[19] In offering to pay, we can encourage more constructive journalism which often reframes negative news positively as problems that need to be solved then considers ideas that could solve these problems.

If there is a movement away from focussing on problems to focussing on ideas that solve them, platforms like IdeaSpies can be successful. Positive ideas and innovations need to be supported and entrepreneurs that develop them need to be encouraged. When news is written from different, more constructive perspectives, showing examples of people making positive changes, people can emulate them.

This is an important point for young people in particular to inspire them to make positive changes necessary to ensure a bright future.

We Are in Control

When we realise that the media has a vested interest in offering us negative news that causes us harm, we can do something about it. While a barrage of bad news can reach us very easily, we need to make an effort to find positive news. The solution to the problem of negative news is a media diet where we read enough news to stay informed and look around for positive news and ideas.

It's never easy to change habits; however, we can redirect our attention because it is under our control. We can give less attention to negative news by not clicking it as much. We can instead click positive news and ideas when we see them and share them with others. If we can't find positive news and ideas we should consider paying to see them. If we are inclined to be entrepreneurial we can also take a positive attitude to problems and come up with solutions that we can develop and share. In all these ways we can create a better world for ourselves and others.

ENDNOTES

1. Beecher, E. (2024). *The men who killed the news*. Scribner.
2. Digital News Report: Australia, 2024. https://www.canberra.edu.au/uc-research/faculty-research-centres/nmrc/digital-news-report-australia.
3. https://pmc.ncbi.nlm.nih.gov/articles/PMC9007765/
4. https://www.independent.co.uk/life-style/social-media-facebook-twitter-politics-b1870628.html
5. https://bpspsychub.onlinelibrary.wiley.com/doi/abs/10.1111/j.2044-8295.1997.tb02622.x
6. https://www.medicalnewstoday.com/articles/327516
7. https://www.australianunity.com.au/wellbeing/-/media/RebrandWellbeing/Documents/AU4355_G_CO_AUWI-s41-PDF-report-booklet_241111.pdf
8. https://www.npr.org/2023/10/24/1208219216/states-sue-meta-claiming-instagram-facebook-fueled-youth-mental-health-crisis

9. https://attorneygeneral.utah.gov/2025/01/03/utah-dcp-and-ags-office-announce-release-of-previously-redacted-information-tiktok-execs-knew-they-were-profiting-off-the-sexual-exploitation-of-minors/

10. https://meo.ca/press/old-news-new-reality-a-year-of-metas-news-ban-in-canada

11. https://www.weforum.org/publications/global-risks-report-2025/digest/

12. https://www.npr.org/2025/01/15/nx-s1-5258510/biden-farewell-address

13. Brown, C., & Handscomb, G. (2023). *The ideas-informed society.* Emerald Publishing.

14. https://www.wisebrain.org/papers/CultPosEmot.pdf

15. https://pubmed.ncbi.nlm.nih.gov/34869835/

16. https://psychclassics.yorku.ca/James/Principles/prin11.htm

17. https://app.adfontesmedia.com/chart/interactive

18. https://www.tandfonline.com/doi/full/10.1080/17512786.2018.1470900?src=recsys

19. https://www.tandfonline.com/doi/abs/10.1080/17512786.2018.1472527?journalCode=rjop20

ABOUT THE EDITORS

Chris Brown is Professor of Education (University of Southampton), Head of the Southampton Education School and Distinguished Visiting Professor, University of Tübingen. He has a long-standing interest in how people go about harnessing great ideas to improve the human condition. Traditionally his work has focussed on the education system, but more recently, he has turned his attention to the 'ideas-informed society' more generally, and how we can ensure ideas are available and used effectively to the benefit of everyone. He has written or edited some 21 books and nearly 100 journal articles in the broad sphere of research, evidence and ideas-use.

Graham Handscomb is Honorary Professor at University College, London, and Visiting Professor at Durham University and the University of Bolton. He was previously Dean and Professor of Education of the College of Teachers. He is a fellow of numerous organisations and universities and editor of a number of journals including *Profession Development Today*. His career involved managing schools and local authority improvement services and he pioneered the concept of *The Research Engaged School*. He now works as an educational and change consultant. He has written and published hundreds of articles and book chapters and edited many books. Whilst most of his work has been in education, he is also currently active in the area of ideas-engagement, democracy and truth-telling.

ABOUT THE CONTRIBUTORS

Arif Anis MBE is a British professional coach, leadership development expert and self-help author. He is a *Wall Street Journal* and *USA Today* bestselling author. Educated in Applied Psychology at world-class institutions including Punjab University and LUMS, and with executive education from Harvard, Oxford and Imperial College, he brings unparalleled expertise to stages across 97+ countries with some of the most influential leaders in the world, commanding attention at forums like the UN, European Parliament and World Economic Forum. His profound impact is recognised at the highest levels, earning honours from Queen Elizabeth II (QAVS) and an MBE for contributions to the field of leadership from King Charles III. Holding London's highest civil honours and a Vatican Knighthood, his influence extends globally as VP of Nobel Fest, Founder of the Institute of Founders and Minister Counsellor to the Andean Parliament. His work has featured in the BBC, ITV, Sky, Telegraph, CNBC and Forbes.

The Revd. Dr John P. Bradbury is the General Secretary of the United Reformed Church. He is the youngest person to be appointed to the post of General Secretary. After studying in Edinburgh, Revd Bradbury undertook graduate work in Cambridge whilst training for ministry at Westminster College. He was ordained in Liverpool in 2004 to work as part of the ecumenical team in the centre of the city, and to minister with Earle Road URC in Picton. In 2007, John was appointed to teach Systematic Theology and Church History at Westminster College, where he ultimately served as Vice-Principal. He has been heavily involved in ecumenism and was elected as one of the three presidents of the Community of Protestant Churches in Europe (CPCE). As well as serving as co-chair of the URC-Roman Catholic dialogue, John convenes the

United Reformed Church's Law and Polity Advisory Group. He is the author of *Perpetually Reforming: a theology of church reform and renewal* and co-editor of *Thinking again about Marriage*.

Andy Braunston is the United Reformed Church's (URC) Minister for Digital Worship; ordained in 1992, Andy worked with LGBT-based congregations in London and Manchester with a particular ministry with asylum seekers before moving to Glasgow to work with four URC congregations there. Now living in Orkney with his husband, he serves the URC creating and curating worship resources. Professionally trained in both theology and history, Andy is active in the Scottish Green Party. He contributed to *Religion is a Queer Thing* (Pilgrim Press, 1988), *Courage to Love* (DLT, 2002) and *Liturgies from Below* (Abingdon, 2020).

Beverley Clack is a Philosopher of Religion. Her interests are in the ways in which a contemporary philosophy of religion might be shaped through engaging with psychoanalytic and feminist theories. She is particularly interested in issues related to death and failure. She has been a local councillor and explores the relationship between philosophy and practical politics. Her recent publications include *How to be a Failure and Still Live Well* (Bloomsbury, 2020), and *Feminism, Religion and Practical Reason* (CUP, 2021).

Sir Les Ebdon CBE had an award-winning career as a Professor of Analytical Chemistry before becoming a distinguished University Vice Chancellor and subsequently a highly successful Director of Fair Access to Higher Education. He is recognised by the media as one of the leading voices in this country promoting the benefits of higher education and social mobility. Three times he has been cited as one of the 100 'most influential' people in Britain by *Debrett's* and *The Sunday Times*. He received his BSc and PhD from Imperial College London and has taught in universities in Uganda, Sheffield and Plymouth. He transformed the University of Bedfordshire during his time as Vice Chancellor. He was awarded a CBE in 2009, appointed Her Majesty's Deputy Lieutenant for Bedfordshire in 2011 and knighted in 2018. Currently, he serves on several boards and as the Chair of the National Educational Opportunities Network.

Robin Ellison is a Solicitor, Visiting Professor of Pensions Law and Economics at the Bayes Business School, City, University of London, and a former Chairman of the Pensions and Lifetime Savings Association. His publications include *Pensions Law and Practice* (4 vols, Sweet and Maxwell), *Halsbury's Laws* Vol 80 (pensions) and *Red Tape* (CUP). He chairs a number of pension schemes including Cambridge Colleges and the Public Service Pensions Board.

Sam Fowles is a Barrister and Author specialising in constitutional law. He is a member of Cornerstone Barristers, Director of the Institute for Constitutional and Democratic Research and a Lecturer at St Edmund Hall, University of Oxford. He has acted in many of the leading matters in modern English constitutional law, including *Miller* v *The Prime Minister* (concerning the unlawful prorogation of parliament in 2019); *Hamilton* v *Post Office* (the unlawful conviction of Post Office workers); and the parliamentary inquiry into the policing of the Clapham Common vigil for Sarah Everard. He is the author of *Overruled: Confronting Our Vanishing Democracy in 8 Cases* (Oneworld, 2022) and writes a regular column for *Perspective Magazine*.

Lee Jerome has published work on the development of citizenship education policy, the establishment of citizenship education as a new curriculum subject in England and deliberation as a pedagogic approach. He is on the editorial group of the journal, *Teaching Citizenship*, and Editor of *Education, Citizenship and Social Justice*. He has also researched character education and the Prevent Duty in education, and is currently conducting research on how to promote active citizenship through schools in the National Citizenship Education Survey. He led a Rights Respecting PGCE at London Metropolitan University, which was founded on the principles of the UN Convention on the Rights of the Child. He led the MA Children's Rights at Queen's University Belfast and coordinated an international research project to establish a baseline assessment of child rights education across 26 countries. With Hugh Starkey, he published a book *Children's Rights Education in Diverse Classrooms* (Bloomsbury Publishing, 2021).

David Lambert is a former secondary school teacher, teacher educator and Chief Executive of the Geographical Association (2002–2012). He is currently Professor (emeritus) of Geography Education at University College London Institute of Education.

Alister Miskimmon is Professor of International Relations at Queen's University Belfast and Fellow of the Senator George J Mitchel Institute for Global Peace, Security and Justice. He edits the Palgrave Macmillan book series in International Political Communication.

Andrew Morris, after researching for a PhD in Molecular Biophysics, he became a Physics Teacher in FE and Sixth Form colleges. He was appointed Director of Marketing and Development at City and Islington College in London. Then he managed educational research at the Further Education Development Agency and subsequently became Director of the National Education Research Forum, located at the Department for Education. This was set up by the Secretary of State to improve the links between research, practice and policy. He continues to work on these issues as an independent adviser and continues teaching science, through informal discussion groups for adults. He is an Honorary Associate Professor at the University College London Institute of Education and, in 2018/2019, was President of the Education Section of the British Science Association.

Ben O'Loughlin (DPhil Oxon) is Professor of International Relations and Co-Director of the New Political Communication Unit at Royal Holloway, University of London. He is Co-editor of the Sage journal *Media, War & Conflict.* His latest book is *Forging the World: Strategic Narratives and International Relations* (University of Michigan Press, 2017). He was Specialist Advisor to the UK Parliament's Select Committee on Soft Power, producing the report Power and Persuasion in the Modern World. He is currently finishing a book explaining the role of narratives in the 2015 Iran nuclear deal.

Matthew Paterson is Professor of International Politics at the University of Manchester and Director of the Sustainable Consumption Institute. His research focusses on the political economy, global governance and cultural politics of climate change. His latest book is *In Search of Climate Politics* (Cambridge University Press, 2021), which explores the contestations over how shifts to a low carbon society produce novel forms of cultural practice and challenge established ones. His previous publications include *Global Warming and Global Politics* (Routledge, 1996), *Automobile Politics* (Cambridge University Press, 2007), *Climate Capitalism: Global Warming and the Transformation of the Global Economy* (with Peter Newell, Cambridge University Press, 2010) and *Transnational Climate Change Governance* (with Harriet Bulkeley and eight others, Cambridge University Press, 2014). He was a Lead Author for the *Intergovernmental Panel on Climate Change's Fifth Assessment Report* published in 2014. His current projects continue to work on the character of political conflicts over climate action.

Vivienne Porritt OBE is Co-founder and Global Strategic Leader of WomenEd, a global charity which empowers aspiring and existing women leaders in education. As a Leadership Consultant, she supports school and trust leaders with vision, strategy, professional learning and development, impact evaluation and Diversity, Equity, Inclusion, and Justice (DEIJ). She is a coach who holds several governance roles as well as an in demand public speaker. She writes for practitioner and academic journals and books and is Co-editor of *10% Braver: Inspiring Women to Lead Education* (Sage, 2019) and *Being 10% Braver* (Corwin, 2021) as well as *Disruptive Women; A WomenEd Guide to Equitable Action in Education* (Corwin, 2024). She is a former Secondary Headteacher, Vice President of the Chartered College of Teaching as well as Director for School Partnerships at University College London Institute of Education and a Chair of Governors.

Anna E. Premo is a Postdoctoral Researcher at ETH Zürich studying educational approaches to misinformation in the Professorship for Research on Learning and Instruction. Her research centres on the creation, use and misuse of data in complex change efforts. Her prior writing focusses on effective creation and use of data to support educational improvement and evaluation. In addition, she has over a decade of experience in technology strategy and transformation in the financial services industry. She holds a PhD in Learning Sciences and Policy from the University of Pittsburgh. She also holds an MCP and SB from the Massachusetts Institute of Technology.

Alexander Ratkovsky is the Director and General Manager of APJ-EMEA Emerging Technologies and Industries for DXC Technology. His 30+ years of global experience in digital and emerging industries, artificial intelligence (AI) and cloud technologies span banking services, institutional banking, capital markets, insurance and mortgage banking. His expertise includes strategy development and implementation, mergers and acquisitions, AI and cloud strategy development, risk and service market operations and global banking operations. He is also highly skilled in application transformation, Application Programming Interface (API)-based platform adoption, Information Technology (IT) governance assessments and IT assets and process transformation. He holds a Master's degree in Resource Economics from Duke University.

Martina A. Rau holds the Professorship of Research on Learning and Instruction at ETH Zurich. Her research team focusses on learning with educational technologies, instructional design and multimodal learning. She focusses on empirical research with an emphasis on multi-methods approaches. Prior to joining ETH Zurich, she was an Associate Professor at the University of Wisconsin – Madison (USA) with her primary appointment in the Department of Educational Psychology and an affiliate appointment in the Department of Computer Sciences. She holds a PhD and MS in Human–Computer Interactions from Carnegie Mellon University and a Dipl.-Psych. from the University of Freiburg i. Br.

Lesley Saunders has worked all her life in education, as teacher, researcher, policy adviser and independent consultant. Her main posts were as Principal Research Officer and Head of the School Improvement Research Centre at the National Foundation for Educational Research; and subsequently as Senior Policy Adviser for Research, General Teaching Council for England. She is a Visiting Professor at University College London Institute of Education and her professorial lecture, given in 2004, was called 'Grounding the Democratic Imagination: Developing the Relationship between Research and Policy in Education'.

Sir Anthony Seldon is one of Britain's leading contemporary historians, educationalists, commentators and political authors. He is currently the Founding Director of Wellington College Education, having been Vice Chancellor of the University of Buckingham, a transformative Headteacher for 20 years at Brighton College and Wellington College. He is author and editor of 45+ books on contemporary history, including the last seven prime ministers. He has been Co-founder and Director of the Institute of Contemporary British History, Co-founder of Action for Happiness, Honorary Historical Advisor to 10 Downing Street, UK's Special Representative for Education to Saudi Arabia, Initiator and Deputy Chair of The Times Education Commission and Institute for Government's Commission of the Centre, member of the Government's First World War Culture Committee, Director and Governor at the Royal Shakespeare Company, Chair of the National Archives Trust, Patron of several charities, Founder of the Via Sacra Western Front Walk and Executive Producer of the film *Journey's End*. Over many years, many writing profits have gone to charity.

Anna Stone is Senior Lecturer, Cognition and Neuroscience Research Group, Department of Psychology and Human Development, School of Childhood and Social Care at the University of East London. She teaches for undergraduate and MSc programmes, focussing on Research Methods and Applied Cognitive Psychology. Her main research interests are political ideologies and their relation to human rights and to animal rights, discrimination on the basis of accent and reactions to people with visible facial difference. She is interested in why people hold beliefs that are not subject to empirical validation, including moral values, religious or political beliefs or belief in the paranormal, for example, alien visitation, telepathy, pre-cognitive dreams, etc. Anna is the co-author of *Anomalistic Psychology: Exploring Paranormal Belief and Experience* with Professor Chris French.

Gopal Subramanium, a former Solicitor General of India, is a Senior Advocate and an International Arbitrator. He was appointed a Foundation Fellow at Somerville College, Oxford, in 2019. In that capacity, he is especially interested in multidisciplinary research on democracy, social inequality, civic education and the applicability of psychology to legal concepts. In his career, he was part of a number of landmark cases, including defending the conviction of the sole surviving terrorist of the 2008 Mumbai terror attacks and protecting the constitutional right to privacy in India. In 2013, he served on the JS Verma Commission, which recommended amendments to Indian laws to safeguard the safety and dignity of women and children and, since 2015, he has served as a Supplementary Judge at the Qatar Financial Centre Regulatory Tribunal. He is also an Ambassador of mental health charity SANE and Honorary Director of the All India Heart Foundation, the cardiac charity.

Steven Warmoes's life theme (1960 Belgium) is the individual and collective human mind. From 1985, he was active in the field of artificial intelligence, and/or with his software company Warmoes & Van Damme from 1987 till 1998. He was also a pioneer in Knowledge Management (KM), coining the term in 1989. Since 1987, he has been an Independent Consultant in KM. He has an MSc in Computer Science (Gent University), Master in General Management (Vlerick Business School, Gent) and studied cognitive sciences and epistemology.

Lynn Wood is currently a student again following a long career in retail and finance and participation in many boards including as Chair. The UTS Transdisciplinary School has accepted her application to study the link between noticing positive ideas and wellbeing. Her Thesis Topic is "Can Entrepreneurial Alertness to Positive Ideas Enhance Wellbeing?" initially as a Master of Transdisciplinary Innovation (Research). Her interest in the topic is reflected in her development of an open innovation platform called IdeaSpies which has shared thousands of positive ideas.

INDEX